M000167010

"A moving and emotional testimony, and a travelogue that is the next most vivid experience to hiking upon the trail oneself." ~ *Midwest Book Review*

"A high-altitude tale of synchronicity, divine providence, begging monks, trigger-happy Chinese soldiers and dehydration." ~ *Pittsburgh Post-Gazette*

Independent Publisher selected *Yak Butter Blues* as a Highlighted Title. "These books are honored each month for exhibiting superior levels of creativity, originality, high standards of design and superior production quality."

"A true pilgrimage, one that plumbs the heart of troubled Tibet and teaches impatient and stubborn Westerners to slow down and appreciate this amazing planet." ~ *Honolulu Advertiser*

"A 600-mile foot slog through Tibet in which you can almost smell the dust and feel the blisters. Worth a read by any adventure or travel-trekking book enthusiast." ~ *Backpacking Light Magazine*

"Even Indiana Jones would have reconsidered the expedition...The Wilson's journey across Tibet serves as a beacon of light for a repressed people held captive within their own country." ~ Jeff Alt, award-winning author of *A Walk for Sunshine*

"... an awesome (in that old-fashioned use of the word) tale...Brave believing people on both sides of this trek...and a tale that deserves the telling." ~ *The Courier Gazette*, Maine

"Wilson leads us through a harsh and beautiful landscape and takes us into the hearts of the people who live there. Time and again he shows us that hardships can become blessings." ~ Jean Aspen, author of *Arctic Daughter: a wilderness journey* and *Arctic Son: fulfilling the dream*

"If you've traveled independently through Tibet, Brandon Wilson's *Yak Butter Blues* will bring back memories...this lively memoir is sure to provide a yak-scented whiff of nostalgia." ~ *Kangri News, International Mountain Explorer's Connection*

"Brandon Wilson is masterful in describing the hardships and trials of his 650-mile journey across Tibet... In this strange paradise, Wilson finds commonality with the Tibetans, yet mourns the continuing disappearance of their culture, noting that soon little will remain of it but their ancient yak butter tea. Fortunately, so will his book." ~ Andrew F. O'Hara, author of *The Swan: Tales Of The Sacramento Valley*

Yak

Butter

Blues

A Tibetan Trek of Faith

Yak

Butter

Blues

A Tibetan Trek of Faith
by
Brandon Wilson

RECIPIENT OF AN
INDEPENDENT PUBLISHER
IPPY AWARD.

PILGRIM'S
TALES

Yak Butter Blues

All rights reserved. © Copyright 2006 by Brandon Wilson
Second edition

**PILGRIM'S
TALES**

For information contact:
Pilgrim's Tales, Inc.
P.O. Box 791613, Paia, Hawaii 96779
www.PilgrimsTales.com
pilgrimstales@yahoo.com

Pilgrim's Tales books are available at special discount for bulk purchases
by corporations, institutions and other organizations.

Library of Congress Number: 2005905469
ISBN-13: 978-0-9770536-6-7
ISBN-10: 0-9770536-6-0 (previously 1-933037-24-5)

Printed in the United States of America

No part of this book may be reproduced or transmitted in any form or by
any means, graphic, electronic, or mechanical, including photocopying,
recording, typing, or by any information storage retrieval system,
without the written permission of the publisher.

Front cover design by Ron Carter.
All photos by Brandon Wilson, unless otherwise noted.

Publisher's Cataloging in Publication

Wilson, Brandon.
Yak butter blues : a tibetan trek of faith / Brandon Wilson.
Portion of Title: Tibetan trek of faith
LCCN: 2005905469
ISBN: 0-9770536-6-0 (perfectbound : alk. paper)

1.Tibet (China)–Social life and customs. 2. Tibet (China)–Description and travel.
3. Wilson, Brandon–Travel

Dedication

This book is dedicated to the people of Tibet, especially those who shared the warmth of their fire, their boundless hospitality, and their whispered hopes and dreams with two weary pilgrims.

May the message from their prayer wheels reverberate in heaven, and may the Dalai Lama, along with their sovereignty, soon return to their sacred land.

This story is true.
However, names have been changed
to protect the innocent.

Contents

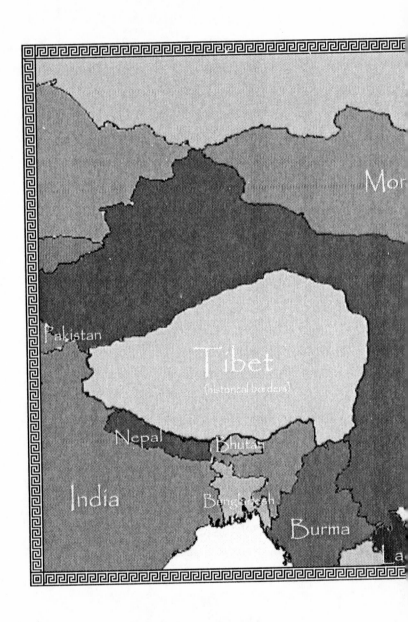

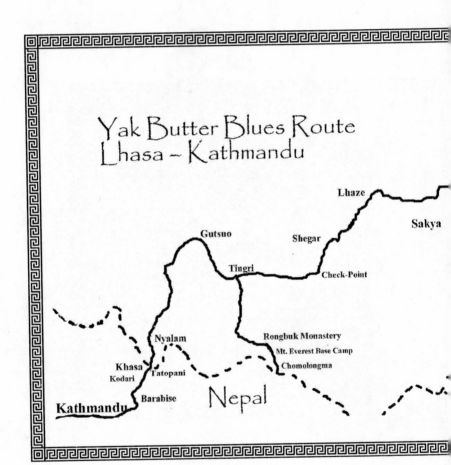

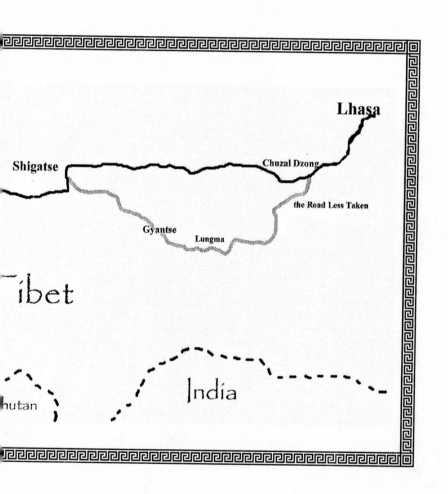

BRANDON WILSON

Introduction

The wind kicks up again. A vast, desolate swath of sand stretches for miles, days in any direction. We are insignificant: insects trudging across a desert. Meager possessions are slung across a patient horse's back. Once-strong bodies buckle under the pervasive wind. We bend double, choking on dust. Sand invades every pore. Pus seeps into stiff socks from sores pocking our feet. Hopelessness, undeniable hunger and unquenchable thirst fill us with a gnawing rage.

For hours or days hatred sustains us. Hatred of self. Each other. The inadequacy of our bodies. The forsaken land we vowed to cross, a ground that consumes our very souls.

Maybe we approached the journey all wrong from the very start, gulping in its challenge in one gigantic breath, like diving headfirst off a cliff into some mirrored pool of unknown depth. It was bound to be a great adventure, we argued, a chance to prove something to ourselves— especially to those who vowed it couldn't be done. But any Western sense of toughing things out, of muscling our way across a land as complex as utter darkness, soon fell by the wayside like exhausted matchsticks.

Survival has somehow become mysteriously linked with the uneasy idea of *letting go*. Perhaps it always has been. But leaps of faith have never given me much personal comfort. Still, this is Tibet; it's unsettling, yet reassuring.

When life is bleakest, magic appears, tenuous at first. It's a strange, exhilarating force, a peace. Obstacles vanish and hurdles disappear. We find water where there is none. Someone arrives out of nowhere offering shelter. Another shares his meager food. Another, his love.

At those moments we have a gnawing suspicion that there is something more to our thousand-kilometer trek, something more than just two weary travelers tracing an ancient pilgrim's path from Lhasa to Kathmandu across the Himalayas.

And that sense of greater purpose, more than any personal tenacity or courage, ultimately keeps us moving.

1

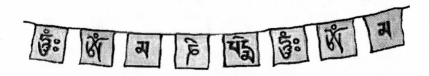

Chapter 1

Never Say "Impossible"

High in the Rockies, in secluded mountain villages like Vail, there were still some things on which you could depend. The mail would already be waiting when I returned home. Still, I was anxious and a little concerned. One particular letter was long overdue. It had been weeks since we'd written. Some days I could just kick myself—what ever possessed us to take that first step, contacting the Chinese Embassy of all places? Then again, why even consider trekking across Tibet?

It all started innocently enough. Sure, my wife Cheryl and I had heard about "Shangri-La," that legendary Himalayan paradise. Who hadn't grown up with the fable? Then, one snowy morning, snuggled deep in a cozy leather armchair beside the library's crackling fire, I became intrigued while reading about an ancient trail once walked by pilgrims from Kathmandu, Nepal to Lhasa, Tibet, home of the Dalai Lamas.

According to this account no foreigners had seen the "forbidden" city until 1903. Borders were sealed after the 1950 Chinese invasion until 1979, only opening for brief periods since.

At that time only 1200 foreigners had ever seen Lhasa, let alone the rest of Tibet, and half of those were with an English army campaign. Most of the others were on more recent, tightly controlled Chinese propaganda tours.

Considering all that, I thought that maybe no Westerner had ever trekked this unexplored path. This was the challenge that initially convinced me to write to the Chinese authorities. The same motivator that has sent other madmen traipsing off to some of the highest, least traveled, most remote corners of a shrinking planet.

Other folks I guess might have been content to stay in Colorado, especially at that time of year. After all, it was a cloudless afternoon. The type of day where the spruce trees, God's own sweet air fresheners, scent the rarefied air with a promise of perennial hope. Besides, who could have guessed such a simple action as opening a mailbox could change one's life forever?

Tearing open an envelope, not from the embassy but from China's "authorized" travel agent, I eagerly read:

> "It is *impossible* to independently travel from Kathmandu into Tibetan Province, nor from Lhasa into Nepal on foot. As far as we know, it is *impossible* to get the permit to stay in Tibet for 60 or 90 days on your own. It is *impossible* to buy local food or find simple guesthouses every 300 km., let alone 30-km. You could hardly come across a soul within a couple of days, if you go on foot." It warned, "No maps of China or Tibet are available…The temperature in Tibet in November is below zero. Snowstorms and avalanches are not uncommon then and there…Conditions in those high and deep mountains of Tibet are beyond your imaginations."

I was thrilled. Its string of impossibilities just made me more determined, especially their bullheaded insistence that it couldn't be done. Still, we prepared for the worse.

"Look, if the Chinese refuse to give us visas," I cautioned Cheryl, my naive accomplice, "we'll be forced to sneak in or bribe our way across the border from Nepal. We'll have to hide in the mountains and slip from village to village."

Plus, I neglected to add, rely on the kindness of strangers.

By the time we'd committed to the challenge, there was so little time to prepare for something so unknown. We feverishly scoured bookshops and found a *Lonely Planet Tibet Guide*. But the book contained no topographical maps, no details on food or shelter, and it was anyone's guess what the Communists would do if they caught us without papers.

Then, unexpectedly, doors began to open.

One day, while ambling through the trendy university town of Boulder, we spotted OLD TIBET, a slip of a cluttered shop. Thinking we might find crucial answers or at least preview some tasty souvenirs, we stepped inside. Narayan, the owner, greeted our arrival like long-lost friends and, in the finest Nepalese tradition, led us into his office with a flourish.

Staring across a disheveled wooden desk, the gregarious fellow began, "So, you want to go trekking in Nepal?"

Obviously that was why most people visited him.

"No," I explained. "Actually, we want to go from Kathmandu to Lhasa."

"No problem," he chirped in his singsong Nepali accent. "The Chinese organize tours. We can put you in touch. Or," he suggested with a grin, "you'll have a very good time hiking Nepal with us."

"No, you don't understand," I elaborated. "We want to trek from Kathmandu to Lhasa...on the pilgrim's trail."

Shocked, he shook his head as if we'd suggested a trip to a far-off planet. "Why, that's over 600 miles! That's impossible."

I tensed. "There's that word again," I thought.

"Impossible? Why?"

Furtively, he glanced around the cubicle, as if it might be bugged. "Because the Chinese will never allow it," he whispered, as though sharing a forbidden secret. "They insist on selling organized tours from Kathmandu to Lhasa. Five or seven-day tours. The border's been closed to independent travelers for years."

"You sure? We'd hoped there was a change with all this détente stuff."

While he adamantly shook his head, I focused on a map thrown across his desk. Then it dawned on me.

"Wait a second! What if we come in from the other direction? From Lhasa to Kathmandu?"

As my suggestion began to register, he smirked at its utter lunacy. "Well, you'd still have to go to Kathmandu and join a Chinese group tour, then fly to Lhasa…"

Nodding, I walked him through our far-fetched scheme. "Right…and…"

"And then what? Disappear?" he asked.

We shot him Cheshire-cat grins. "Melt into the crowds. Vanish."

Intrigued, he affectionately stroked his bushy mustache. "It just might be possible…"

"Look, it'll be close to winter," I reminded him. "They'd never suspect anyone would be crazy enough to take off over the Himalayas at that time of year!"

Neither could Cheryl, but she cautiously joined our tag-team lunacy.

"Sure. If anyone stops us we'll invent some excuse. 'Hey, we just got separated from our group.'"

"They'll probably figure you'd head to Beijing or Hong Kong anyway," he chuckled, caught up in our gambit.

"What's the chance of hiring a guide in Lhasa?" I wondered, far from thrilled at the prospect of getting lost. "Can we find someone to lead us back to Kathmandu?"

"Doubtful. Maybe you'll find a Nepali eager to return there," he suggested, intently leaning forward in his chair. "But never a Tibetan. They're reluctant to travel farther than the next village."

"What about visas?"

"You can get them faster in Kathmandu."

"Say, can we buy a yak or horse in Lhasa?" my partner asked, nervously twisting her long, auburn hair.

Narayan was incredulous. "You really want to do this like Tibetans, don't you?" Our stares told him we were dead serious. "Well, maybe you can find one in the Barkhor Market," he suggested. "But don't count on it."

After an hour, we had more questions than answers. Still, I was hesitant to leave so much, virtually our lives, to chance if we could possibly avoid it.

"Isn't there anyone in Kathmandu we can talk to? Someone with contacts?"

A terrified look flashed across the Nepali's eyes. "Don't tell a soul what you're doing," he warned. "You don't know who you can trust!" Then, he reconsidered. Leaning across the desk, he confided, "On second thought, talk to my brother, N.D. His travel agency's in Thamel. That's all I can suggest."

Grateful, we stood to go, but he offered one last kernel of wisdom.

"Look, you two, I don't think this has ever been done before—and there must be more than one good reason why."

Those last, simple words sealed our fate. The chance to become among the first Westerners to capture a bit of history, while beating the Chinese at their own bureaucratic game, convinced us. We'd give it our best shot.

Looking back, we should have taken a year to plan for our harrowing journey. There was equipment to buy, test and break-in; food and supplies to order; maps to study; lives to put in order; physical conditioning to achieve. But we knew if we were to complete our trek before the ominous November snows, we had only three months to prepare.

"If we wait until next year," I figured, "good sense will probably prevail. Physically, we're in good shape, but we're far from being mountaineers," I thought. "Living at nearly 2743 meters (9,000 feet) this past year will speed our acclimation. Still, when you get right down to it, there's little we can do now to prepare for a 35-kilometer (22-mile) hike each day, which is exactly what we need to cover if we hope to make it to Kathmandu before the last 5182 meter (17,000 foot) pass is hopelessly blocked by a ton of snow and we're stranded until May."

Kathmandu, Nepal

October 7-12

It's easy to forget the subtleties of a place like Kathmandu. But, like meeting an old lover on the street, those exhilarating sensations and musky memories quickly stir and reawaken.

It begins with an on-rush of a dozen desperate urchins with their frantic curbside hustle, screeching, "Taxi, Misstah! Taxi, Sir?" Then there's the ritual cramming of two size ten bags into a size five trunk. Once loaded, those taxis take off and swarm with all the frenzy and heated determination of wasps in a jar. Incessant bleats, peals and joy buzzer rasps of ten thousand horns punctuate fits of starts, stops and swerves.

It's an intricate ballet. Motorized *tuk-tuks*, hand-pulled rickshaws and dilapidated Datsuns career down crowded streets, blaring at gawking tourists, persistent hawkers and wayward cows. They follow a well-practiced weave, fake and swerve through an orchestra of sheer chaos and overpowering odors. All that's missing is a conductor's baton to direct the symphony of shit.

"Official trekking season" attracts those who dream of Himalayan quests, like vultures to an African roadkill. The French roam murky alleys, narrowly skirting ambushes by mock-gracious merchants. Brits scour streets in search of legendary cakes, while Americans suck cold brews to tunes from pizza joint jukeboxes.

Now, as if that wasn't already enough to throw the typical traveler off balance, a two-week Nepalese religious festival added to the madness. Dasain, the most lavish of Hindu holidays, spilled frenzied throngs into already undulating streets.

During our last visit after a month spent roasting in Rajasthan's summer desert, Kathmandu was an oasis fulfilling fantasies of food, comfort and relaxation. Yet, even then she was enigmatic. Her face changed like masks in a Balinese barong: one moment beautiful and enchanting, the next bizarre and revolting.

Unfortunately since then, fame aged her more than centuries past, and her virginal innocence, an honest wanderer's welcome, was deflowered.

We were saddened by the loss, but this time Kathmandu was just a staging area. Its score of trekking supply shops, groceries, banks and one-star (or falling-star) hotels only promised to hasten our departure. We needed all the help we could get since everything was uncertain. All except our steadfast determination.

"Right now," I thought, "we don't even know they'll allow us into Tibet. Will they issue visas? Will the border be open for independent travelers? Will we just waltz right on through? Or will we be forced to fly to Lhasa, join a tour and escape into Tibet unfettered and alone?"

"All we can do is have faith," I kept reminding myself. Yet, at that point in my life, the concept of faith was abstract to me, ethereal, best relegated to love, religion and the life hereafter.

N.D.'s travel agency was set among a hundred other one-person shops in Kathmandu's teeming Thamel district. We approached it reluctantly since after flying halfway around the world we arrived to find our hotel hopelessly filled. He had never reserved our room. Still, he was our only contact. Perhaps our last hope.

Anxiously we peered through the grimy glass door to a chubby fellow scrutinizing a newspaper, spread like a crab-fest tablecloth across his desk. As we entered, he casually cocked one eye from under an American baseball cap in our direction. Mumbling a disinterested "Namaste," he immediately returned to his reading.

Unwilling to let him off the hook that easily, we returned his traditional Nepalese greeting then pulled up chairs, encircling his desk and closing in for the kill.

"Narayan suggested we see you when we arrived."

"Ah, yes," he sputtered, slurping milky mint tea. "He was just here a week ago."

"And he telexed last month," Cheryl reminded, "asking you to reserve a room for us at the hotel across the street."

"Hmm, don't remember any telex." Glancing up from his paper, he half-heartedly grabbed a tattered notebook from the shelf and lazily leafed through it. "No. No telex here…"

"Anyway," I interrupted, careful not to antagonize him, "we're planning a special trip and your brother thought you could help."

N.D. grinned while his head bobbed back and forth in that unmistakable Nepalese wobble—like a plastic dog in the rear window of a '65 Chevy.

"Not to worry," he chirped, already mentally tallying commission from another lucrative Nepal trek. "I will try."

At this mere mention of business, our host sent the "boy" scurrying for more tea then leaned back with a confident smirk.

"Can we speak frankly?" I whispered, after turning to confirm the door was closed.

Our plans had been shrouded in secrecy since that first meeting. Narayan's hushed tones and wary glances made it seem like Chinese spies lurked right beneath his desk. Since then, we were extremely cautious about sharing our plan with anyone for fear the Chinese would catch wind and refuse us entry.

"Of c-c-course," he stuttered, now becoming intrigued by his mysterious strangers.

Exasperated by our labored ritual, Cheryl impatiently blurted out, "We want to go to Tibet."

"We want to fly to Lhasa," I added, "then, trek back to Kathmandu."

"Trek back?" he clucked, shaking his head. "Nooo... Impossible!"

After traveling so far, I refused to accept *impossible* as an excuse anymore.

"Why? Buddhist pilgrims have done it for centuries."

"But no Western couple ever has that I know of," he replied, snickering at the prospect. "Do you know how far it is?"

"Over a thousand kilometers (621 miles)," Cheryl deadpanned, used to that tired old argument.

"Yes and it's a long way between villages," he reminded us, as cautious or frightened as his brother.

"We know," my partner assured him, "but we have plenty of dehydrated food."

I nodded in agreement, although *plenty* was certainly stretching it. Actually, hoping to lessen the weight in our packs, we had foil packets for ten meager meals.

"And we have maps, too," I added, having picked up the "very latest" showing the thin, ragged route from Kathmandu to Lhasa. Although the kid hawking them on the street promised it was "just five-days old," I had my doubts since travelers are expected to be mighty gullible in Kathmandu.

"Hey, maybe we can buy a yak or burro in Lhasa," Cheryl suggested, figuring that hiking that far was hard enough without lugging forty-pound packs. "Or we can even hire a guide to lead us from one village to the next."

Although N.D. was fascinated, his practical nature (or daily experience with the Chinese) warned him that our scheme was pure craziness. It took several glasses of creamy tea to finally convince him it was worth at least one phone call to China's "official" travel agent. One call and he could prove us wrong, get rid of us, and get back to his newspaper.

As he slowly dialed the number, I almost stopped him. Reluctant to reveal our plans, especially to the Chinese, I was afraid we'd never get in. "It's still not too late to hop an organized tour," I figured, "then disappear into the Himalayas." But to be honest, I wasn't anxious to run into some overzealous, pubescent Chinese soldier waving an Uzi, eager to shoot "spies."

While all those doubts crossed my mind, N.D. reached the airline office. Although neither of us speaks Nepali, it was easy to decipher his conversation with China South West Airlines.

"I have a couple who wants to trek from Lhasa to Kathmandu," he started. Then in a patronizing tone, he snickered, "I told them it was impossible, but..." He suddenly stopped.

Our hearts raced. Were we finished? Did they just flatly refuse?

"Yes, they know they'll have to book a Lhasa tour, but...What? You'll consider it?"

Stunned, he shot us a quizzical glance. Then he apologetically blubbered, "Why, yes, yes, I'll send them over right away."

The staff at CSWA was surprisingly cooperative and more than surprised that two Americans were serious about trekking through Tibet.

"Your timing is fortunate. Most fortunate," the slight supervisor pronounced, sizing us up with wide-eyed curiosity. "You see, the border officially opened just yesterday."

"Yesterday?" I thought. "What incredible luck!"

"However," he continued, "it is only open from the Tibetan side. You must first fly to Lhasa on our mandatory five-day tour."

Cheryl and I shot each other incredulous looks. Grins started to surface as we thought, "Hey, we can deal with that."

"Afterwards, you can continue on your own."

On our own? We nearly leapt from his sofa. Then, reluctant to let him glimpse our explosive, hallelujah-excitement, we calmly asked that one question, one last time.

"Has this ever been done before?"

The pensive supervisor hesitated only a second, assuring us, "No. To my knowledge, no Western couple has ever walked Lhasa to Kathmandu."

"There, we've heard it three times," I thought. "It must be true. But does that only mean that no one's been so mad?"

"It just hasn't been possible," he added, de-emphasizing our luck. "The border's been closed many years now."

Although he promised to send our request to the Chinese Embassy, we remained skeptical that they would issue visas for the sixty days we needed. Or that they'd allow two unsupervised Americans free rein to trek across "their" Tibet. That was unheard of.

I could just hear them chuckling, "Americans want to trek through the Himalayas this time of year? Wa ha ha! Imagine them trying to talk with Tibetans? Wa ha ha ha! Or find a hotel? Impossible!"

Then, as if to allay all those unspoken fears, a displaced Tibetan clerk secretively shared something with us, a truth which eased our minds.

"Why worry?" he asked, with a cryptic smile. "If it is meant to be, if Lord Buddha wills it, it will be."

And so it was. One telephone call, a change in policy one day earlier, the unlikely consent of a few officials, and suddenly it was willed.

It was pure synchronicity. If we had never stumbled into that Tibetan shop, or had arrived in Kathmandu one week earlier, or never dared to chase our outlandish dream, our lives would be different now.

Chapter II

A Hundred Yak Butter Lamps

L anding at Lhasa's incongruously modern Gonggar Airport, we excitedly joined an international group of five other travelers on our mandatory, propaganda-laden, organized tour. We were a little nervous approaching customs since we'd secreted a stack of photos of the Dalai Lama into our luggage.

His Holiness had lived in forced exile in Dharamsala, India since 1959 while the Communists waged an untiring campaign to wipe out any memory or remaining allegiance to Tibet's god-king. Although we knew photos were strictly forbidden and their presence might have caused us to be expelled immediately, we decided to risk bringing them in. Not only would they be a sort of holy currency, they'd serve as a treasured gift of faith to any of our local hosts.

Our photos remained undetected. After breezing through customs we were met by two politely grinning Chinese appointed guides who herded us into a mini-van. Then, signaling the start of our ninety-six kilometer race, the coach electronically bleated, *"Bong schwei! Bong schwei! Bong schwei! Bong schwei!"* before spinning down serpentine roads toward our long-awaited vision of the Tibetan paradise.

As a fleeting barrage of images sailed past, everyone anxiously pressed noses against the smoked windows. Gui, a bearded Barcelonan professor, craned to snap photos as Elyse, a winsome Parisian, feverishly drew on her notepad. The rest of us struggled to mentally sketch a composite of it all as it swirled past.

13

At first, it looked just like another god-forsaken wasteland with monolithic, stark boulders sprouting atop a desolate, dusty plain. Then, upon closer inspection, we could tell it wasn't entirely foreboding. Sparse green fields were polka dotted with shaggy black yaks looking like sheep dogs on steroids, and squat, sugar-cubed adobe huts. A glittering swatch of snow crowned surrounding peaks while swirling rust-hued dust clouds engulfed black-robed pilgrims. And then, for an instant, a brilliantly surreal rainbow even garlanded the otherwise bleak, coffee ground terrain.

"That's a good sign," I thought, hoping and desperate to believe that luck had flown over those impenetrable Himalayas with us. We needed all the help we could get.

It was nearly two hours later when those tidy huts transformed into clumsy, cookie-cutter, concrete block houses hidden behind thick, foreboding walls. This was Lhasa.

At first glance, that "Place of the Gods" was unsettling in its bland newness, unnerving in its pervasive Beijing persona. Family-run shops, their facades plastered with hand-lettered signs, stretched for miles. Rickshaws clogged pockmarked streets, while packs of soldiers scavenged town squares. Tons of Chinese troops in olive-drab, one-size-fits-all uniforms flirted with Szechwan go-go girls and hookers decked-out in '60s beehive bouffants and spiked heels. Standing and smoking, spitting and gawking, they leered with distaste at the once-sacred city where fate had dumped them.

In that crowd, spotting a Tibetan was like finding Waldo, since China's resettlement of ethnic Chinese into Tibet has been horrifyingly successful. Beijing knows exactly what buttons to push, billions of times.

Social and economic incentives for resettlement include substantial perks: pay up to four times what they would earn back home; favorable loans; better housing; longer leave; exemption from the hated one-child-per-family rule; and the ultimate "golden carrot"— the chance to live where they want when they return. Consequently, Chinese pioneers outnumbered Tibetans within the pre-invasion borders, five million Chinese to only four million Tibetans.

Already, I could clearly see it wasn't the ancient "paradise" everyone imagined. "Where is the legendary city that withstood foreign invaders for so many centuries?" I silently wondered.

As if in answer, the concrete curtain parted, if only for an instant, and the Potala Palace rose in transcendental splendor from atop nearby Marpori Mountain. For a heartbeat I was relieved. Then I wondered in horror if the Dalai Lama's former home was all that was left of Tibet after forty plus years of occupation?

Khada Hotel became a humble base for our five-day escorted tour. As you might expect, it was rustic by Western standards (or any standard for that matter). Our room, a dazzling psychedelic parrot green, overlooked a courtyard parking lot while sagging twin beds faced a battered black-and-white TV flickering Kung-Fu films. The sink was a simple affair: a tin wash basin and crimson thermos of boiling water in the corner.

At least it was warm. Our room was bone chilling, since nights already plunged to freezing and there was no heat. Those "modern" communal showers they had bragged about were two floors down and rarely offered hot water. Sadistically, even the Turkish squat toilets were two halls and a very long jog away.

Funny. Although it seemed primitive to us then, looking back, we would soon miss its relative luxury.

Khada's restaurant was a pompous cavernous hall, splashed the same gaudy shade with an immense incense pot planted in the center of the floor. A golden altar flooded an entire wall with bottles of whiskey, brandy and imported cigarettes shanghaiing sacred positions once occupied by photos of the Tibetan god-king and the benevolent Goddess of Mercy. Lhasa's new gods silently reflected in a cracked and peeling mirror, offering numbing communion to those few who could afford their nightly redemption.

That first evening, the seven of us reluctantly joined our guide in what was to become a frustrating daily ritual, a kind of culinary Chinese torture. After laboriously deciphering the jumbled menu, we carefully pondered our slim options and cautiously ordered, only to be scolded, "We're out of that!" And so we started our frustrating guessing game again. Each night we salivated as visiting dignitaries (Lhasa Rotarians?) were plied with piled platters of delicacies. As spicy aromas wafted and mingled with nauseating rose incense, each man ate his weight in meat and vegetables, *momos* (stuffed dumplings), noodle dishes and pastries. Then, with a loud belch, they casually flung empty beer bottles to the floor.

"Hey, we'll just have what they've ordered," quipped Tedd, our gregarious Swiss club manager. With a noncommittal smile our guide shook his head then vanished behind beaded curtains into the kitchen–only to eventually return with yet another bland plate of noodles or rice or an omelet traveling incognito as scrambled eggs.

Meanwhile, Mandarin waitresses, clicking back and forth in high heels and even higher teased hair, graciously kept cups topped with an endless stream of sweet jasmine or yak butter tea.

We'd read about that traditional Tibetan staple: how a pressed block of strong black tea is brewed in a huge pot with a fistful of salt for hours over a dung-fire. Then, just before serving, a dollop of rich, freshly churned yak butter is added, creating a cloudy soup. Since we figured we'd practically live on the brew like local Tibetans for the next few months, we might as well try some. So those waitresses graciously poured us cup after murky, swirling cup.

Unfortunately, the Khada Hotel's recipe lost something in translation. That rancid yak butter concoction kept weak Western stomachs brewing and churning all night.

The next morning, anxious to discover the remnants of that endangered culture, we set off for the Jokhang Temple, center of Lhasa's religious and social activity. However, to reach that fortress-like complex, we needed to maneuver through and survive a living, swarming maze. For one fleeting instant, a moment frozen in time, a few wayward travelers became part of an eon's old spectacle.

Everyone had something to sell; everything had its price. We skirted pushy jewelry vendors screaming, "Come look! Come look!" while tugging sleeves of reluctant passersby, and wove a path between rickety food carts stacked with a mosaic of colorful produce and squatting, sun-ripened women pushing pyramids of seeds piled high on yellowed newspapers.

As much as we tried to downplay our Western presence, we were as invisible as skinheads at a Hasidic temple. Beggars who hobbled past on a wobbly crutches cased out the strange-looking foreigners, while rickshaw drivers cried out in *Chenglish*, "Hey, take you somewhere, Misstah?"

Even religion was peddled, with prayer flag merchants and ceremonial *khata* cloth salesmen hawking holy offerings by the yard or strand to frenzied shoppers and Western heathens alike.

Outside the temple's seventh-century facade, shrouded, gnarled men bought aromatic boughs of juniper and sage-like herbs, which they ceremoniously tossed into the smoky pyre. Then, heads bowed, they fervently chanted amid swirling white smoke, engulfing both the pious and not-so-holy in pungent wafts of incense as clouds billowed and surged from twin immense urns.

Their reverence was contagious and carried upon the wind.

Beneath fluttering strands of multi-colored prayer flags, a hundred Buddhist pilgrims feverishly prostrated onto the temple's entryway, sliding well-worn calluses across polished bare stone. While a few fell on tattered straw mats, others wore cardboard squares on weathered hands. Trance-like, their rhythmic reclining and chanting repeated again and again. No beginning. No end.

A massive cylindrical prayer wheel the size of a Volkswagen guarded the temple's monumental portal. Its metal inscriptions were rubbed smooth by hundreds of thousands of pilgrims over the centuries who had traveled far to spin the missive millions of times, sending its prayer of *"Om Mani Padme Hum!"* soaring to the heavens.

We, too, drifted on a cloud of incense to an expansive inner court where flickering rays of a hundred pungent yak butter lamps cast eerie illumination across the grounds. We joined humble throngs shuffling through the temple in a clockwise procession amid maroon-robed monks chanting a mystic drone of devotion. Eager hands turned scores of prayer wheels mounted beneath exquisitely graphic *thangka* murals, tempting with the pleasures of *nirvana*, shocking with the agonies of hell.

Swept up in a tide of cherubic-cheeked pilgrims, we left the light-streamed courtyard, and wandered past a solemn inner sanctum holding the treasured seated Sakyamuni, Gautama Buddha. Then, climbing stairs, we ducked inside a tiny chamber and plunged into a stifling total void.

The walls oozed grease. The floor seemed to have a life of its own. There was an overpowering stench, a sickening scent of sweat, musky incense, and putrid yak butter matured over fourteen centuries. As our

17

eyes adjusted to the murky light, we found ourselves pressed into a five-by-eight chamber with sixty others who reverently filed past the Medicine Buddha, as they rubbed brass plates and mumbled incantations to ensure their good health.

From there we meandered on several levels through another twenty crowded chapels dedicated to a confusing array of deities, royalty and saints; the only foreigners to be seen among hordes of joyous Tibetans. Although awe-struck by the temple's craftsmanship and astounded by the tremendous devotion, we couldn't help but feel intrusive, strangely out of place, as if we were missing something.

Envious, I searched the blissful faces around us, thinking, "These people have come huge distances and sacrificed greatly for this once-in-a-lifetime trip to their Mecca. Some, I've heard, have even crawled like human inchworms the entire distance! Unfortunately for us, this part of our trip, although uncertain, has been almost too easy. We don't deserve to be here. If only the Jokhang was at the end of our journey…if only politics didn't dictate Kathmandu as our destination, we could join them here in celebration…perhaps even as pilgrims."

Feeling insignificant, I fled the temple alone, swept up in a sea of civilization, swimming clockwise through the crowded bazaar on an inner pilgrim circuit. I became lost in a crowd, enveloped by nomad women, *drokpa*, garbed in black robes and turned-up felt boots. Their braided hair and blushed cheeks shone with yak butter pomade. I was surrounded by statuesque, fearsome Khampa warriors whose hair was looped in red braided rope; austere, wandering monks in burgundy robes; Amish-looking Muslims in battered straw hats and wisps of beards; gnarled women spinning miniature prayer wheels and bundled in ten layers of rags; wizened men with skin the texture of dried earth, curiously gazing out from under floppy felt hats.

And, it would be safe to say, the goods sold there were as diverse as the buyers were. Lhasa's ancient trade center was a street market goulash of mostly imported goods, peddled mostly by imported Han merchants and peppered with unbridled enthusiasm. If it could be bought in Tibet, you could buy it there: everything from fresh yak carcasses to boxes of apples, pears, chili peppers, persimmons and raisins; from barrels of dried or shredded yak cheese to dusty bags of *tsampa*, ground barley flour. Ladies hawked yak butter by the block, while Han shops offered every expensive import: flapped fur hats, bolts of material, thermoses, rice pattern dishes and tin plates, kerosene stoves, herbal remedies, beers and brandies.

It was a grand spectacle, much as it ever was, except for one frightening detail. As Tibet's hub, it is not surprising that the Barkhor is also one of the most closely observed areas of that occupied capital. Video cameras and plainclothes police provide ever-vigilant eyes, ensuring protests are short-lived and retribution severe, as evidenced by the hundreds of political prisoners.

Sadly, even the hallowed Jokhang provided little sanctuary. During the 1959 uprising Tibetan freedom fighters took refuge there, reasoning the invaders wouldn't dare desecrate the premises. They were wrong. After suffering a shelling, tanks rammed then rolled through its crumbled gates. However, we soon discovered that Tibet's recent tragic history lesson only began there.

That afternoon our guide took us to Sera Monastery, former home of the 5,000 famous fighting monks. Once trained in the martial arts, many gave up their vows to fight for freedom. All that has changed. Today, most skirmishes are between young monks debating in the courtyard.

We, too, were flooded with unanswered questions. Cruising past an exhausting collection of temples and shrines, we probed our well-meaning, but ill-informed guide for more information, asking, "What's that statue?"

"One of Buddha protectors," he'd cough.

"Which Dalai Lama is that?"

"Yellow Hat," he'd mumble.

"What's that?"

"Very old…" he'd whisper, shuffling off.

Finally, frustrated with his non-answers, we supplied a few our own. Chasing after him, we spotted another brooding statue. "Oh, that must be a Yellow Hat!" I proclaimed. Pleased with his students, he nodded in agreement.

From that day on, we fondly called him Wrong Job. As Cheryl explained, "Nice guy…wrong job."

19

Over the next few days Elyse, Gui and Conrad, a German banker, diligently fought frantic mobs at the China South West Air office. For some unexplained reason the airline hadn't booked return seats on the once-a-week flight back to Nepal and the trio was reluctant to overstay their welcome. So, while they battled the bureaucracy, Cheryl, Todd, Fredo (the Italian) and I joined Wrong Job wading through a confusing hodgepodge of Tibetan history, which only created more unanswered questions.

Our first stop was Drepung Monastery, once the world's largest with 10,000 monks. Now its halls and kitchens ring silent, testimony to Beijing's Chinese Religious Bureau. This state-appointed committee controls all aspects of the once-thriving monastic life and reportedly limits monk recruits to those who "love the Communist Party." Consequently, Drepung's dogs, thought to be reincarnated monks who've failed to karmically advance in life's cycle, were more visible than its holy men. Far from the seat of wisdom it once was, all Drepung could muster was a state-orchestrated, Disney-esque diorama of religious tolerance for the traveler's benefit.

Still, in some ways, we felt fortunate to even step across its massive portals. During Mao's Cultural Revolution, thousands of Tibet's temples (perhaps 90 percent) were pillaged and tens of thousands of monks or nuns were killed or sent to concentration camps.

Our next stop, the Norbulinka, was once the Dalai Lama's pristine Summer Palace. Today, it is a neglected garden complex and the Holy Man's former quarters were locked. However, after great persistence, a caretaker understood our wildly animated requests and led us to the hollow shells of two 1927 Baby Austins. Tibet's first cars, the Dalai Lama's pride and joy lay rusting among weeds. Originally carted over the mountain passes in pieces by the 13th Dalai Lama, they were reassembled in the 1950s by the present Dalai Lama then demolished by mobs during the bloody revolt.

Disheartened by Norbulinka's lackluster condition and the temple's cultural sideshow, we approached the Potala Palace, a last visible reminder of the Lama's power, with trepidation.

"What if it, too, is ransacked?" I thought. "What if just a shell remains?"

Fortunately, as we entered, any fears quickly vanished. Spiritual significance aside, the building remains an architectural wonder. Built in the 17th century without steel frames or even nails, the Potala towers thirteen stories, contains 1,000 rooms, 10,000 shrines and 200,000 statues. A monumental achievement, it was built entirely with human and animal power, since the wheel was still unknown in Tibet.

All afternoon we aimlessly wandered its chapels and meditation halls. Fascinated, we explored silent shrines and towering mausoleums whose *chortens* contain dried remains of former Dalai Lamas. Each gargantuan urn was extraordinarily exquisite, studded with precious jewels, turquoise, diamonds, coral, and plated in gold and silver.

But for us, the most fascinating feature was the rooftop apartment that overlooks the sacred city, the chamber of His Holiness Tenzin Gyatso, 14th Dalai Lama. In its simplicity and frigid, symbolic loneliness, it supposedly remains in the same condition as when he fled into exile to India in 1959.

For an instant, huddled atop the gusty rooftop, surrounded by the sweeping, snowcapped panorama of the Himalayas, Cheryl and I were deeply chilled by the challenge confronting us.

Then, mysteriously, we were blanketed with a warm, reassuring comfort: a feeling as though we would never be alone on our journey. And any doubts we had vanquished in the wind.

Our days in Lhasa quickly passed. We learned to go inside the hotel kitchen and point to what we wanted to eat. Our companions eventually found passage back to Nepal, and even Wrong Job, thinking his nickname was one of affection, started to brush up on his Buddhism. Still, we faced one final hurdle: securing the dreaded Alien Travel Permits (ATPs).

There were horror stories about how, in the past, if travelers were stopped in a city not on their permit, they could be fined, expelled or worse—forced to write a "self-criticism" about how their ancestors would be ashamed of their actions.

For a moment, I considered bluffing our way through, but was convinced there were already too many unknowns. I didn't want to leave any more to chance than was absolutely necessary. Who knew if permits were actually needed? Nonetheless, I hated the prospect of trekking halfway across Tibet, only to be sent back by some Uzi-toting soldier just because we didn't have the right papers.

When we first arrived in Lhasa, Khada's manager promised to talk to his *very good friends* at the Regional Police who issued ATPs for Gyantse, Shigatse, Lhazê, Tingri, Mount Everest and the border at Khasa. He did and just two days before our departure we received ATPs—valid for only ten days. We were devastated and simmered on a slow boil.

"We can't walk across Tibet in ten days!" we fumed.

The manager, the perfect *functionaire*, just shrugged, mindlessly shuffling papers on his desk.

I appealed to our ol' friend, Wrong Job. "Please, can you explain this to him?"

Although aghast that I dare ask him to question a superior, he hesitantly conferred with the bureaucrat, then announced, "He told you to get another one in Shigatse."

"We can't even trek to Shigatse by then!" Cheryl countered. It was anyone's guess how far ten days would actually carry us, but it seemed that that metropolis was out of the question. It was nearly 340 kilometers (211 miles) away.

As they spoke again, a nervous Wrong Job did most of the listening, obviously intimidated by the local dictator. Then, with a sudden hush, a final pronouncement was made. "Sorry," Wrong Job mumbled, turning inside-out in shame, "That is all he can do."

"Look," whispered Losang, our other nearly absent guide, "I'll take you to the Regional Police. Maybe you can trade this permit for another."

Although a temporary reprieve, it meant there was still hope in a country where, already, grasping at straws seemed like a way of life.

Shortly after, the three of us arrived at the police station, which looked sternly officious outside and was nearly deserted inside. Tiptoeing through the lobby, we gingerly climbed upstairs to find someone, anyone, and proceeded until a pissy-assed voice out of nowhere whined, "You waiiit downstair!"

Scurrying back to ground level, we waited. And waited. Then tried three more times at three different offices to find THE official.

"Yoo waiiit, yoo!" each clerk screamed with crane-like squawks, shooing us away.

We continued pacing for nearly an hour. Finally Losang, with frustration and shattered nerves equal to ours, disappeared, only to slink back a few tense moments later. "Police station closed today. Saturday," he explained with a weary shake his head.

"Then who are these people?" I sighed.

"Their office open. Yours closed…at least till Monday." It seemed the Lhasa Police Department closes to foreigners on weekends. Losang's defeatist tone implied we might be delayed even longer.

Hearing the bad news, Cheryl ceased her vulture-like circling and pleaded, "Does anyone else issue ATPs?"

"Well, we could go City Police."

That's all we needed to hear. We were off. Thirty minutes later, we reached another nondescript office staffed by another single mousy clerk suggesting, "You may find Duty Officer at Holiday Inn."

Though she sounded dubious, what choice did we have? Bolting out the door, we bounded over to Lhasa's luxury hotel.

With its synthetic sameness, the inn could have been in Lima, Peru or Lima, Ohio. The only noticeable difference was the Duty Officer, fingering a long knife in the lobby. Apparently there had been an "ethnic" fight in the bar the night before and he was putting the final touches on another open-and-shut case. As one might expect in Lhasa, where Tibetans are outnumbered, ethnic tensions simmer just below a frosted Himalayan surface.

However, he willingly led us back to the station and quickly issued the necessary papers—this time good for a month. "Pick up another in Shigatse," he echoed. "Theirs will take you to the border." Then, reflecting on our unpredictable journey, he whispered a fatherly concern. "You really want to walk?"

Nodding with unshakable certainty, I prematurely breathed a sigh of relief, certain we'd cleared the final hurdle. What a mistake. The one last problem, one we couldn't count on, surfaced the very day we left.

Each of us, except my partner, had battled fevers and lingering chest colds since our arrival. Perhaps it was the lack of heat. Or maybe it was the altitude of 3,658+ meters (12,000+ feet). Still, after five days in Lhasa, just as I started to shake mine, Cheryl succumbed, awakening in a damp, feverish cloud. Although a 1000-kilometer high-altitude trek was the last thing she needed, the clock was ticking. The Himalayan snows would never wait. We'd press on.

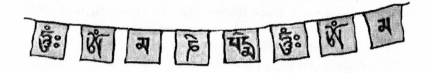

Chapter |||

So Long, Shangri-La

Be generous.
Travel lightly. All in life is a gift.
What you don't need, give away.

October 18

Our trek began in earnest, a yak stew of minor successes, major failures. The trouble began early in the day when we simply tried to pay our hotel bill. It took the intractable manager nearly an hour to eventually find change in the local FECs, Chinese tourist currency. But I couldn't blame him. It really wasn't his fault.

Blame the government since they adamantly insist on having two currencies in a rural country that survived pretty well for centuries on barter.

The problem begins when travelers exchange their hard foreign currency at banks and can only receive FECs, the money required in Lhasa for visitor transactions. Unfortunately, the rest of Tibet had never even seen them since they spend RMBs, fondly called "remmie-bees." Essentially, FECs are worthless except for splurges on overpriced imports at government Friendship Stores. Since it's impossible for locals to buy those treasures anywhere else, they're forced into accepting FECs if they want to buy demon-capitalist luxuries like soft toilet paper, chocolate, foreign soaps and cigarettes. Both locals and travelers are forced into patronizing a booming black market blatantly operating from Lhasan street corners.

Eventually, with perseverance, this underground system succeeded. Finally, with a fistful of FECs stuffed deep inside our moneybelts, we blurted out *"Ghale zhuu"* to our first Chinese pen-pushers and excitedly headed west.

Traffic was light, which was a blessing. If we had to dodge cars and weave through *tuk-tuks* while loaded like mules, our pace would've been even slower. Those packs were heavier and more cumbersome than we remembered. We would soon suffer the consequences.

Wending through a paradise gone mad, we passed dusty, tattered-robed pilgrims who had no inkling of our mission. After their long journeys, viewing the sacred Potala Palace for the first time, those devout wanderers threw themselves down right in the street.

Although we didn't join them, we at least stopped for one last glimpse of the sacred icon, hoping that it would give us strength. Then sauntering past a bridge festooned with prayer flags, we bought a strand of those red, blue, green, yellow and white pendants to fly from our packs, figuring we'd need all the help we could get to reach Kathmandu.

Finally, whispering a hopeful prayer, we set off on the first steps of our odyssey.

God, help us.

Row after row of drab concrete block Han houses lined that main thoroughfare where troops wasted their day as soldiers anywhere do: washing cars, listening to music, eating, visiting families, and generally wishing they were somewhere else. But soon, all those familiar treats and trappings of a city disappeared, as we stepped back onto a bleak, lonely landscape—a dustbin dissected by black ribbon. It was the same foreboding sight that welcomed us a week earlier.

"Only now," I thought, "now it's one step at a time."

We trekked in silence across a parched plain leading to infinity. Absolute desolation stretched as far as the eye could see, farther than we could trudge in any given day. The sun's rays were relentless, as constant as the wind that slashed like wet bamboo across our naked faces. Both forces slowly sapped our energy. Both quickly made us question why we were out there to begin with.

For hours there was no glimmer of life. Then abruptly, we'd spot the shaggy shadows of yaks nibbling sparse, cow-licked grass in a meager meadow, or a startled pilgrim, surprised by backpacking Westerners. With a conciliatory smile, a wave, and cheery greeting of *"Tashi delek,"* we passed all too quickly on to our solitary mission. Before long, they melded into just another smudge on a fanciful horizon.

With plodding progress we pushed ourselves leaning into the wind. Until in late afternoon, panting, Cheryl stumbled onto the gravel shoulder muttering, "I'm ready...to stop."

The 3,657-meter (12,000-foot) altitude, an 18-kilometer (11-mile) hike, 35-pound pack and cold had all taken their toll. Clearly, I wasn't faring much better. Fortunately a cluster of adobe huts stood just ahead.

"Come on. Just a little farther," I promised. "Maybe we can camp over there."

Carefully easing Cheryl to her feet, we staggered that last hundred yards together and nervously approached a woman whose face glowed with the same ochre patina of the potato fields where she stooped. Since we had never had any personal contact with Tibetans before, it was anyone's guess how open or friendly they might be.

Desperate to lick our wounds, I shouted, *"Tashi delek,"* trying to sound both genuine and harmless.

She paused digging for a moment. With an incredulous grin, she replied, *"Tashi delek."*

"Well, that's encouraging," I thought. We had purchased a Tibetan phrase book in Kathmandu and it was a relief to know it wasn't some obscure dialect only spoken in one remote village. Today it seemed the slim volume and pantomime were the only things separating us from *pung-gus*, the donkeys in her field.

Approaching, I sketched a tent in the dirt for the startled farmer. Although confused, she quickly caught on and inferred, "Well, if you really want to sleep in my potato field."

Now normally, one might consider that an inconsequential victory. But in the Tibet, we'd soon learn to savor every little success, appreciate every minor breakthrough along the way. Unrolling our nylon two-person tent, the spirited elder pitched-in, as if she knew exactly what she was doing, and soon our tiny shelter popped up between narrow furrows in the field.

Searching the horizon, I pointed skyward in my best TV-Indian sign language, asking, "Rain?"

She cocked her head, as if more bewildered by my ridiculous sign language than my garbled Tibetan. Quickly I thumbed through the book, the first of over a thousand times. "Where," I thought, "are those easy-to-learn, snappy Tibetan repartees when you need them?"

I tried again, asking, "*Chaa-ba deng-giy re-bay?*" Will it rain? Should we put up our rain flap?

Politely smiling at my silly attempt at her tongue, she shook a weathered head, assuring us it would be a clear night or so I understood.

After carefully scrutinizing us, one by one, other bashful villagers slowly emerged from modest adobe huts across a tiny stream. Curiously they stared at perhaps the first Westerners they'd ever met face-to-face, certainly the first to sleep in their field. Soon we found ourselves surrounded by a swarm of twenty kids ranging from five to twelve-years-old. Only then did "Grandma," a serene, toothless woman who looked to be about eighty, shuffle over. Peering inside our futuristic tent, she spotted Cheryl, already pitifully curled up in her sleeping bag.

"What's the matter with her?" Grandma mimed.

Again I frantically leafed through our book, searching for the right word, until I finally declared, "*Cham-ba!*" hoping it meant a cold and not something insulting.

Grandma understood. Hacking, as if to confirm my barefoot doctor diagnosis, she scurried off to her crude adobe hut at the speed of a woman half her age. Moments later she returned, toting a thermos nearly half her size.

"*Cha!*" she declared, thrusting the bottle at me.

I nodded, a little confused. "Yes." Sure, whatever *cha* is…

"*Cha!*" She repeated, emphatically shaking my sleeve, insisting I wake Cheryl.

We quickly learned that *cha*, or tea, was the Tibetan cure-all: a Himalayan chicken soup. But that was just the beginning of my lesson.

While Cheryl gingerly sipped the steamy brew, Grandma lectured me, as near as I could tell, on how crazy it was to travel with her in such a sad state, how our packs were too heavy, how she wasn't guzzling enough tea. Then thrusting a gnarled finger at my neatly trimmed beard, her wrinkled face curled into a gremlin's grimace. Well, I couldn't argue with her first points. Although it was crazy to start such a journey when you're half-dead, picking on my furry growth was not fair game. Still, I bit my tongue, humoring her, "I know. My grandmother always said the same thing..."

At just that instant, inexplicably interrupting our "tea social," Grandma made an ominous sound, a deep primeval growl and mimed a monster, seeming to warn us that someone...or something...was going to cross the road and harm us.

Frantically I looked around. There was nothing, nothing at least that I could see. Then, just as suddenly, the grizzled little woman excitedly leapt to her feet, shuffling off to gather stones to throw at whatever it was. I still didn't have a clue what she was so afraid of.

Meanwhile the twenty ragged urchins who'd circled for an hour took that as their cue, swooping down like vultures to a Parsi funeral. Insatiably curious, those kids gingerly poked and inspected everything, fascinated by the simplest items: a tent zipper, cook stove, zip-lock bag. They even studied me with unconcealed glee. Giggling, they brushed the hairs on my arm back and forth in amazement, since Tibetans are nearly hairless.

Over the next few hours those potato patch pals and I became best friends while my companion dozed. I taught them how to count in English and they chirped back in Tibetan, "*Chig, nyi, sum, shi, nga, thru, dun, gyay, gu, ju.*"

Later, giving each of them a Tibetan animal name, they jumped at the chance to bark, shriek, squawk, moo or buzz. Saving the most graphic for last, I pointed to myself growling, "*Miy-go!*" Abominable snowman!

By sunset, both our limited phrase book and I were exhausted. Those kids were starved for outside contact and we covered all my book's handy phrases, except an extensive list of illnesses and "Please take these suitcases to my room." I didn't think we'd need those.

With night spilling over the silhouetted mountains, it was time to fire up the cookstove. Unfortunately, by the time I switched to the right fuel jets, I had almost set the fields ablaze. Oh, what a pathetic display of Western ingenuity! I was glad the kids had already scooted home for their supper of *tsampa*, more yak butter tea and precious potato nuggets, so I was able to salvage what was left of my dignity. However, news of strangers spreads quickly out on that remote Tibetan plateau.

Those urchins were replaced by the equally inquisitive shadows of farmers who kindly offered us a place to spend the night. Maybe it was my cookstove struggle that prompted their generous offers, but I declined. Cheryl was already in hibernation and I thought it'd be too rough striking camp in the dark. Before long, I regretted that hasty refusal.

The woman's "no rain" forecast proved disastrous. Just after midnight, the sides of our tent were furiously whipped by almost gale-force winds. It beat so hard that I expected our tent to be tossed into that nearby stream. Then the rains pounded like a natural tympani, followed by blinding hail which pelted our thin shell for thirty minutes.

"This is the acid test," I thought. "Will our tent hold? It's the first time we've ever used it. How much can it stand? How much can we?"

That chaos grew in intensity, threatening to soak us to the skin, until eventually I whispered, "Cheryl, you awake? Cheryl? Think we should we put on the rain fly?"

She didn't reply, not even a groan. Anyway, I already knew her answer. Neither of us was ready to rush naked into that deluge. No one wanted to battle the roaring wind to attach a nylon cover. It was futile, like flying a kite in a hurricane. Besides, it was clearly too late. So we lay there, silent, hesitant to move, afraid to touch the tent ceiling and risk drowning in a potato field.

"Next time," I swore, "next time we're going to take advantage of anyone's kind offer to follow them home."

Eventually the winds did die down and we trusted the worst was over. But no such luck. At two in the morning, the hail returned to slash with blinding force. The sides and roof, weakened by the first barrage, leaked like a sieve and all we could do was hang on tight. Luckily we'd slipped our down sleeping bags into nylon bivys that offered some protection. But it was three tense hours before the tempest finally passed.

Although it could have been much worse, our limp bags were left cold and damp. Nevertheless, the tent didn't blow away. We'd learned a few critical lessons in planning. We'd survive.

October 19

Just past dawn we were awakened by tiny voices and fumbling fingers struggling to unzip our tent fly.

"Hey!" I groaned, still in a daze. "Stay out!" After last night, it was too early to provide any more entertainment for our eager hosts.

At the grating sound of my voice, Cheryl rolled over, awake from the dead, adding, "Go awayyy!" But they persisted, relentless and impossible to ignore.

Reluctantly we climbed out of our battered blue balloon and stepped onto a soggy field shrouded in light mist. The sun rose and filtered through slender trees baking our private potato patch. With the kid's enthusiastic help, we spread and dried our dripping tent, bags and bivys in its graceful rays. After helping repack our nomadic home, the boys, some looking as if they'd slept in a haystack, horsed around and cracked woven yak hair slingshots like whips.

Nearby, a beautiful girl with doe-like eyes timidly watched our antics, waiting, chewing a chunk of dried yak cheese until we finished. Then sloshing over to her house for yak butter tea, *po-ja*, she returned with the milky brew which quickly warmed our wet bodies and soaked spirits.

"Now this," I thought, "this is real yak butter tea!" Savoring it much more than the Khada's sickly imitation, we were soon ready to trudge on, except for one final detail.

Before leaving, we sneaked past a pack of growling mongrels and climbed over a pattern of swollen furrows to Grandma's whitewashed adobe. Finding her at her gray weathered door, I gently handed the generous lady a postcard photo of the Dalai Lama.

"Here, we wanted to give you this."

At first, she stared at the photo as if she didn't recognize him. After all, he'd fled Tibet over thirty years before, and anyone, even a god-king, ages. Finally, tilting her wrinkled head, she brought the photo to within two inches of her brown eyes that suffering from glaucoma but were still so full of life. She beamed.

We resumed our trek down the dusty road toward the bridge leading to Gonggar Airport. Even if the hostile surroundings remained the same, it was surprising how quickly the weather could change. One minute we were roasting under a harsh sun, while virtually the next we were shivering in shade. Sadly our pace was more sluggish than the day before, as we plodded into a stiff, near freezing head-wind. There were no villages or stores, no trucks, few people. The only Tibetans we passed stared in awed disbelief, heads cocked, silently wondering, "Why would foreigners hike out here?"

"Will the rest of the country be as stark and unforgiving as this," I asked? "Maybe it's truly as desolate and impossible as those Chinese Embassy naysayers warned." As if that wasn't enough to worry about, our bloated packs became more of a ball and chain with each labored step.

"What can we sell?" I pondered. "What can we leave at the next village? If there ever is a next village." It was like that Zen riddle, "What is the sound of one traveler collapsing?" I kept coming up empty.

We had so little considering what we faced, with only enough food for five days, ten at half-rations. Puzzled, I searched for an answer in our original plan.

"Maybe we can buy a yak or mule in Gyantse? There must be something we can load these packs onto and just walk a thousand kilometers. That's got to be hard enough."

As I struggled to find an answer, that tiny voice in my mind suggested we were paying back some strange pack animal karma...

Late that afternoon, bone-tired and bone-dry, we stumbled past Netang, a Buddhist monastery the size of a roadside café. Hailing monks who huddled in a circle, we were waved over. While they surrounded us, each inspecting our packs and marveling at my partner's high-tech, expandable, aluminum walking stick, a young initiate with close-cropped hair asked that inevitable question, "Where are you going?"

Did we dare answer? Would it infuriate some local official? Or merely jinx us? Cautiously eyeing them, Cheryl hesitantly mumbled, "Kathmandu."

Astonished, another gasped, "Where are you from?"

"America," I offered to more astonished "Ahhs!" Quickly changing the subject, since I was unsure if Americans were welcome in China's Tibet, I asked, "How far is the bridge? *Zampa?*" That question had been on our minds for miles. We desperately needed encouragement and the overpass marked the airport turnoff. Plus, there was sure to be water and our canteens had been empty for hours.

"Six kilometers (four miles)," they replied, wondering why I was looking for a bridge.

God, I hope water's closer than that. Thinking maybe there's a well nearby, I continued, "Village? *Dhrongsay?*"

"Six kilometers."

We'll never make it.

Tired of me beating around the monks, Cheryl pleaded, "Water?" through cracked lips. "*Chu-coma?*"

In her unmistakable condition, they realized what we really wanted and instantly fetched a shiny red thermos, filling our one-liter plastic jugs with boiled *chu*. Although we thanked them profusely, words alone seemed insufficient. Never had something so simple meant so much to us.

With another essential word for Tibetan survival under our belts, we continued toward that bridge. We trekked alone until we were pleasantly surprised a kilometer later by an eight-year-old monk who joined us for five or six kilometers more. Patiently he endured my one repeated question, demanded like a squirming, bladder-bloated kid on a family outing. "How far is the village, now?"

That miniature holy man was equally kind in his concern for Cheryl, who diligently struggled fifty yards behind. For a while, out of concern for her safety, I slowed down to drag along beside her. But as she reminded me, we agreed from the very beginning to set our own pace and, "Not," as she bravely joked, "hike the entire thousand kilometers joined at the hip."

It was probably better anyway since I had my own problems, and I'm not convinced that misery always loves company. Only inertia kept me moving. Already my back throbbed from that unwieldy pack. Four blisters on one foot and six on the other forced me to constantly shift weight to skirt the piercing pain.

Yet even though each step brought searing agony, we trudged another ninety minutes to that village *just around the next bend*. Every turn on the distant horizon promised relief, but they were empty promises. Exhausted and losing the sun behind the valley walls, we finally stopped. As near as anyone could tell, we were still two kilometers (1.2 miles) from the village when we set up camp at the base of a sheer rock face, barely protected from the perpetually ripping winds.

At first, we assumed we were as alone as we'd been for kilometers. Nevertheless, just as we started to heat water for dinner, two smirking Tibetan girls popped their heads out of a nearby trench where they'd been working. But at that point, we were too tired to care.

October 20

By the time we gobbled our hot porridge and instant coffee, it was late in the morning. It was hardly the breakfast of marathon trekkers. By then it was already a stifling 80°F. Groggy, I stumbled down to the icy, glacier-fed river to dunk my head into its churning waters and refill our canteens.

As I pumped its silty fluid into each bottle, I couldn't help but wonder, "Is this filter actually going to do anything?" It was another high-tech wonder we bought before just leaving. Any accolades were reserved for later when only our bowels would tell.

Eventually we left in search of the elusive bridge that promised us a meager measure of success. Our pathetic pace was even slower than the day before, as we shuffled in a wretched rhythm. My feet were half-covered in seeping water blisters drained the night before, and Cheryl's cold steadily worsened, making her lag behind even my labored pace. Just as I began to believe the village was some cruel hoax, three kilometers (nearly two miles) past our campsite, we spotted a sight to feverishly spur us on—a bridge sprouting fluttering strands of prayer flags!

Thrilled, we hobbled at a full tilt run to the hilltop, only to scan a vacant horizon.

"This isn't the bridge to Gonggar!" I yelled. Anger had already teased and goaded me the edge. "This isn't *our* bridge, the *right* bridge, the one we've spurred ourselves so hard to reach. There's no village here! Just a pack of soldiers, shouting, 'Herrrr-o! Herrrr-o!'"

Cheryl flopped onto the sand at the river's edge as we cowered on the shore. Our heads reeled with disappointment, questioning the lunacy of our plan. Still, without saying another word, we faced what had to be done and set off again.

Desert sand flowed from the road, disappearing into craggy monoliths rising to either side. Sea gulls, far from any ocean, circled overhead. Boatmen lunching by the swift river waved and offered us a lift downstream in their yak skin ferry, but we reluctantly declined, insistent on journeying alone by foot.

Soon the river vanished as in a dream. Alone in our thoughts and fears, we eventually passed a fortress-like village where sturdy adobe walls surrounded squat one-storied huts. Burros sought shade beside that bastion, motionless like Mexican yard ornaments sweltering in the scorching heat. Ragged children rolled in a sandpit beside the road until they spotted us, easy prey.

All ten charged like crazed trolls screaming, "*Kuchi! Kuchi! Kuchi!*"

Saddled with my useless pack, I swaggered, trying to keep a steady pace as wee fingers grotesquely wriggled and the kids demanded sweets–their toll for letting us pass.

"Do I give them something?" I wondered. "What, and teach them to beg? That has to be one of the worst things a traveler can do."

So I shuffled through their gauntlet as quickly as I could. I was barely halfway across when I felt tiny hands tugging at the sleep pad strapped to the bottom of my pack.

Enough! Wheeling around, I towered over them, shook my fist, screwed my face into a ferocious scowl and howled a menacing, "Arrrgggrowllll!"

Shocked, they retreated, but only for an instant. Cheryl was a better target because she was slower, and they'd lost some of their inhibitions with me. She, too, tried to ignore those monsters until she felt rocks pelting her pack. They were stoning her!

Furious, she spun around waving her shillelagh and wailed, "All right, you little pests! Take your best shot!"

Scared "dungless," they scattered.

Heat waves rose from a tabletop road. Dust swirled off the parched plain in miniature twisters, twirling into a cloudless sky. Solitary, we resumed our pitiful shuffle, consumed by sadness in what had just happened, until we noticed blurred figures inching toward us.

"Are they two kilometers away? Ten? Who can tell?"

Within an hour those stick figures gradually transformed into a spry old gent and his grandson herding their cows. There was something truly remarkable about them. Even at a distance, his weathered eyes appeared to radiate from beneath an embroidered fox fur hat.

We continued to approach, fascinated, and we were just an arm's length away when the herder extended two sinewy arms, palms up, in universal welcome. Instinctively, I set my hands on his and became mysteriously transfixed by a magnetic power emanating from his eyes. For a long moment, he held my hands, glowing. I swear I felt his raw energy pulse into my open palms, a surge of human electricity, a power to combat the brutal strength of that fierce wind. With that, leaning slightly forward, the venerable stranger lightly cracked his forehead into mine before repeating his mystical ceremony with my partner. Then broadly smiling and politely bowing, he seemed to bid us safe journey.

Confounded, yet energized, we set off more reluctantly, examining our flurry of emotions. To the kids we were a curiosity, a traveling sideshow offering treats and entertainment. But to their more enlightened elders, we were all just weary pilgrims: sweaty, dusty, all trekking the same path.

By late afternoon, searing aches and gasped breaths consumed our every thought again, as our pace slowed to a crawl. At one point, two boys glided up on bicycles, generously offering to carry our packs. It was a grand temptation. Still, we refused. Like silent sentinels, they insisted on walking bikes beside us for the duration of the next kilometer as we struggled to find a solution. It was difficult forming words in the dry blasts of desert air.

"We can't go on like this," I gasped. "We're growing weaker every day."

Gathering her strength, Cheryl panted, "These packs…there's no way we can carry them…thirty kilometers a day."

"Can't leave them behind either." I was certain of that, since I'd considered little else since leaving Lhasa. "Look, we've got two options. We can find something to carry them and walk alongside."

"I could get a four-wheeler in Lhasa…to carry everything…and drive ahead." My lover shifted her load from sore shoulders to aching lower back one more time. "I can have camp set up…before you arrive…" There was a hopeful tone in her voice, as if she thought I might consider trekking alone.

"If she drives," I thought, "this'll be one lonely journey. At this pace, it could take me sixty days to cross Tibet. More if it snows. No, that's impossible. Now I'm starting to sound like them."

"Look," I suggested, huffing, "we'll find someone in Chuzal Dzong with a cart. He can carry our packs as far as Gyantse or Shigatse. We'll just find someone there to take his place. Or maybe we can find a mule or yak?"

"Maybe…" she muttered, staring down at the ground inching by.

We both knew the other option, but weren't willing to even consider it…not yet.

Although Chuzal Dzong boasts only one main hotel, after potato patch camping, its simple concrete block room with five steel frame beds was sheer luxury. Its long front window (or where the glass would have been if it hadn't disappeared years ago) overlooked crimson, naked mountains. Last cleaned during the Chinese invasion, its squat toilet reeked, and until we insisted, the floor hadn't been swept in decades judging from heaps of rotting scraps and empty bottles scattered beneath the beds. Yet given all that, its restaurant was a welcome oasis that served icy Lhasa Beer, our fondest desert fantasy.

As an enthusiastic waiter popped two bottles, creamy foam cascaded into an amber pool onto our table. Laughing, he nonchalantly wiped it onto the bare concrete floor where it was eagerly lapped by two scrawny, appreciative restaurant hounds.

BRANDON WILSON

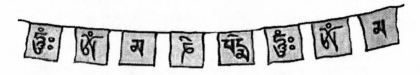

Chapter IV

If Wishes Were Horses...

Be a friend.
Folks on the trail impact your life, if just for a moment.
All too soon they leave to follow their own path. Bid them good journey.
Thank them for their gift.

October 21

Chuzal Dzong was three gritty, unpaved streets, boasting a couple of general stores all touting the same Chinese goods; a pool hall; a smaller café frying more spicy Szechwan and an audio cassette cum sweet shop. It wasn't much. But I figured it was our only chance to find something with four legs to carry our packs and someone with two to guide us to Gyantse. Unfortunately, at first glance there were few horses, ponies, donkeys or mules in that smudge of a town—let alone any for sale.

All morning, like a highwayman, I ambushed each infrequent startled donkey cart driver plodding that main dirt thoroughfare, quizzing them on the run in wild, comic pantomime and broken Tibetan. Most simply snickered and kept on clopping. In no time at all, it was clear I was getting nothing accomplished except perfecting a routine as the new village idiot.

Eventually I spotted a donkey and his owner resting in the shade of the hamlet's pathetic outdoor market. "At least," I thought, "they're a captive audience. It'll be harder to escape."

Sidling over to the gaunt, spiritless man propped against the whitewashed wall, I smugly offered a cordial, *"Tashi delek!"* It was the one phrase I had down pat. After that, well, it was all touch-and-go.

Glancing over at me, he smirked beneath a beat-up felt hat, amused by my childish grasp of his difficult language. *"Tashi delek,"* he reluctantly replied.

Hey, it was a start. So I continued in herky-jerky Tibetan, "I…want… donkey…go… Gyantse. *Yuan?"*

At that, my reluctant prospect began to lead his sturdy cart away.

"Wait!" I continued to mime, blocking his path. "We've walked from Lhasa…Potala…Dalai Lama…go Gyantse." I pointed west.

He paused for a second, wistfully scratching a sparsely whiskered chin.

"He seems interested," I thought. "Can't let him slip away."

So I continued acting out, "Packs too heavy!" as I hoisted an imaginary backpack and fell to my knees. To that he merely snorted in vague interest. So I shifted tactics and began appealing to his empathy while still blocking the way, just in case he tried to make a run for it!

"My wife," I explained, gesturing that familiar hourglass shape, "has cold, *cham-ba.*" (I hoped it wasn't the word for rain.) "And me," I added, pointing to my soles, "bad feet." Then smiling, I nodded to his precious cart imploring, "So we need your donkey."

It was harder than any game of charades and the stakes were definitely higher.

Shaking his head, he chuckled. Whether he was laughing at my antics or our situation, I couldn't tell. But I took it as a good sign.

"My feet…no good either," he countered, casting lively eyes down to his plum colored, swollen toes gruesomely poking through remnants of battered Chinese Army sneakers.

"We walk," I insisted, strutting off like Groucho Marx down the road. Then, pointing at him, I patted the cart seat promising, "You ride here." Shrugging off my imaginary bag, I gestured to the cart's bed adding, "Packs here." But that dubious tilt of his head told me he was far from convinced. My suspicions were quickly confirmed when he led his cart into the street.

"*Whey! Whey!*" I shouted, since that was the extent of my Chinese and I wasn't ready to start all over with someone else. "How much… *pung-gu*…seven days…Gyantse?"

He stopped, bewildered, as though trying to piece it all together.

Quickly I gestured as though paying him. "I give you 100…*gya yuan*."

"That's a fair price," I thought, ready to seal the deal. Then thumbing through our handy phrase book, I added, "*Diy ya-go du-gay?*" ("Is this good?")

Although hesitant, he relented, mumbling, "*Diy ya-go du.*" ("It's good.")

"Great! We leave in two days," I announced, drawing a finger twice across the sky as I'd seen done in so many westerns. "Friday." That pleased him even more. "Eight o'clock." I sketched an eight in the sand and, pointing down the street, added, "Meet us at hotel."

"He seems to understand," I thought.

However for good measure, I asked one last time. "*Diy ya-go du-gay?*" to which he responded with a languid nod, "*Diy ya-go du.*"

As our new partner turned to leave, I remembered to ask his name. "*Kyo-ray ming ka-ray ray?*"

"Patron."

"Patron, *ya go*," I shouted after him, only hoping his name matched his character.

October 23

Well, no Patron appeared on Friday. We finally found him nursing his swollen foot in town, clearly unable or unwilling to join our journey. So while Cheryl took advantage of the delay by restoring her health with the hotel's specialty, yak filled *momos* in hot pepper sauce, I continued my quest for the hard-to-find horse.

It became strikingly clear that Chuzal was the epitome of the "one horse town." And they weren't selling. Once I came very close. A sympathetic shopkeeper agreed to sell her white pony and cart for 1200 RMBs. But as luck would have it, I was seven hundred yuan short and she refused to take dollars or those worthless FECs, neither of which she'd ever seen before.

So I sprinted out to change money, but even that became a chore. There were no banks, not one. Not even one of those pesky, "Psst. Psst. Hey Misstah. Change money? Change money?" blackmarket dealers.

By the time I returned, our horse trader had already closed up shop and vanished. Discouraged and cursing our fate, I returned to the hotel thinking that maybe our wheeler-dealer manager could change dollars. She seemed savvy enough. Then I could meet the merchant in the morning.

"Sure, how much do you want change?" the pompous queen of Chuzal Dzong clucked, as she picked her yellowed front teeth with a pinky nail.

"We need to buy a horse, so probably…"

"Why you not buy mine?" she seductively offered, turning and thrusting a chubby digit towards a healthy dappled mare grazing behind the inn.

I was open to that. Why, I was open to almost anything.

"How much?"

That one naive question was the starting gun for a haggle-athon that lasted nearly an hour. Until finally, exhausted, we agreed on 1500 yuan. Sure, it was more than the other lady wanted, but I was relieved and felt we got a decent price on a good mare. Besides, I already sensed a horse would mean the difference between success and failure of our mission.

Unfortunately, any hope for celebration was immediately dashed. For as soon as we entered the kitchen, inexplicably, it was no longer her mare. It was the chef's! So frustrated negotiations began anew with a slight serious man in between the cacophonous caterwauling of waiters, simmering soups and frying noodles. Talks finally stalled at a figure three hundred yuan higher than her last offer. And he refused to budge.

So with great reluctance everyone agreed to, "Sleep on it and talk tomorrow—Saturday."

October 24

During breakfast, for some unknown reason, the capricious cook avoided us and any further negotiations. We silently fumed and stewed in the dining room, wondering how to resolve our problem.

"Like our brother," we vowed.

As reluctant as our new horse, or *da*, was to leave his country home, it soon became equally clear how hesitant he was to exchange his hefty horse cart for our backpacks.

Back at the hotel, while Cheryl held Sadhu, the cook and I gingerly eased seventy pounds of attached packs over his head and onto his wobbly saddle—a big mistake. As soon as he saw that load, Sadhu reared up and snorted with a maniacal glare. Snapping the worn leather lead tying him to the post, he deftly shook Cheryl loose and stormed toward the courtyard gate!

"Stop him!" I screamed. I lunged for his saddle, which easily wrenched off in my hand and sent me sprawling in the dirt. Jumping up, I joined Cheryl, the chef and his four assistants in a galloping chase down the street with everyone frantically screaming, "*Daaa! Daaa! Daaa!*"

Several villagers gossiped at a nearby *chang* or barley beer booth. Hearing us, one grizzled man calmly set down his grog and stepped forward. Inexplicably, that wild gelding stopped dead in his tracks. Gently, the bystander reached up, grabbed Sadhu's bridle and casually handed him to me, as if that sort of thing happens all the time in a one-*da*-town.

And, after another more cautious loading, this time from his rear, we finally set off for Shigatse.

Sadhu's outburst aside, I was proud our expedition had increased to a threesome. I was fully convinced, with nearly a thousand kilometers (621 miles) and several 5000-meter (17,000-foot) passes ahead, Sadhu would soon become our most valued friend.

"Sadhu? Wait..." The great cosmic pun suddenly hit. In Tibetan his name meant chestnut, the color of his hair. But in Nepal, where we were headed, a *sadhu* is a wandering holy man. Call it coincidence, but I like to believe he was meant to join us.

In late afternoon we spotted two silhouettes meandering down the windswept road. It wasn't until we pulled alongside that we recognized the two young, burgundy-robed monks we had met the night before outside our hotel. They had been peddling meager possessions to buy food until Cheryl insisted on buying them *momos*.

Instantly they recognized us, cheerfully miming that they, too, were bound for Shigatse. So we trekked together nearly twenty kilometers (12.5 miles) until, weary and famished, we neared a cluster of low-set mud houses. As Tenbo, the taller twenty-year-old monk, cautiously approached the first hut to beg for shelter, his companion, Thubten, kept a wary eye out for the region's notoriously vicious dogs.

Asking people to sleep in their home was new to us, since we'd either camped or stayed in run-down inns so far. But I was intrigued about everyday Tibetan life and eager to learn what went on behind those high adobe walls.

At the first hut, Tenbo was politely turned away and he tried another. Although a chained snarling mutt with piercing yellow eyes guarded the next house, he narrowly slid past. In short measure, he convinced a frail, bent woman to provide shelter for four ragged travelers and their *da*.

Then she personally escorted us past the demon-dog that howled and snapped, furious that he couldn't rip into us.

We couldn't help but be impressed by the woman's genuine hospitality. Although I'd read somewhere that Buddhists consider welcoming travelers one of the greatest services they can perform, I'd never actually seen it.

"Imagine a Westerner letting strangers into their home like this?" I mused, as we stepped across her wooden portal.

Inside, goats, sheep and yaks were tied around the wide dirt corral. Mounds of straw were piled to one side under a small roof, while an unpretentious two-room cottage was set to the other. Immediately we unsaddled Sadhu. Luckily, removing his packs was easier than putting them on, especially when hay or a bucket of *tsampa* and water completely distracted him. After tightly tying his thick canvas bridle to a wooden stall post, the four of us collapsed on the nearby porch.

Famished, the monks immediately scrambled to pull wooden bowls and *tsampa* from hidden crevasses under multi-layered robes. We were hungry too and dug deep within our packs for a foil packet of dehydrated food to split. Then our generous hostess shuffled back and forth to her small fire, as she served us a bowl of roasted barley, a sort of Tibetan popcorn, followed by a thermos of *cha-dang* or black tea.

Our companions were eager to show us the correct way to make a Tibetan standard called *pag* and shocked that we didn't already know how. What were we living on, anyway? Shaking just the right amount of *tsampa* into their bowl, they added a little steaming brewed tea and kneaded it all together. Then using fingers, they gobbled the cookie-like dough with undisguised gusto.

Well, after that, our dehydrated food seemed blasé. But our instant packet dinner equally intrigued those monks. We were happy to nonchalantly play the role of trail galloping gourmets, saying, "Just add boiling water. Wait ten minutes." They were duly impressed.

Shortly after sundown, taking the hint from our hostess, we spread out sleeping bags on her front porch. Meanwhile, the monks retreated to a private corner of the corral to meditate. After our nerve-racking day, the setting was tranquil and still. The frigid night air and starry sky were perfect for a good night's sleep. Still, we spent hours tossing in our bags like two new parents, listening for a kick of the metal feed bucket, every snort and each whinny.

At about midnight, just as I dozed off, there was a blood-curdling scream. *"Da! Da!!"* It took a moment to sink in. "What's a *da*?" Then it registered. "Oh no, it's our horse!"

Sadhu had slipped out of his bridle and headed out the unlocked corral door!

What might have been a complete disaster was narrowly averted. Fortunately our host's son heard Sadhu and found him wandering and stumbling around in the dark. After he led our sleepwalking equine back inside, I eased the confused gelding's head back through the bridle, this time tightening it.

"How easily he entered our lives," I thought. "How easily he can disappear."

The woman carefully made sure to bolt the heavy corral door and fed him once again. Then, with my Swiss Army knife, I severed the protective white *khata* cloth encircling his neck.

"Your home's on the road with us now my friend," I reminded him.

Sadhu stoically stared up at me through brown saucer eyes. Questioning and bewildered, his eyes reflected like pools of sorrow.

October 25

At dawn we gingerly led our wandering holy man through the corral gates and past that growling mutt to load our packs outside. After the fit he threw at the inn, I cautioned everyone, "Move slowly. We don't want him to take off again." So while Cheryl held his bridle, Tenbo and I gently eased the packs up over his rump and across the saddle. "Easy now. Easy," I whispered under my breath.

Well, Sadhu no sooner felt the weight of the bags than he reared up on his hind legs and Cheryl was sent sailing like a spinnaker, screaming airborne.

"Hold on," I yelled.

Although she grabbed on tightly, while we were busily distracted with our want-to-be Pegasus, that sinister guard dog sneaked up from behind and lunged at my partner, catching her high on the thigh!

"Yeeee-ahowww!" she shrieked, still tenaciously hanging on like a soaring pit bull.

As Thubten rushed to wrestle off the vicious hound, Tenbo and I grabbed Sadhu, trying to calm him.

Meanwhile, Cheryl was doubled-over and moaning in pain and disbelief. "He bit me. The little shit bit me!"

Frantic, I rushed her inside the compound to more closely examine a purple wound already swollen to the size of a ripe pomegranate.

"Did it break the skin?"

"No, no, I don't think so," she sniffed, choking back tears.

"Maybe we should get you to a doctor?"

She shot me a glance, as if I was kidding. "Here?"

She was right. The closest medical help was probably days away in Lhasa.

"No, I'll be all right," she bravely assured me, more embarrassed and scared than hurt. Fortunately, it was just a bad bruise and there weren't any puncture wounds that I could see. So with cleansing, antiseptic and her recent gamma globulin shot, we could only trust she'd survive.

Still, taping gauze over that ugly bite, I couldn't help but joke, "I'll let you know if I catch you frothing, okay?"

Later that morning the monks left us, hitching a ride to Shigatse's Tashilhunpo Monastery. Whether it was all just too much excitement for them, or they were leery of rabid trekkers, we'll never know. Although we were on our own, I sensed our paths would cross again.

All day we sweated over an exhausting series of 4,600-meter (15,000-foot) passes in broiling heat, tracing what we figured was the Yarlung Tsangpo River. For hours there was no traffic, no life on that only road across Tibet. Occasionally a swirling dust storm on the horizon would transform into a convoy of raucous, rattling trucks. Honking their horns like geese headed south, drivers cheered us on, as open trucks of pilgrims and nomads enthusiastically waved and shouted in chorus. Then, the canyon rang silent again.

Through it all, Sadhu's hoofs set a steady clop-clop mantra that only seemed to accentuate how slowly we moved, how badly we fared. My partner and I were in rough shape, barely keeping pace with our eleven-year-old gelding. Cheryl's wound was searingly painful and she struggled with a poorly disguised limp. My feet were ragged. Arid slashing winds left our lips split and bleeding in their wake. Worst of all, I fought impromptu bouts of diarrhea and bronchial hacking fits, a deadly duo.

Until eventually, with seven brutal hours and what we guessed were thirty hard-earned kilometers (18.5 miles) behind us, we literally stumbled into a tiny village.

Mules, harnessed to long poles, trod in circles to separate grain from stalks. Singing women, faces bright and aglow, winnowed wheat to a syncopated beat, while animated prayer flags seemed to wave a welcome.

"It's got to be Pede Dzong," I thought in my dizzy stupor. "We've passed nothing else all day. It's the only village remotely near where we must be…sure, let's stop here…we've gotta stop…we've been out of water for hours…"

Dehydrated, we collapsed in heaps beside what appeared to be a store. Hopeful, we glanced up and struggled to focus, only to discover it was closed. Momentarily, something towered above us, blocking the sun. Slowly I tilted my head back, screwing my eyes to concentrate on that blurred shadow.

49

BRANDON WILSON

"What? It looks like a man in a broad felt hat and sunglasses...can't be a Tibetan...must be hallucinating...Tibetans don't wear hats like that or wear shades...but what the heck...I'll play along."

"*Chu?* Water?" The apparition nodded.

Weary, Cheryl placed parched, folded hands against a raw, sunburned cheek and choked out, "Sleep?" He nodded again. Then that unusual but very real Tibetan farmer virtually lifted us into his fly-ridden corral. After staking an equally exhausted equine in the yard between chickens and yak, he escorted us to their balcony.

There his comely wife served us as much *chang*, the local beer, or *cha*, as we could possibly hold. Until at last recovered, or at least pleasantly numbed, we were led to their daughter's cozy chamber in a detached cottage.

Two simple wooden cots draped with rugs lined adjoining walls. Photos of the Dalai Lama serenely gazed down from beneath a ceiling dotted with a smattering of simulated sparkling stars. At last, under his benevolent gaze, we could lick our wounds in peace.

The only drawback for me, my diarrhea (and hungry parasitic friends) was the obscure location of their latrine: through two wooden gates, past another snapping mutt, up twenty narrow, unlit stairs, and inside a puny three-sided adobe pen which had seen no light since Creation.

There, a dark narrow slit awaited, while all the world passed by.

Chapter V

A Crooked Little Finger

Be humble.
Walking on dirt is easier on the feet
than walking on pavement anyway.

October 26

Early the next morning we set off, following the meandering jade river and feeling remarkably better. The swelling on Cheryl's leg had already subsided. Not only could I walk without a Quasimoto swagger, but I even hoped that antibiotics would soon cure my bout with the unpredictable giardia.

Stoic, we trekked in tranquility, trudging through a craggy lifeless basin. To either side, Utah-like desert peaks sharply popped from the valley floor, while Sanskrit prayer etchings, a holy graffiti, mysteriously appeared on sheer rock faces for the benefit of pilgrims past and present.

For endless hours, an eternity, there were no other pilgrims. No birds, animals or beings of any shape shared our desolate stretch of road. It was Zen nothingness personified.

Then without warning, for one brief moment, we entered a reserve of life, a color intermission in the midst of that otherwise bleak film noire. We were heartened by a splash of golden butter patties dripping from birch trees, the whitewashed welcome of a primitive adobe house, scraggly goats and fuzzy tufts of sheep grazing on hardy grass, and the shimmering turquoise jewel: life-sustaining and inviting Lake Yamdrok Yam Tso. Tibetan women in floor-length *chubas*, robes of heavy black wool, even waved to us from atop flat rooftops.

We reveled in the midst of our Andy Warhol-promised fifteen minutes of celebrity until suddenly a car skidded to a halt.

Two Chinese hopped out, snapping photos of us from every angle. More than a little paranoid, I suspiciously eyed them and muttered to Cheryl, "What do you think? Military? Police?"

As if on cue, one of them, sensing my anxiety, gingerly offered me his business card. To our relief, we discovered they were merely Shigatse reporters—keen in their interest, unabashed in their amazement.

For a while they circled our trinity, noting every detail and questioning us in sign language. Cautiously, we mimed the tale of our trek, ever-diligent not to supply too much information, leery of who might decide it was their duty to stand in our way.

Until at last, their inquisition completed, one man slightly bowed. Unclipping a circular medallion from his lapel, he reverently handed me his well-worn Panchen Lama pin for luck. Then with a smile and a thumbs-up, they zoomed off.

"This trip's getting stranger all the time," I mused, little knowing how true that was.

It wasn't until late afternoon that we passed the largest hamlet we'd seen all day. Studying our useless map, I thought, "This should be Nagarze, since we've been climbing beside that lake all day."

Yet something just wasn't right. Everyone we asked called it "Kumu," and there was no Kumu on the map.

"Nagarze can't be more than another five kilometers," I reasoned. So we decided to begin what became our daily race with the sun, rushing past both the quiet settlement and usual military barracks.

Before long, we spotted a Jeep stalled in the middle of the road, where eight Westerners took turns "Vogueing" for snapshots. Although it all looked too silly to believe, especially given our current condition, they were the first foreigners we'd seen since leaving Lhasa. So, what the heck.

We approached, excited and bursting with questions, anxious to compare travel notes. Still, it only took an instant for us to discover those

Dutch, English and Americans were on an entirely different trip. They'd just spent ten days on their organized tour with a Chinese guide who spoke no English. So they could offer little advice, except to warn us about the weather at Mount Everest base camp which was extreme this time of year.

Well, flash! As with most Tibet package travelers, they'd traveled halfway around the world to experience the wonder of Mount Everest, only to spend an hour there before hustling on. For a once-in-a-lifetime experience, it was sadly pathetic.

I'd seen it all too often: some fat guy carrying a bright umbrella in Piazza San Marco, decked out in polyester with a matching Velcro moustache, screaming, "People all together now. Follow me. We have to be back on the tour bus in fifteen minutes. Ladies, pleease!"

No, that's not my idea of traveling.

"Pass any villages lately?" Cheryl asked, always hoping for the best.

"Maybe twenty kilometers back," blurted a stocky Brit, expedition-suited in a yellow *Tin Tin in Tibet* t-shirt.

Solemnly we eyed each other, knowing what that meant. We were forced to stay in "Kumu" or "Nagarze" or whatever that last town was. Already out of necessity, we tried to pace each thirty-kilometer day to reach shelter at the end. Already it was too cold to camp, too difficult to find hay. Besides, we looked forward to our lively impromptu conversations with Tibetan families.

"Say, you guys hungry?" one of the Dutch punkers innocently asked.

Little did anyone know what paltry dehydrated food sustained us.

"Always!" Cheryl was quick to admit, and with that those generous travelers rummaged through boxes, donating leftover tins of dace fish in black bean sauce, two day-old bread and pickled mustard shoots. I didn't know what to do with much of it, but figured anything had to be better than our limited foil packet menu.

Then, anxious to get settled in before dark, we wished each other well, as Cheryl and I began our tedious saunter back to the village.

Approaching the nearest field, I called over to a handsome man, looking classically Tibetan (or at least how I imagined a classic Tibetan to look) in his traditional high felt embroidered boots with yak hide soles.

"Nagarze?"

Pausing from his hay stacking chores, he nodded. Cheryl then shot him that now-familiar other hand gesture.

"Sleep?"

The farmer nodded again and we trustingly tagged along behind him past a cluster of buildings and around a corner, only to run headlong into a police car.

"Oh no! This is it," I thought. "They're gonna send us back to Lhasa! Or worse!"

Yet it was too late to do anything but follow.

With a kick-in-the-groin trepidation, we ducked inside a simple adobe hut where two Tibetans and two Chinese were seated around a crude wooden slab table in the midst of a heated mah-jongg tournament. For a few long, tense moments we watched in nervous anticipation until there was a lull to their turbulent tile slapping.

Slowly an obese, dour man with reptilian face, wrapped up like an egg roll in a too-tight Mao jacket, momentarily glanced up.

In a flush of over-anxious zeal, I readily confessed, "We're going to Shigatse," in a neighborly, yet upbeat voice, which only thinly masked my overpowering urge to rush back out the door.

Waving officiously like some Supreme Pubah, the fellow merely garbled something I didn't understand and glared in our direction. We must have looked totally baffled because a quizzical old fox, in a hat to match, drew out his tattered yellow papers in a "See, like these," gesture.

"Oh, passport?" I guessed, reluctantly tugging my battered blue book from my money belt three layers deep. Quickly flashing it, I held on tight, not wanting to risk him perusing the sixty other stamps inside. Who could guess what he'd find to raise his bureaucratic dander? I only handed him our ATP, naming Shigatse as our destination. With that, I made a stamping motion in the air, as if it were all official.

Somehow, I doubted this would've normally satisfied that petty potentate, who was obviously flexing his muscle to impress his comrades. But it appeared he was more anxious to continue his game, for he summarily waved us outside where three inquisitive villagers led us next door to a deserted schoolyard.

There, behind sturdy walls, Sadhu was fed, watered and tied. From our early calamity, we'd learned the importance of removing his bridle and tying him by the foot. That was the only sure way to stop our "wander-horse."

After spreading our sleeping bags across the primitive wooden benches in a classroom, the four of us were soon joined by a myopic village schoolmaster and his paunchy supervisor, a Party appointee from Shigatse. For awhile in that cordoned-off courtyard, we shared "talk, talk" and *chang*.

Proudly those educators, or more correctly re-educators, discussed life in their "Tibetan Autonomous Region," as the Communist Chinese have dubbed it. It was an eerie lecture. Even though the *chang* flowed freely, through all their hospitable show of "nice, nice," we felt an alarming undertone of tension like a grating of fingernails on a Beijing blackboard. That uneasiness didn't disappear until the boss and instructor did.

Then those simple villagers candidly shared heartfelt feelings, even though by doing so they may have put their lives at risk. We'd read and now we saw for ourselves how villages such as theirs had suffered during the oppressive occupation. Everywhere we turned we encountered haunting reminders, from omnipresent army bases to the rubble of monasteries, thousands of which had been destroyed.

Today, the few rebuilt lamaseries, once cornerstones of Tibetan society, no longer admit school-aged children, although reportedly one in six boys still vainly try to enter. Now who will teach the masses? Reportedly, most settlements still offer no electricity or running water— let alone education. Yet the humiliation doesn't end there. Unfortunately today, public schools, when they do exist, teach only in Chinese and reportedly, in one populous county, only 22 percent of the girls are even educated. So Tibetans face a triple-threat. They're in grave danger of losing not only their religion and independence over the next generation, but their language and culture as well.

Oh, how we wished we could speak better Tibetan with them, but we were delighted to learn how far sign language could take us. For example, at one point I motioned to the crimson Chinese flag flapping just outside the walls. Furtively glancing around, one wiry peasant made sure no one was spying, while another screwed up his weathered face in disgust. Another, snickering, crooked his little finger in an obscene gesture. In a universal language, that gesture about said it all.

October 27

Bright and early we were awakened by the drone of a radio broadcast echoing from monolithic speakers just outside the compound. Although in Chinese, it was easy to decipher as the "Good Morning Comrade Show" live from Beijing. A combination of classical music and classic propaganda, it sounded identical to the one aired in Chuzal Dzong at eight every morning, eight each night. In each small village, that monster's presence was inescapable and all-pervasive, a mean-spirited, gossiping neighbor.

After a quick breakfast, we thanked our friends, saying, "*To duo chay!*" and with hands clasped we bowed, discreetly wishing them the Dalai Lama's blessing as we set off toward Gyantse.

We had no idea where we were exactly. There was a jade river, a stark desert, a brilliant turquoise sky, but little else. Although our map showed the river in a slightly different position, we blamed that on the inaccuracy of our "latest map of Tibet."

Why, it didn't even show Lhasa's airport built years ago!

"We're heading west on the only road we've seen," I thought. "We can't be too wrong and the villagers we'd stayed with finally agreed that the last town was Nagarze. We should be in Gyantse in a few days, Shigatse a week later."

Hiking in a sinister silence across a land that seemed to suck the life out of our very marrow, I kept chewing one thought over and over like a nugget of dried yak cheese.

"What ever possessed the Chinese to take this stretch of parched inhospitable land? And why?"

I knew the Chinese had long claimed it was part of their original country, their Fatherland, in a notion reminiscent of the excuse the Nazis had for invading Poland. "But if that's true," I wondered, "why do

56

Tibetans look so different, speak a different language, tell different legends, eat different foods, wear different clothes and even worship different deities?"

Although early twentieth century political scholars claimed Tibet was captured to provide a military buffer zone to a powerful British-backed India to the south, to me it appeared that greed was the more plausible reason for Tibet's conquest.

Why, the Chinese have even historically called Tibet "the Western Treasure House."

Walking alone, sometimes 500 meters apart, we encountered little all day except the lone goat, distant shepherds and relentless sun. Finally, in late afternoon, we approached a narrow concrete bridge surrounded by a pack of snarling dogs and eight adobe hovels carelessly lettered in Chinese characters. We were exhausted. Sadhu was sweaty and since the tattered town sat beside a bridge, I figured it would probably have a police station.

"Maybe they'll be able to tell us where we are? How far it is to Lung ma? But God," I thought, "this place is ominous."

As if on cue, Cheryl quietly began whistling the music from the film *The Good, The Bad and The Ugly*, while I approached four lifeless cops leaning against their car. Mustering my best *excuse-me-but-we-must-be-lost* smile, I mimed the usual pleasantries. But as luck would have it, they only spoke Chinese and I had no phrase book.

So I pointed to the map pleading, "Where...are...we?"

All that raised was their silly grins. I tried again. Pointing to the ground I suggested, "Lung ma?" It was the only place remotely close to where I guessed we were.

They stared back with an *I know he's talking, but I don't have any idea what he's saying, so I'll just nod and smile* sort of look. It reminded me of that Gary Larson cartoon where the guy is intensely lecturing his dog and all the dog hears is, "Blah, blah, Ginger. Blah, blah, blah, blah Ginger."

"I'm getting nowhere," I thought. "Time to change tactics."

Pointing down the road, I offered, "Gyantse?"

They enthusiastically shook their heads, gurgling, "Gyantse!"

"Ah, now we're getting somewhere," I figured.

"How far? Kilometers?"

A mumble rose through the group and I ended-up with estimates of eighty to 120 kilometers (fifty to seventy-five miles). Little help. While we wallowed in gestures, a crowd gathered. As that entire prying village scrutinized Sadhu and Cheryl's every detail, the five of us scrutinized that map (including Nepal and India) in a sort of bizarre, fruitless geography lesson for twenty minutes. More police came to their rescue, yet we still had no idea where we were.

Finally I tossed in the charts. As the sun quickly disappeared, Cheryl and I forced a grim smile and waved, masking a sneaking suspicion that the next village was still four hours away.

Fortunately, God watches over travelers and traveling fools. Not three kilometers (two miles) later we spotted a family winnowing grain far below. A mule was led in circles around a paddock, knocking grain from flaxen stalks. Chanting women tossed grain from straw baskets into the air, while a farmer forked hay from one pile to another. Hoping for the best, I gave it my best and gestured to him. "Sleep?"

The seemingly genial fellow nodded or seemed to, since it was difficult to tell at that distance. Trustingly we followed where fate led us.

What could have been a disaster became an encounter to remember. The three of us were quickly ushered inside their massive, multi-level compound. Sadhu was in horse heaven with all the hay his ample belly could hold. Meanwhile, upstairs we were led to two simple beds consisting of hay filled sacks set within wooden frames on the porch.

We no more than sat down than the couple's teenaged daughter, Gyaltsen, graciously served us steaming *cha*. We no sooner sipped than our cups were re-filled to the brim. Their son, a tousle-headed kid with eyes full of mischief that we nicknamed "Chang-boy," hurriedly fetched homemade barley brew. And, as inquisitive neighbor kids showed-up, I showed them how to make a telephone from two cans and string.

"Ah, Western technology finally reaches Tibet," I mused. "Via two scraggly backpackers! That's doing our part for civilization."

That simple toy fascinated them for hours, especially since they'd probably never even seen a real phone before. They also explored other simple wonders we'd taken for granted, including the marvel of a tea bag, a mini-kerosene cookstove that doesn't require sheep dung and the mystery of a jacket's Velcro. Like missionaries toting the gospel of the twenty-first century to their doorstep, we shared our treasures with pint-sized converts. Finally their Mother, a serene lady who looked about thirty-years-old, invited us inside for dinner.

Stooping through their low wooden doorway, we ducked into a combination living, dining and bedroom area. In the diffused evening glow, Mother squatted over a tin washbasin scrubbing her face and arms. Father broke dried yak dung patties and gingerly fed them into a small stove which vented through the roof, while Gyaltsen, her hair braided and smiling coyly, nervously shuffled sneakered feet beneath the low table.

A perfect hostess, the delighted mother served a mouthwatering concoction of noodles and sheep cheese, or *thugpa*, which everyone enjoyed with unabashed gusto, slurping noodles straight from the bowl. Teacups were refilled each time a sip was taken and that generous family even feigned mock disappointment when we could only finish two huge bowls of the rich steaming stew.

While we wallowed in that rare feeling of both physical and spiritual fullness, a smoky yak butter lamp was lit. Then by its warm glow, we acted out our trip to the Potala Palace, boasting how we'd actually seen the Dalai Lama's throne. That was a feat most Tibetans will never enjoy, since visits to the Potala are tightly controlled by the government.

Then, eyes aglow with excitement, that kind family tearfully reminisced about their own special trip to the holy city as they shared a few weathered snapshots of their special pilgrimage.

At some point in the evening, after earning their trust, Father stood and proudly parted ancient, dusty black curtains, revealing a tiny sacred Dalai Lama altar surrounded by photos taken during various stages of His Holiness' remarkable life. Then something equally brazen happened.

For the first time with any Tibetans, we dared to divulge our scheme of trekking to Kathmandu. For the first time we dared to call it a *pilgrimage*, for that was what it had become.

To us it was now more than just another trek, another physical challenge along another trail. It was our chance to prove to the Chinese that if two Western *heathens* could trek a holy route to a sacred site, then certainly Tibetans should be allowed to trod that same lonely path in search of their souls. Unreasonably, both the Chinese and Nepalese governments had imposed stringent border controls for decades, even for the devout.

Our journey had been transformed, as were we. It was a cherished chance to combine our energy, our *ki*, with that of thousands of pilgrims past along a trail now nearly empty.

October 28

When we awoke the next morning, our kind hosts were dressed in their best outfits. At their request, I snapped a series of family portraits, feeling a little like Edwin Curtis on his trip across Native America in the 1800s. I was particularly honored, as it might be one of the few photographs that family would ever have taken of them.

Normally we planned to offer several dollars worth of yuan to our hosts for their shelter. Not enough money to transform hospitality into a business or kindness into greed, but just enough to buy something special or ease a special need. But that compassionate family accepted nothing for their room or kindness—except a photo of the Dalai Lama that they reverently placed beside the others.

Their friendship had warmed us more than any *thugpa* and I instantly felt a frigid pang of loss the moment we departed.

All day we wound through towering, impenetrable mountains. Gold-plated sand dunes rose along one side while the river meandered on the other. Sadhu's pace was less motivated than usual. It could have been his age, but I suspected his lethargy was from standing awake all night eating. All in all, I was convinced our daily treks simply interrupted his sleep.

"Cheryl, why don't you lead Sadhu for a while," I suggested, "so I can apply a little encouragement to our friend's backside if he starts lagging."

She shot back a glare that left me cringing.

"I know she thinks it's cruel," I thought, "but then again she's someone who moves worms off the road so they won't get squashed. I know for a fact that Sadhu eats and sleeps better than we do."

"Look, I just can't start pulling him thirty kilometers (18.5 miles) every day," I complained. "It's sheer torture and I don't have the energy. Besides, what if he starts dragging like this during some mountain blizzard?"

She shot me another sarcastic sneer, muttering, "Right..."

The seriousness of what we faced still didn't register with my partner. Not yet. But those approaching winter snows and the nearly impassable 5,182-meter (17,000-foot) passes weighed heavier on my mind with each passing day.

Switching positions, we yawned, missing what we were assured was "Lung ma." All those whizzing cars and thundering trucks made a more lasting impression. Dodging them every few minutes all afternoon became a Laurel and Hardy farce.

I screamed, "Car to the front!" or spotting a swirling tornado approaching from behind, "Truck to the rear!"

Cheryl led Sadhu onto the shoulder, just as an another overloaded truck or bulging bus barely crowded past, dodging potholes along the way. All day long, trucks, suspensions long gone, careened sideways heading straight for us. At the last second they swerved, shooting past in a cacophony of blaring horns and haze of debris and exhaust.

Hours later, it was a relief when the mountains finally melted away. For the first time in days we scanned the horizon, depressed. There was nothing. Stopping stock-still, I desperately searched for some sign of life.

"So...where do you think we'll end up tonight?" I sighed, expecting no reply. Our joke-of-a map showed nothing between Lung ma and Gyantse. Despondent, Cheryl looked up. Then as if in answer, we spotted two monks deliberately shuffling toward us.

"Hey, it looks like our friends from the other day!" I shouted. "See, I knew we'd run into them again."

More coincidence? Or serendipity?

Greeting each other like long-lost pals, I mimed, "Where are you headed?"

"Back to our monastery outside Lhasa," Tenbo replied.

"You've already been to Shigatse?" Cheryl asked, envious of their speed and luck at hitching. They nodded and broadly grinned. Then I remembered their knack for finding places to stay.

"Any idea where we can sleep tonight?"

They glanced around, chuckled at my garbled Tibetan, and pointed at a house just up the road. "Just say '*Kuchi, Kuchi!*'" Tenbo reminded me. "It always works for us," he bragged, and waving they walked away.

Unlike the last time, I knew our paths would never cross again, at least in this life.

"*Kuchi, Kuchi...Kuchi, Kuchi,*" I repeated that mantra to myself, hoping his magic words would work like some weary traveler's *open-says-a-me* on the farmer and his family who I spotted stacking hay in front of their house. We prayed they'd have shelter for or pity on three ragged wayfarers.

Nearing them I bowed slightly, humbly offering, "*Tashi delek!*"

The tall, emaciated man took this as his cue to stop work and plopped down next to his disheveled wife as he muttered a reply. Encouraged by his rapt attention, I set both hands against my sunburned cheek suggesting, "Sleep?" He simply stared.

"Not a good sign," I thought and tried again.

"*Kuchi, Kuchi...*sleep."

Nothing. No glimmer of recognition. Desperate, I performed our complete pantomime of five minutes since his was the only house it seemed for miles.

"Sleep...tired...walk...Lhasa...Potala...Dalai...Lama..."

Still nothing. Finally after ten more frustrating minutes we gave up, discouraged, beaten. Shaking our heads, we turned to wander back down the road. But hearing approaching footsteps, we spun around.

That granite-carved farmer stood facing us eye-to-eye and stoically placed folded sun-creased hands against a leathered cheek. Then he resolutely motioned for us to follow.

They led a marginal existence. That farmer in his thirties, his wife and seven small children (the eldest was maybe seven-years-old) lived in a bleak adobe compound. Scrawny donkeys, sheep and chickens scratched for food right outside their door. Children ran about in layered rags. They were black from dung fires, as though they hadn't washed in months. Even worse, one child's swollen belly protruded from malnutrition.

I was deeply saddened by our obvious intrusion, once I realized, "That's why they took so long to answer."

Slowly the family joined us in what appeared to be their feed room. Birds flew in from an open window, nesting on rafters above our bags. Children cried and ran around, their tiny brown peckers poking through crotchless pants. One squatted and peed beside our pack as we unrolled our sleeping pads and bags.

They watched us. We boiled water. They stared. We split a packet of dehydrated food. They gawked. Conversation was minuscule. For once, simple sign language failed and they only looked confused at our brainless attempt to speak Tibetan.

Until finally, I was dead-tired and frustrated by their unwillingness to communicate, disgusted by our filthy surroundings, sickened by their awkward stares and silent intrusion.

"Maybe it's just better if we just turn in early," I snapped, sliding off sweat-encrusted boots.

Finally in one last effort, I offered a cigarette to our mute host. Suddenly, as if by magic, a bottle of *chang* appeared. The howling babies vanished and we shared a tepid brew from the same tin cup in that rustic hovel. Then it all hit me like bad yak butter tea.

"This isn't their tack room. This heap of hay sacks, bird droppings and fetid confusion is their bedroom! Because of us, this family of nine is forced into the one dingy stall, much smaller than this, next door."

Once again I was humbled by the kindness strangers had shown, and repulsed by my own reeking odor.

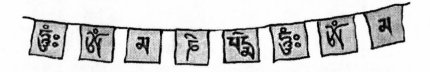

Chapter VI

The Road Less Taken

Be flexible.
Sometimes trails just vanish.
That doesn't mean you're on the wrong path–
there's just a better one now.

October 29

The next morning just three kilometers (1.8 miles) from where we slept, we heard swift footsteps pounding the gravel behind and directly below us. Quickly we spun around, half-expecting to see another grizzled shepherd and his goats. Instead we faced a quirky little guy toting a miniature overflowing backpack as he bobbed up the mountainside. That chance encounter with another Westerner, the first we'd seen hiking since we started, completely threw us off guard.

"What is someone else doing out here?"

Curious and admittedly lonely, we slowed down, anxious to speak to someone, anyone, in something other than our usual feeble-minded sign language. As the short, wiry stranger crested the small rise behind us, we examined his unusual appearance more closely.

I was truly baffled. First, the eccentric interloper hardly looked equipped for high altitude trekking in his long-sleeved white shirt, thin vest and sneakers. Second, the little fellow seemed to pop out of nowhere, since it was impossible to hide for long out on that flat, treeless plain.

Even when he finally approached, our suspicions were far from relieved when, slightly winded, he gasped, "Hi there!"

"Hello. Where'd you come from?" I replied, in a tone less than cordial. "Didn't see you in that last village."

"It's only ten in the morning," I thought. "If he didn't stay in our settlement, why, he's already hiked over twenty kilometers (12.5 miles)!"

The neatly trimmed stranger pulled a cheap flannel covered tin canteen from his rucksack. It was similar to Chinese jugs we'd seen in the Barkhor.

"Oh, I just slept under a small bridge down there," he explained, pointing down toward the valley. "You know, the ones over those dry stream beds?"

"Yeah, they're about a meter high and the same wide," I recollected in disbelief.

"It's not bad," he continued, stomping his spotless white tennis shoes to keep warm. "At least you're out of this wind."

"You must have a very good sleeping bag," I suggested.

"Meanwhile," I thought, "this guy's truly insane. It's midmorning and still only 45°F. I know it dips down to freezing every night because we watch our breaths."

"Nah, just a blanket."

"He *is* crazy." As we surveyed him up and down, something seemed very unusual. Maybe it was the way he looked so clean compared to our already grotty condition, especially for a troll sleeping under a bridge. Or maybe it was the fact that he was traveling so light, too light to survive for long up there.

"I heard about you two a couple of days ago," he continued, as he carefully inspected Sadhu. "Some Chinese truckers were talking about the two foreigners with a horse."

"Oh, really?" Part of me was proud we were noticed, part afraid of what that implied. I still half-expected to be interrogated at a Chinese roadblock. After spending seven months crossing Africa not so long ago, we knew dicey things could and do happen while on the trail.

"Where you two going?" he asked, tossing back his canteen to down some water.

"Kathmandu," Cheryl proudly proclaimed. "We're walking the pilgrim's path from Lhasa. You?"

"Oh, I've just spent two months in China...and I'm headin' to Nepal. My Chinese girlfriend's there."

"Chinese girlfriend, huh? Why doesn't that surprise me?"

"So, how far is Gyantse?" I inquired, itching to reach the "big city" before sundown.

The stranger looked confused. "You mean Shigatse?"

"No, Gyantse. What is it? Another twenty kilometers?"

"Sorry to disappoint you," he replied with a sly grin. "This road goes to Shigatse. You'll never reach Gyantse on this."

Cheryl and I stared at each other completely dumbfounded. If someone had told us the edge of the world was right around the next bend, we couldn't have been more baffled and crestfallen. I was certain for the past three days we'd sweated up mountain passes in a west to west-northwesterly direction. Sure, our heading was slightly off at times. But I figured that small difference was to skirt the surrounding Himalayan foothills.

Desperate to convince that busybody that we were on the right path, I pulled out our ragged map. I was certain that he was the one off-track.

"Look," I explained, pointing to the hills surrounding us. "These mountains are here..." I argued, showing him their corresponding position on the map. Then I traced the map's vague blue lines, adding, "And the lake follows along this road..."

Unconvinced, he shook his disheveled head while nodding below and countering, "That's Yarlong Tsampo River. Not the lake."

At that, he tugged a slick Chinese topographical map from his small daypack.

"Hey! Where'd you get that?" Cheryl wondered aloud. We'd scoured nearly every bookshop halfway around the world looking for one, from Colorado to London to Kathmandu..

"Oh, China," he answered, a little too smugly. "You guys missed the turnoff three days ago."

Cheryl glared at me. "Turnoff? What turnoff?" she cried, sounding betrayed. Neither of us had seen anything resembling an intersection—or any other road for that matter.

"Well it's not much. Just a dirt road off to your left. You could easily miss it if you don't speak Chinese."

"You speak Chinese?" I demanded, growing more suspicious of that weird intruder every second. With its subtle intonations, I'd heard it was one of the world's most difficult languages to learn.

"Uh-huh," he nonchalantly bragged. Oddly, the shape of his entire face changed as he rattled off something in Mandarin.

"Only two months in China? I'm no expert," I thought, "but this guy sounds like he was there a little longer than that."

"Look," I started, still desperate to convince him, or mostly us, we were right, "We've asked 'What village is this?' in each town we've passed."

I remembered, only too well, how frustrating those attempts were. At times, I figure we could have said anything, like, "Is this really the road to hell," and those Tibetans would have agreed just to be polite.

"We even asked a bus driver."

"Both in Nagarze," Cheryl chimed in, "and those policemen in Lung-ma."

"Well, sorry," he sarcastically chirped with a shrug. "But if you're on this road, you weren't even in Lung-ma!"

We were devastated by the implications.

Frantic, I weighed our limited options. "We've only got two choices," I thought. "We can retrace our steps all the way back down this mountain for three days and hope to catch some unmarked, dirt trail. That's gotta be grueling. I don't look forward to crossing that desert again, especially now that we know how far it is from one village and water to the next. Besides, Cheryl's been spitting green phlegm non-stop. Or, we can press on," I figured. "Why couldn't we have discovered this mistake two days ago? Now there is *no* real choice. We must go forward—or risk failing altogether."

With that realization weighing heavier than our packs, we marched on. Our bizarre escort scampered along with us for the next few hours, like the March Hare in *Alice in Wonderland*. I half-expected him to hum, "I'm late, I'm late, for a very important date…"

Still, we kept each other company as Sadhu was put through his gaits. Meanwhile, I planned to take advantage of the opportunity to probe a little deeper and find out more about our unusual companion.

"Say, why don't you sleep with locals in villages like we do?" I innocently teased. "Got to be more comfortable than sleeping under bridges."

"I've no interest in meeting the locals," he confessed. "No interest whatsoever!" Then again, he muttered a footnote in Chinese.

I was shocked. "Why's he out here then? After weeks on the road he's had no local contact?"

"When'd you say you left Lhasa?"

"Oh, four days ago."

"Four days? This is getting more fantastic all the time," I fumed. "This guy's walked over 200 kilometers (125 miles) in just four days? He's slept under bridges in freezing weather? He's still squeaky clean? Speaks fluent Chinese? Chinese topo map? Something's odd. Something's very odd."

Unable to resist, I pressed a little harder, asking the one question that I knew could seal his fate. "So, what do you think about the Chinese presence in Tibet?" It was a trick question offhandedly asked, like, "So, what about those Mets?"

"Oh, it's nothing worse than when the U.S. took New Mexico."

"Well maybe so, but that doesn't necessarily make it right. Besides, that was a hundred years ago. The world was different then."

"Say, how are you on water?" he interrupted, abruptly changing the subject as we approached a Chinese military installation. "I always like to stop at these posts for boiled water. Besides, it's a good chance to practice my Chinese."

Any suspicion that I had was confirmed. In an instant, my growing sense of self-survival took over—along with supreme doubts. "Oh, God. Maybe he was sent out here to ask us questions. If so, I'm afraid we've told him too much already. But there's no way that he's going to get us to follow him behind those adobe walls. Not even if we were totally out of water with nothing in sight. No way!"

"No, we're okay," I calmly replied. "We'll probably see you up ahead!" We hoped not.

The rest of our day was a slow torture. We descended the foothills and began a painful crawl across the arid, lifeless basin. The sun, high in a cloudless sky, beat down relentlessly. Steam rose off the desert floor. Sweat evaporated as soon as it surfaced on our skins, except for the occasional burning salty drop that dribbled into our eyes. Ever at nature's mercy, we drew bandanas tightly across noses and mouths in a last-ditch effort to keep sand from invading our lungs as it had every other crevice of our toasted, sandblasted bodies. We rationed water. One puny one-liter bottle had to last each of us until the next village, wherever that was…

However, by midafternoon I had drained the last steamy precious drops with no town in sight. Then the predictable afternoon winds picked up again, leeching moisture from our skin, scorching our faces, parching our lips…frying our brains.

For a while, to take my mind off my thirst, I fantasized aloud about the perfect meal.

"Cheryl, imagine this…a cold, fresh fruit salad…Lobster Thermidor…steaming baguette with real butter…green beans in a creamy cheese sauce…a bottle of single malt scotch…and a pint of chocolate chocolate chip ice cream!"

"All on a windy jungle cliff overlooking the South Pacific!" she crooned.

Together we moaned, peaking in a simultaneous orgasm.

For an hour, or what seemed like days, the subject of water solely occupied our every thought: Hawai'i's beaches, tropical showers, cool turquoise pools, running through sprinklers as kids, a squirt gun, all the spit we'd wasted in life. Until finally, as my addled half-boiled brain struggled to still function, choking and sputtering like a Model-T, I spotted the symmetrical square blocks of a village on the horizon.

Still, all I could wonder was, "Is it real? Or just another seductive mirage?"

At our steadily deteriorating pace, it took nearly an hour to reach those ten houses that promised relief. But approaching that vision, the ramshackle village appeared about as inviting as a dilapidated ghost town. We encountered no one until we'd almost trudged through the eerily silent settlement. Just then, we spotted a windswept shadow of a man leaning in the inferno's one slim sliver of shade.

Sidling over to him, I hacked, "Water?" to which Cheryl translated, "*Chu ko-ma?*"

Immediately he led us into the black, cool interior of his rustic home. There, a plump gentle woman glowing with sun-blushed, yak-buttered cheeks ladled bubbling black tea from a simmering iron pot into one of our bottles, while our rescuer poured *chang* from his brown plastic jug into our other.

Saved once more, we thanked those benevolent phantoms and shuffled off again.

After several hours, and nearly thirty kilometers (18.5 miles), we began our daily search for a place to spend the night. It was a task we never looked forward to throughout our entire odyssey and it was faced with humble apprehension.

At first Cheryl took the lead, smiling and waving to three stern women in a drowsy village courtyard. "Sleep?" she pleaded, with an innocent *gotta-love-me* kind of grin.

Sneering with suspicion, the peasants somberly shook their braided heads in unison and waved us up the road another five kilometers (three miles). In Tibet, it was always up the road, never down.

Now, five kilometers (three miles) is nothing when you're driving. It's a couple of minutes. But for two people leading a lagging horse, who've just spent seven hours crossing a desert, it's an eternity—or at least an hour.

Reaching the next settlement we immediately drew a curious crowd of gawkers. That became more common the farther we strayed from Lhasa. It was my turn to beg, so, with the usual apprehension, I approached two cheerful ladies spinning wool as they sat outside an adobe wall.

"*Tashi delek!*" I cried, with all the forced sincerity of a door-to-door salesman. But they just glowered.

So I clasped my hands together in that pillow-like gesture suggesting, "Sleep?"

They just stared.

"Maybe I'm over-simplifying our request," I thought…

So again, I pantomimed our tale. "Lhasa…pilgrims…walking…Kathmandu."

There were a few snickers and then one slight man pointed a gnarled finger at yak hair tents flapping by the roadside. Laughing, he suggested we camp there. A few girls joined in, tittering at the prospect of us setting up our tent amidst the nomads.

"We might seriously consider it," I thought, "except there's nowhere to tie Sadhu. No feed or place for him to graze and I don't want to have to worry about him all night."

At last, after several futile tries to communicate, we reluctantly gave up on the simple villagers and their mocking silence. It was obvious we were in deep trouble. No other town was in sight. It'd be dark soon and, after trekking for what seemed a thousand miles through that Tibetan Death Valley, we were physically and mentally frazzled.

"Please, let us find a place to sleep," I silently prayed.

Just across the dirt courtyard, multicolored prayer flags fluttered from poles, *darlog*, atop corner turrets on a nearby adobe wall. "Maybe," I thought, "maybe that's a good sign. Maybe someone so religious has a place in their stable for three wanderers."

So on a hunch, we quietly led Sadhu alongside the compound to the hefty wooden door. With little idea what was one the other side, I cautiously ducked my head inside, whispering a timid, "*Tashi delek?*"

Hearing those words, a hellish nightmare of a black hound with bark to match bayed and snapped, while a small boy hysterically cried, "*Kiy! Kiy!*" (or "There's one big hungry dog over here, ready to chomp your head off!").

Rushing to grab their sentry, that tiny lad wrapped a cloth over the mutt's shaggy head while his brother led us through their gate and into a vast livestock yard. I handed Sadhu's rope lead to Cheryl then followed the kid, sneaking past their snapping Minotaur into a peaceful sanctum.

Inside, a man with closely cropped hair sat cross-legged on a straw mat. With profound reverence he droned, reciting passages from the holy sutra while turning sheer, yellowed, wood-blocked pages with strong, slender hands. For a few awkward moments I patiently waited, not daring to interrupt his devotion.

Until finally, during a pause in his chanting, I screwed up the nerve to whisper, "Papa…"

The serene sage glanced up.

"Sleep?" was all I said, all I needed to say, as he motioned for me to sit across from him. Finishing his scriptures, he folded ocher fabric over nearly transparent, well-worn pages, then set them aside.

Just outside, the chaos continued as thirty prying villagers who'd followed us into the courtyard waited for the drama to unfold. As they poked and probed Sadhu and our packs, the son kept his howling dog at bay until he spotted his father and me. Then catching his father's discrete nod, the boy pretended to unleash that frothing hound and snickered as the pesky crowd nearly fell over each other as they scurried to escape through the door.

With little ceremony, our bags were spread in the inner courtyard where we could finally relax over shared glasses of *chang*. Soon we were invited to join the former monk, his wife, mother, two sons and three daughters around the warmth of their dung-stoked fire.

While Mama cooked a simple supper of tender marshmallow-sized potatoes, the lads showed off, imitating all the birds and animals they knew. Eager young girls, separating fuzzy lumps of freshly sheared wool, patiently showed Cheryl how to spread the fibers without using a wire brush.

The surprise of the evening was meeting their sweet, deaf daughter, who, although injured as a child, perfectly understood our ridiculous sign language. Although she was obviously delighted to finally have someone to talk with, it pained us to see how, even in that generous family, she was regarded as an embarrassment, a village outcast. It was tragic. With her handicap she'd always be just outside her culture. Chances are she'd never find a husband, raise a family or do more than fetch water for her parents.

After warming ourselves around their smoky fire and sharing their simple fare, we shared stories as best as we could. While tickling his squirming sons, Papa fondly reminisced about his days as a novice in

Shigatse. Hearing the tale of our own personal pilgrimage, the kind ol' gent's eyes positively glowed. But that flicker was dim compared to the one that sparked into flames when we eventually presented his family with a Dalai Lama photo.

His eyes sparkled like the Tibetan sun on the river as he committed to memory each wrinkle of that image, as though it was the most wonderful treasure he could receive. After reverently touching it to the top of his head several times, the holy man bestowed that same simple blessing on each family member. Then he carefully placed it in an unadorned wooden frame along with other well-worn symbols of his endangered heritage.

Later, as we snuggled out in the frosty, starry stillness of a heaven-illuminated courtyard, Cheryl and I reveled in a family's pure love which blanketed us yet another night.

October 30

The next day we pushed on to reach Shigatse before another nightfall. Kilometer posts slowly ticked by as we inched closer with resolute deliberation, one minuscule step at a time. Cheryl's chest cold grew increasing worse. Only adrenaline kept her moving.

"Sadhu's sluggish too," I groused. "I've had to almost pull this equine zombie the last twenty kilometers. With my partner so far behind, there's no one to even switch his backside to help keep him awake."

We'd looked forward to reaching Tibet's second city for weeks and I'd made a mental list of everything I wanted to do. I could already taste the searing, spicy Szechwan restaurant food, feel the pulse of a sizzling hot shower, smell the crisp sheets on that long-awaited bed. Then again, there was the new ATP hassle, as well as the joy of getting our wander horse shod for the first time, neither a pleasant task.

Just as I was adding to my checklist, far-off on the horizon, I detected the shimmering golden roof of Tashilhunpo Monastery.

"Whoa! Cheryl. Look!" I screamed back down the road to her, about a hundred yards away. "It's Shigatse. We're there!"

74

Anxiously, I waited in anticipation with Sadhu for what seemed like hours before Cheryl joined us. Then, our trio complete, we excitedly paraded toward that amber beacon, as a real city blossomed before us.

At first, I was inexplicably nervous. Then I realized how long it had been since we'd seen so many people, shops or streets.

As we self-consciously mingled with a lazy, never-ending procession of donkey wagons and horse carts, sheep and goats, pedestrians and pilgrims, only two questions ran through my mind. "What's the best hotel in town?" and "Do they take horses?"

In search of the first answer, we sauntered up to the Shigatse Hotel, reputedly the finest. I dusted myself off. Straightened my hat. Checked my haggard face in the doorway glass. Then with great anticipation, I bounded inside toward a cheerless Han receptionist perched behind an inviting glass case, chock-full of Capitalist delicacies.

"Room please!" I announced, feeling like Donald Trump swaggering into his Towers. "The best you have!"

"No rooms!" the gum-popping comrade snapped.

"I have dollars!" I declared, as though greenbacks, those skinny world treasures, would make her cut to the chase. In the past, even in Eastern Europe, hard currency could always convince reluctant innkeepers to re-check their registry. Dollars could vacate the fullest of hotels. "Besides, this one looks nearly empty," I guessed, scanning the deserted lobby.

This time it was different. China plays its own odd game. The Shigatse Hotel must have been reserved only for high-spending organized Western tour groups and party-line hotshots. Totally indifferent, that *functionaire* with her chubby face and pageboy haircut tossed her head then callously ignored further pleas.

Amazing. Even there, back in *civilization* we were stranded, temporarily defeated, hopelessly staring into a case brimming with all the chocolate, brandy and other hard currency goodies we'd never enjoy.

Having found the brutal answer to our first question, we set off in search of the Teinsin Hotel, hoping it would provide the second. Luckily, finding the fabled traveler's hotel was easier than expected. First we met an English couple staying there and then stumbled upon its gregarious manager dragging potential guests in right off the street.

At just ten yuan, Teinsin was a bargain, if less than luxurious. Two floors of rooms were arranged around a central courtyard dissected by laundry lines. Narrow stairs led to tidy, brightly painted concrete rooms, complete with steel-framed beds and a welcome tin wash basin. Although there was no shower, there was plenty of freezing water for an exhilarating sponge bath—once you chipped away the ice.

Sure, it may not have been a steaming shower, but after that long-awaited brush with soap and water I almost felt human again. After the last grimy, sand-choked weeks, it was such a sensual relief to wash that I was totally unaware of the erotic floorshow I provided for the giggling schoolgirls across the alley.

Best of all, the Teinsin was as accommodating to our wandering holy man as the rest of Tibet had been. Wherever we stopped, villagers always made sure Sadhu was well fed, watered and bedded down first. True to form, Tiensen's genial manager found a cozy spot for him right in the hotel entryway beside their family yak.

Like I said, it's important to take the small victories whenever and wherever you can.

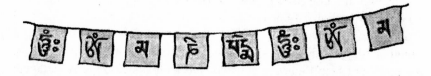

Chapter VII

Showdown in Shigatse

Be focused.
Never look back. "Sempre diretto!"

October 31

Shigatse promised us absolute comfort. Maybe it was its manageable size, its broad tree-lined streets, its near absence of cars, its more discrete military presence or its people's friendly attitudes. Perhaps it was the companionship of other Westerners after weeks of near isolation. Or maybe it was simply the mystic peace radiating from Tashilhunpo.

"But three days here," I thought, "will give us a second glance at Tibetan "big city" life. While Cheryl finally conquers her cold in a real bed, I'll handle all the nagging details: shopping, trading, shoeing Sadhu, renewing ATPs and, God please, perhaps even find a real shower."

Our permits had already expired and one quick trip to the local police station landed us new ones for the towns of Lhazê, Xegar, Tingri, Nyalam and Khasa on the Nepalese border.

"But no Mount Everest base camp," the rotund officer with the childish moon face cautioned. "Or Rongbuk Monastery."

"Why?"

Cocking her head, she curiously stared, as if to ask, "Where have you been the last forty years? In a cave? Perhaps in the U.S.?"

"Rongbuk closed to foreigners," she blurted, spouting the Communist Party hard-line.

I'd heard that villagers "re-educated" by the Communists destroyed Rongbuk, the world's highest monastery, during the Cultural Revolution. It's just one of six thousand cloisters and temples which were pillaged, and its monks and nuns were some of the tens of thousands murdered or sent to concentration camps. Its wood was used for fires, *stupas* were smashed, holy treasures stolen, murals destroyed. No building was left unscathed.

Since then, however, I'd heard the temple had begun to rise like a sacred phoenix from the ruins. Even a few monks and nuns had already returned, out of the hundreds originally inhabiting the valley called the Sanctuary of the Birds.

"And," she added matter-of-factly, "You get permits for Everest only from Mountaineering Association in Lhasa."

"Back in Lhasa?" I cringed. "No one ever mentioned that to us when we got our last ATPs..."

Remembering back to that debacle, it was a wonder we got any at all.

"Well," I thought, "there's nothing to be gained by arguing. Hey, at least her office was open and maybe there's still a way for us to slip in to Mount Everest. Besides, it's nearly November. Depending on how soon the winter snows hit, we may be sprinting for the frontier by the time we reach the base camp turnoff at Tingri."

That afternoon I explored the main market flooding the street across from the Teinsin. The blocks-long Shigatse Mall consisted of a line of rickety tables under corrugated tin roofs. The bazaar was ringed by black-robed men selling their menagerie of freshly butchered goats, sheep and yaks with severed heads prominently displayed as totems of freshness. One table sold kitchenware, another bolts of brilliant Chinese fabric. One peddled bridles, saddles and harnesses, and still another offered bottles of *chang* in identical tan plastic jugs.

Serious Shigatse shoppers hustled from stall to stall stuffing treasures into straw or neon plastic baskets. Scrawny dogs in packs nosed for bloody butchered scraps. Dung smoke-blackened kids jostled and hollered. Men, gawking and crooning to themselves, walked rickety pony carts by, while monks shuffled past, pretending to be oblivious or immune to it all.

In the very center of the din and confusion, under a series of tin awnings, sat another thirty tempting stands appearing each morning, vanishing every night.

As I passed through their gauntlet, women yanked at my sleeves, cooing, "How much you give me?" "Best price!" Persistent, they thrust huge strands of turquoise nuggets, strings of freshwater pearls, wooden prayer wheels, intricately designed silver temple bells, conch shells, silver-trimmed human skulls and pillboxes in my face. They were ever eager to trade for yuan or dollars. Or even swap for sunglasses, watches or calculators. They hadn't seen many visitors lately, just the occasional tour bus of day trippers, who swarmed their stands like locust then flew off just as abruptly.

Returning to the Teinsin in late afternoon, I traded travel tales and maps with an odd entourage of four bicyclists sunning on the hotel's flat rooftop. It turned out that they were also en route to Kathmandu.

Marley, a wild-eyed, dreadlocked Chicagoan, and Billie, a willful Southerner, were in the middle of cycling around the world. Two unlikely partners joined them. Hans, the tenacious Bavarian, was consumed with the quest of hiking Mount Everest to advanced base camp, whatever the cost. While Jacob, a wooly, light-hearted Israeli ex-tank commander, was so devoted to his mountain bike that Billie swore he'd make love to it if only the handlebars didn't get in the way.

It was fun just unwinding and comparing notes with that quartet. In some small way, their interest and concern in our journey made me feel like we'd already accomplished something by just coming that far. Eventually, all those nagging loose ends would soon fall into place.

Returning to our room, I crept in and leaned over Cheryl, gently feeling her clammy head.

Slowly she cranked open hollow eyes, whispering, "If I don't feel better soon, I'm catching a ride back to Kathmandu."

Any optimism I'd savored just moments earlier immediately vanished.

79

November 1

With Cheryl still bedridden, I joined Billie, Marley and Jacob on a tour of Tashilhunpo Monastery. Set high on a hillside, just west of the crumbling fifteenth-century ramparts of Samdup-tse Dzong, Tashilhunpo looks down on all Shigatse in gold-domed splendor. Built in 1447, it's the traditional seat of the Panchen Lama, the second highest incarnation in Tibetan Buddhism.

Historically the Dalai Lama and Panchen Lama have routinely been set against each other, at least since 1720 with the early Chinese domination of Tibet. In 1959, after the Dalai Lama fled to India, the Communists seized that opportunity to appoint the Panchen Lama Chairman of the Preparatory Committee for the "Autonomous Region of Tibet." In doing so, they hoped to make him their official mouthpiece. But that was short-lived. Crying out for independence in 1964, the holy man suffered house arrest, torture and it was even rumored that he died in prison. So, it came as some shock in 1978 when the "re-educated" Panchen Lama resurfaced and was appointed a Vice-Chairman of the National People's Congress Standing Committee, China's pseudo-parliament. Tragically, the Panchen Lama, China's reluctant political pawn almost since birth, died in 1989 at the age of 51. Fittingly, just before his passing, he denounced Tibet's destruction by the Chinese.

Predictably enough, the Chinese quickly declared they had to recognize his successor, since, according to Buddhist doctrine, his soul would soon reincarnate into the body of his replacement. The Communists, far from being ardent Buddhists, also unilaterally declared that "lamas could only be born into Chinese territory."

Today many Tibetans revere both the Panchen Lama's memory and his reincarnation, recently discovered in the form of a young boy in a distant eastern Tibetan village. He was secretively whisked away by the Dalai Lama's hierarchy. However, in yet another brazen move to destroy religious freedom, the Chinese Communists kidnapped his successor, the 11th Panchen Lama and his family in 1995, and placed him in detention—his whereabouts uncertain. Just six-years-old at the time, today he is surely the youngest prisoner of conscience in the world.

While waiting two hours in the sweltering heat for that monastery to open, we witnessed a remarkable display of devotion as rows of earnestly chanting pilgrims lined up outside Tashilhunpo's vast wooden gates. Pious women, eager children and ancient men fervently threw themselves forward in humble prostration, yak-buttered braids flying into vermilion dirt. Flat on the ground, they continued chanting melodic prayers as constant as the turning of their prayer wheels. Then, rising barefoot and dusty, they dove again. And again.

Eventually a whisper arose and all forty pilgrims and monks formed lines in front of the portals, while an orange satin banner-like prayer cloth was reverently passed hand-to-hand. Burgundy garbed monks and black-robed pilgrims, in school-photo fashion, stood on the steps, kneeled or sat on the ground. Marley and I were asked, and honored, to snap their portrait. Then rising, the cloth draped about their shoulders like a Tibetan ceremonial dragon, they turned and humbly passed through the welcoming sacred gates.

We eagerly joined their silent procession. Our wandering tour wended through the Hall of the Maitreya with its towering three-story Buddha of the Future, the *Champa*. Next, enveloped in pungent burning incense and acrid yak butter lamps, we shuffled through chambers surrounding the Great Hall, weaving past magnificent frescoes and jeweled funerary pagodas containing remains of former Panchen Lamas.

At last, an hour later and world away, we marveled at an amazing factory-sized kitchen, emitting an overwhelming stench of centuries old yak butter. Behemoth copper cauldrons, six-meters (twenty-feet) high, fifteen-meters (fifty-feet) around, bubbled an endless supply of *pö-ja* for thirsty monks.

That monastery once housed as many as four thousand holy men, who worked as artisans, operated a college and printed religious sutras. Presently only seven hundred remain due to the China's Religious Bureau's complete control over restoration of monasteries and the admissions of monks.

Tashilhunpo, one of the holiest sites in Tibet, once fulfilled a vital aspect of spiritual life. Today it mainly survives as a tourist attraction with its monks posted there for window dressing and propaganda purposes.

81

Since the Chinese authorities consider monks "Tibetan reactionary lamas," their numbers are strictly controlled, presently limited to three percent of the country's population. Of those, according to leading pre-invasion monks, the majority know little about the teachings of the Buddha. Many novices are just there for an easy life and secure income.

With Tibet's future religious leaders subsisting on Beijing's wages, one can only wonder, "Can a monk serve two masters? Can one be a devout Buddhist and ardent Communist at the same time?"

November 2

Early the next morning I set off to find shoes for our hoofed friend. "Surely," I thought, "with all the horses here (many more than cars), hiring a blacksmith is going to be as easy as finding good Szechwan food."

Oh, how wrong I was.

Figuring I could use all the help I could muster, I recruited a hotel hang-about, the spitting image of Dustin Hoffman in the film *Papillon*. Together we scoured narrow streets, stopping at stalls, bushwhacking men leading donkey carts and chatting-up contacts in the marketplace. Still, it took at least two hours before we found our man: an angular Chinese Muslim sporting a wisp of a Fu Manchu beard who worked incognito from a covert smithy right outside our hotel door.

With high hopes we led him to Sadhu, naively pawing in the freshly scrubbed hotel courtyard. In an instant, his assistant, a chubby little fellow with a rosy inquisitive face and six more meddlesome men sprung out of nowhere to join us. With the cast finally assembled on stage, the curtain went up for a simple shoeing destined to snowball into a comical Chinese opera. One man blocked the door. Another inspected the horse, parading around with a puzzled look. Each gave approving nods. Then one fellow ran off in search of horseshoes, again and again, before bringing the right size. Another helped the assistant tug back and restrain Sadhu's front leg, something our friend didn't appreciate in the slightest. Meanwhile the others, including Papillon, "oohed," "ahhed" and laughed in chorus without a single cue card.

At first, they tugged Sadhu in a push-me, pull-you manner. He didn't know what to think. He just indulged them, staring over at me with a *here we go again* glare. Our wander-horse was used to constant inspection by well-meaning villagers.

When it came to horses, every Tibetan was an expert. At every village, at each crossroad, at every cart we passed, villagers either appreciatively smiled or, more than likely, nit-picked some flaw. They criticized his slightly split hoofs, his age, his lack of teeth, the way we tied his packs, the way his saddle rested, the number or quality of blankets on his back, the way his bridle was either too tight or not tight enough. They even lifted his tail for a more personal inspection! Ironically many, after just demeaning him, insisted on trading their horse and cart for good ol' imperfect Sadhu. So he and I quickly learned to bear all their well-meaning indignities with a sense of humor.

However Sadhu had never been shod before and he didn't take the operation lightly, especially with their unorthodox style. Now I'm no expert. But when they started driving nails through his entire hoof, even I wondered if they really knew what they were doing.

Noting my foot-shuffling anxiety, Papillon shook his finger assuring me, "Don't worry," while the incessant pounding continued accompanied by cringing and wincing by both the patient and me.

Finally, the confident Muslim bent over the spikes on the top of Sadhu's hoofs and clipped them off.

"Not very cosmetic," I thought. "I just hope they work, since there's rougher road ahead."

Well, ol' Sadhu endured fitting his front shoes well. But as soon as they began on the rear, a look of undeniable terror shot across his startled face. As he started to twitch and quiver, the smithy's assistant spun the jumpy gelding around by a leather snare clamped to his soft, rubbery lips. Then, bending up Sadhu's hind leg, he wrapped the horse's floor-length chestnut tail tightly around it.

Big mistake. Sadhu totally lost control. He struggled and jerked to straighten his leg, fought to free his head and tried to snap at the Muslim. To complicate matters, his front hoofs, now fitted with new, slick metal shoes, skid across the wet concrete floor. Skating off in opposite directions, they knocked over two gawking locals like wooden duckpins, and for one horrifying instant I was certain Sadhu was going down!

Just then, the door opened and three Brits poked their fuzzy red heads into the courtyard, whingeing, "Can't we go upstairs?"

"No!" the chorus cried in unison, struggling to keep our diva from toppling over on someone, as we reached a crescendo to our awkward equine opera.

Eventually, God only knows how, Sadhu found his balance. The Muslim persevered until all four shoes were in place and all that was missing was the proverbial fat lady's song.

Except for dealing with the two weeks of grit still plastered to my body, even after my "luxurious" ice bath, we were ready to hit the road. I'd looked forward to a steamy shower. No, I'd lusted after it for two sweaty weeks. It was just what the doctor ordered to boost grubby spirits. I knew Shigatse has a public shower, so grabbing a nearly recuperated Cheryl, we set-off to indulge in our well-earned fantasy.

We'd only walked half a mile before spotting what we were to discover was a rundown curbside clinic. Since Cheryl's cold had lingered too long, we dropped in (which wasn't hard since its door was flung wide open) to a closet-sized room straight out of the 1960s furnished in the finest Naugahyde splendor.

The sight of us clearly startled an eager young doctor, garbed in his starched white lab coat and gauze mask. With profuse apologies, he motioned for Cheryl to come over. Bowing ever so slightly, he began an animated routine reserved just for foreigners.

As our less than *barefoot* physician mimed a litany of symptoms one by one, his odd routine made our usual sleep skit seem like it was ready to take on the road (which I guess we already had).

He began by exaggerated hacking.

Cheryl nodded. Encouraged, he placed his hand against his forehead, then removed and waved it. "Hot?"

"Yep."

"Head hurt?" he asked, throwing his back in mock misery.

"Uh-huh," she deadpanned, wondering what was next.

With that he swiftly reached to a shelf packed with clear medicine flasks. Pulling several down, the doctor poured out a mosaic of fifty multi-colored pills, then resumed his intense interrogation.

"Sneezing?" he mimed, snorting an unmistakable "huh-chew!"

"Yea."

He jabbed fingers to his cheeks. That one had us stumped for a second. "Sinus pain?"

Cheryl finally nodded in recognition, pointing to the left side of her head.

Hearing that, he grabbed several more jars from the wooden shelf. After stuffing two folded paper packets so full they could barely close, he bowed again. Then he gently handed my companion a virtual mound of medicine.

At first, she was hesitant to accept since so much medication would amount to fifty dollars or more in the States, certainly more than we carted around with us through downtown Shigatse.

"How much?" she nervously asked. "Yuan?"

Embarrassed, the doctor scribbled "11" on a crumpled paper sack. Then he sheepishly peered up, as if to ask "Too much?"

It was all less than two dollars. At last, we'd found something something positive about the Chinese presence in Tibet.

Those magnificent showers awaited nearby at the end of a long birch-lined drive, and spotting no one else waiting in front of the utilitarian concrete bunker, I was ecstatic.

Even Cheryl perked up. "No chance of running out of hot water today!" she chirped sweetly. With her illness, it was the most excited she'd been in weeks.

We stood there an hour…patiently…in the blazing sun…in anxious anticipation. Finally, a stout middle-aged Tibetan woman strolled past scrutinizing us, then bellowed something, while ominously waving us away.

"What's that supposed to mean?" I wondered aloud, hoping in Tibet there was some less obvious meaning to her gestures. "Maybe she's bragging about how great the showers are? How we'll shed all this crud from our bodies?"

Cheryl shouted after her, "Hey! We're just waiting for the showers!" But the crony just shook her head and kept walking.

"This isn't a good sign," I thought, "but we're not budging. We're relentless. We've waited too long, come too far."

Within an instant a massive military flatbed truck tore down the road headed right at us, throwing a hurricane of dust in its wake. As it slammed to a stop, fifty grinning soldiers eagerly piled out of the back and formed a ragged line in front of the open shower door. There they were sternly briefed by their pint-sized "general" before hightailing it into our waiting warmth.

"Hey, wait just a minute! Don't they have showers on their base?" I swore.

As any hope of a hot shower was doused with each passing second, our resentment grew. Indignant, I finally approached the officer. Forgetting that he probably didn't speak English, I started insisting, "Excuse me, but these are public showers!"

To which Cheryl sarcastically reminded him, "And we've waited the past hour."

The pompous officer glared up at us, his pencil-thin mustache stretched to a smug lizard-like smirk, as he shrugged, "So?"

"So can't we work something out?" I figured there must be a way for everyone to win. "Look, there are just two of us—and fifty of you. We'll only be five minutes," I promised, willing to settle for almost anything after all we'd been through.

He casually lifted dark aviator sunglasses. His sinister eyes narrowed to slits and with a condescending sneer, he hissed, "No!"

That was in English!

As I barely contained my rage, Cheryl continued to plead, "After your men are done? Please? My husband really needs a shower!" And she ought to know…

Callously, that conniving excuse for an officer slowly shook his puerile head and I knew it was a lost cause.

"Come on Cheryl," I fumed, ushering her away before we took on the entire local regiment over a damned shower. "Let's not give this snake spit the satisfaction of watching us grovel."

Dejected, we shuffled silently down desolate streets. The wind was a little more relentless, the sun more stifling, the dust more suffocating, the few folks we passed more distant and hollow. Depressed, we trudged back to our inn, a little wiser about life in that cruel "Land of Impossibilities."

His sadistic pleasure had disturbed me. "Probably," I thought, "just probably, all those gruesome rumors we heard are true: the ones about Tibetans being skinned alive...hundreds in slave labor camps...nuns serving seventeen years in prison for singing pro-independence songs...Tibetan nuclear missile deployment sites."

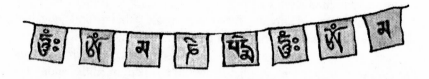

Chapter VIII

Village Of Fear

Be patient.
Going that extra little bit can make all the difference.

November 3

Shigatse's respite was hesitantly packed. I grew more concerned as each day drew us further into November and with it the increased probability of battling heavy snowfall. Crawling out of our down bags each morning, which we'd used since the hotel's blankets were threadbare, we could see our breath freeze in midair. Already we'd delayed our departure an extra day waiting for the Chinese medicine to take effect and hoping Cheryl's hacking and even more debilitating depression would be left behind.

Unfortunately, both were still with us. We could wait no longer.

Before leaving, I passed Billie a hastily written note for N.D., since traveling by bike, she'd arrive in Kathmandu long before we did. Our "message in a bottle" gave N.D. our estimated date of arrival, asked him to reserve a room for us in Thamel and find a place to bed Sadhu. Those simple requests would make our arrival that much easier, especially if we pulled-in late at night. I even dared to suggest that he talk to all those "family contacts" of whom Narayan boasted back in his office in Colorado.

With any luck he could arrange for us to meet his "friend," the King of Nepal. Since we'd already discovered most Tibetan and Nepalese Buddhists are prevented from crossing borders to worship in Kathmandu or Lhasa, we'd decided we wanted to present the monarch with our Lhasan prayer flags. Perhaps if he'd agree to fly them in Kathmandu, that simple act might help persuade both governments to reconsider pilgrimage policies. Sure, I realized it was a long shot, but worth a try.

Billie readily agreed to become our courier. Tucking our wax-sealed letter deep inside a hidden jacket pocket, she boasted, "Even if they search me, the Chinese'll never find it here."

Surprisingly, our hotel departure became a poignant ceremony. The cheerful owner, his daughters, sons and Papillon all helped us down to the courtyard with our bags, saddle, bridle and bizarre provisions.

While in town, we'd stocked up on Chinese noodles, a few green tins of unknown mystery meat and some *761* bars. Weighing nearly a pound each and wrapped with an illustration of a saluting Chinese soldier, every bar promised over two thousand calories of quick energy. Unfortunately, they tasted like rancid graham crackers, since most of the calories, as in much of the local Han diet, were from pork fat. They were a far cry from the luxury of Western high performance protein bars. They were but another far-fetched fantasy.

Although we merely tolerated *761s* for their size and convenience, Sadhu absolutely loved those foul wafers.

After his vacation, our wander horse was fit and surprisingly eager to hit the road. Eyes alert, ears erect, and rotund with hay, he practically pranced in the courtyard. Although Sadhu had reveled in the attention of fellow travelers who had secretively slipped him apples and other goodies, I could tell he was tired of his nightly bouts fighting that ornery family yak for space.

In a solemn ceremony those kind hosts strapped our stuffed packs onto our friend's broad back. Then leading us through the waiting portal and into the bustling thoroughfare, with hands folded, they bowed slightly and bade us a safe journey.

As we sadly ambled down Shigatse's now-familiar streets, many kind folks, complete strangers, approached and wished us well, or flashed that universal "thumbs up" sign. Somehow they knew what an arduous journey lay ahead.

As yet, we could only sense the worst was yet to come.

After sauntering past the reassuring gilded rooftops of Tashilhunpo and those few wobbly streetside carts selling gold *khata* cloths, both trees and pavement abruptly vanished. The road disintegrated into sand. We were thrust back into that arid high desert terrain which tested every step. Even our one constant companion, the river and its life sustaining force, evaporated. We were alone except for distant flocks of scrawny sheep or wayward goats, those cartoon caricatures nibbling sparse green flecks on nearly barren hillsides.

Occasionally the absolute silence was broken by a hoarse, infrequent, "Hello! Hello! Hello!" as a curious village lad drew near, then glided past on his black one-geared steed.

Traffic was always a mixed blessing. "At first," I thought, "it's comforting to see other traces of human life."

But each twister swirling in from the horizon enveloped us in a lethal cloud. It didn't take much coaxing to heartily agree with the wisdom of the early Tibetans who'd banned cars until the late 1950s believing that they "scarred the earth."

Although our mouths and noses were tightly wrapped with gingham kerchiefs like Jesse James and his gang, nothing stayed that brutal sand. As each barreling military truck careened past, we flew into coughing fits, while Sadhu grew more jumpy at each passing jitney. One crazed kamikaze attack led to the next. Without time to even clear our lungs between assaults, those whirlwinds did nothing to help my bronchitis and Cheryl's hacking and spitting increased, finally progressing into convulsive vomiting.

Then to make matters worse, her knee, never a problem before, started throbbing acutely. One pain led to another all morning, until finally she collapsed in a heap, moaning, "I told you I didn't want to leave today."

"Hey, don't blame me for the trucks."

"Not just the trucks..." she whimpered, choking back tears. "For this. For all this."

"Maybe she's right," I thought. "Maybe I shouldn't have insisted we leave. Maybe I shouldn't have even brought her along. Maybe neither of us should be doing this. Maybe it's just not worth it. What difference will it ever make…"

Weary, I tugged a canteen from the side of my pack. Towering above her, blocking her just a moment from the relentless elements, I gently passed the water down and wished that somehow I could offer more.

"It'll be all right. We can make it," I assured her. "We just need to have faith."

Yet even as I uttered those words, I realized they offered little comfort, standing as slender as my body had become. But words, love and boiled water was all that I could spare.

We trudged and stumbled like drunken fools in that infernal heat all day, motivated by the dream of food, hatred of each other, disgust with ourselves and a raw will to survive.

By late afternoon, thirty kilometers (18.5 miles) closer to Lhazê, we neared a small settlement just east of Ne. Spotting a ramshackle adobe hut that seemed to rise and float above the pulsing heat waves, I croaked in disbelief, "That a hotel?"

"Might be…" Cheryl sighed, hopeful, yet growing more skeptical with each passing kilometer.

A fractured Chinese hand lettered sign dangled on its outside wall. Although I couldn't read it, it boosted our spirits with the promise of a bed and hot food. After our showdown in Shigatse, I'd given up on enjoying that simmering hot shower until we reached Nyalam.

Three massive mongrels prowled the enclosed yard and I approached cautiously, stooping to pick up a fistful of stones in case they attacked. "Cheryl's already had one run-in," I thought. "Besides, we've heard about Tibetan dogs and their uncanny ability to smell a foreigner. My lack of a pervasive yak butter odor is still a dead giveaway."

With growing apprehension, I hailed a slight woman squatting inside the thick walls, shouting "*Tashi delek!*" Immediately I wished I could reel back that greeting since, as soon as she spun around, it was obvious she wasn't Tibetan.

No, that comrade wore a black Maoist jacket, blunt, bobbed hair and kung-fu slippers and was as severe as her surroundings. Glancing up, she scowled in our direction. Still, I convinced myself there's no harm in asking.

"This is a government rest house, isn't it? And we could definitely use some rest."

"Sleep?" I naively hollered, careful to remain out of leaping range of her ferocious dogs. But she simply shook her head and coolly waved us on, her sentiments punctuated by the snapping and snarling around her.

As we reluctantly set off again, Cheryl whispered, "I just don't know how much farther I can go…"

"I know. We'll find a place soon," I promised, trusting it was true. "Faith…"

Our prayers were soon answered. Nearby, miraculously, shelter did materialize. Just down the cratered road, a family winnowed grain in front of their whitewashed adobe house. Spotting us, they immediately waved us over without me having to utter a single syllable. Like inquisitive children, they excitedly led us inside their courtyard. After unsaddling, feeding and watering Sadhu, they proudly led us to their tack room.

Sinking to the floor amongst their wooden Tibetan saddles, brass yak bells and decorative donkey bridles, my stalwart companion immediately revived, began rubbing lines of creamy liniment into her knee and unexpectedly broke into a zany, off-key song to the surprise of their charming kids.

Meanwhile, I tugged sleeping bags, cook kit and flashlight from our packs. Upon seeing those unknown marvels, the family poked and prodded our down bags with delight.

Cheryl, interrupting her song, plucked a feather from their packed dirt floor. Pointing to our bag, she explained, "Same, same."

They stared in wide-eyed wonder, sighing in amazed unison, "Oooo!" They'd never seen goose down before.

Playing along, I grabbed our fuel bottle, attached it to the pocket-sized stove, lit it with a "woosh," and adjusted the knob until a blue flame appeared.

"Ooooh," they cooed, doubly impressed.

But our flashlight caused the most astonishment. They repeatedly turned it off and on, making its beam dance all over their simple mud walls for a full ten minutes.

I sensed that our arrival was a little like a strange UFO setting down in a suburban neighborhood. I wondered if bizarre looking creatures pulled fantastic items from their sacks, impressing us with their gadgetry, would our lives ever be the same? Would they inadvertently create envy where there was none? Change the course of our technological progress? Sadly upset the natural order of our lives? This was our *Star Trekian* dilemma.

November 4

Throughout the next day we trekked another thirty kilometers (18.5 miles) across a nearly identical landscape—with one exception. The village waiting at the end made it regretfully memorable.

As it grew late in the afternoon, we began our daily search for shelter. All day long, the scarcity of villages warned us we might only have one chance to find a warm place to sleep and that opportunity lay just ahead.

Approaching first one house, then another, our simple request was flatly refused by each and every farmer, who merely pointed to the government rest house up the road. The last even insisted his daughters lead us there. I didn't need to remind myself that yesterday's experience with a government inn was less than successful.

"Maybe," I hoped, "maybe this will be different…"

The rest house yard swarmed with a mob of flatbed trucks, dirt encrusted travelers and the usual roaming dogs. Cautiously entering the shabby grounds, we were instantly the center of attention, and I was summarily escorted to the manager: a short, abrupt Chinese fellow sprouting a wisp of a goatee, enthroned in front of whitewashed adobe rooms. From the looks of things, I'd obviously interrupted his card game.

Not wanting to start off on the wrong foot, I sidled up beside him, like a dog that's just been hit on the nose too often with a newspaper, and sheepishly asked, "Sleep?" in English. Half expecting him to fly into a rage as in our last fracas, I hesitantly suggested, "Room?"

"How many?" he replied in perfect English.

"Two. And our horse." Then again, Sadhu was already snoozing standing up.

"No rooms!" he snorted, slamming well-worn playing cards upon the flimsy aluminum table.

"None?"

"Dorm only!" he insisted, rising to leave.

"Wait! Let us take a look," I relented, too frazzled and frustrated to argue.

Reluctantly he led us to a puny cell jammed with six beds, baskets and belongings of what appeared to be twenty other luckless local travelers. Already I longed for our plain, private tack rooms, porches and potato patches.

"How much?" I asked, secretly hoping the amount was outlandish, ready for any excuse to refuse.

He looked me up and down, as if to determine my weight in yuan, then declared, "Eight!"

"Eight?" Indignantly I shot back, "No thanks!" and abruptly waking Sadhu, we stormed out.

Still silently optimistic, we soon entered a hamlet that was forbidding in its eerie silence, foreboding in its deadly tension. We swaggered down the village's desolate one main street, a derelict drag where high whitewashed walls seemed intent on hiding secrets and safeguarding houses that were strangely identically painted. Orange, white and blue stripes bordered each window or lined every doorway.

Before long we approached a square reassuringly more alive with activity. Tibetan men and women sifted barley, bagged it, then hauled it off. However, upon our intrusion there was an awkward pause. For an eternity villagers whispered amongst themselves as we gingerly approached. I just assumed they were shocked to see foreigners off the main road in the center of town. While we stood stock-still, a few fearful men cautiously approached Sadhu, not us, with a basket of straw and began their expected equine inspection.

Early admiration, smiles and "*Yago dos,*" led to mimed comments like, "He's very old," "There's not enough blanket under his saddle," and "Look, his ankle's bleeding!"

"Yes, I know," I tried to explain. "New shoes." His rear hoof had clipped his ankle. Impatiently cutting to the chase, I asked the eldest, "Sleep?" as I re-enacted our ridiculous nightly game of charades.

Appearing to understand our dilemma, the village elder discretely nodded, quickly imitated by the others, and implied that we'd talk about it later.

While I pantomimed equine tales with those guarded peasants, Cheryl joined the ladies rolling barley kernels in a screened basket to a rhythmic "shooka, shooka" beat.

After nearly an hour as the novelty of playing the human grain machine wore off, she asked the eldest, a woman whose skin mirrored the patina and texture of the earth, one simple question. "Sleep?"

Smiling sweetly, the sympathetic matriarch nodded and seemed to assure her, "Don't worry."

Relieved, Cheryl and I unwound for the next hour, laughing, "talking story" and sharing *chang* and tea with the twenty villagers. Until finally, with the last barley "shookaed," bagged, and hauled away, everyone abruptly stood and started to leave.

"Wait a second," Cheryl frantically demanded, looking over to me for support. "How about a place to sleep?"

"Maybe," I thought, "we've been too subtle in our approach."

"Sleep?" I begged, signing that universal symbol to the fellows I'd partied with all that time.

One by one they averted their sorrowful eyes or stoically shook heads and shuffled off, while we only grew more distraught.

Cheryl confronted the lady who'd taught her how to sift grain, the one who'd convinced her not to worry, pleading, "Sleep, Mama?"

The grizzled gentlewoman cast her eyes to the ground.

"There's something very wrong here," I thought. "Very wrong. People have never been this skittish or reluctant before."

In desperation, I finally invoked those magical words that had never failed us in the past. "Pilgrims...Dalai Lama!" I sighed, clasping hands in prayerful fashion. But it was useless.

With a weary sadness reflected in her eyes, our reluctant hostess pointed an invisibly shackled hand at yet another government rest house, collected her battered red thermos and hobbled off. We were abandoned, forsaken in an empty square. It seemed so strange, since just an hour earlier we were welcomed as family.

"Why?" I wondered. "What could we say or do to offend an entire village?"

In answer, we spotted the now-obvious black sedan with police emblem parked across the square and we shuddered in its implication.

The wind grew frigid. The sun was setting and our options faded with it. "Come on," I whispered, jerking a reluctant Sadhu by his lead. "Let's check that other guest house they suggested."

Just inside the hotel gates, we ran into a chubby, droll innkeeper, eyes poking out from under a floppy, beat-up cowboy hat.

"Sleep?" I sighed.

Lethargic, the gerbil-like fellow waved a stubby paw toward his one dorm room.

"What about those?" I countered, gesturing to six other chambers.

Pointing to laundry lines hung outside each one, he snorted, "Filled!"

"Come on Cheryl," I relented. "Let's take a look at his dorm." We stormed up the concrete steps and onto the creaking, sun-baked porch, figuring, "What other choice do we have?"

Poking our heads inside, we slowly scanned his six-bed warren, until our eyes froze on a cot beside the soot frosted window. There, an obese woman was stretched out across tattered blankets. She personified death. Glazed eyes were set back in her head, hair matted across her sweaty, flushed face and she babbled and trembled in delirium.

Ripping out of the room, rushing back down the stairs, we confronted the shifty host. "She's dyin' in there," I whispered. "You can't expect us to stay with her."

"Either that or she's crazy!" Cheryl swore. "No way I'm sleepin' in there. You can if you want, but not me."

I'd never seen her so adamant.

"I don't want to be stabbed in my sleep by some madwoman."

For an instant, the manager quizzically stared at us, as if to say, "What's got into them?" then merely shrugged. It seemed like a typically Han way of dealing with foreigners.

I glanced over at the kitchen suggesting, "How about in there?" With that, I strode over and performed a quick inspection of the dank chamber, murky and reeking of decade-old yak. Although the thought of sleeping on greasy stone slabs was as enticing as a night curled up on a butcher's block, the raging cook, waving a wooden spoon over her head, quickly burned even that idea.

So we were left with only one option, one neither of us relished. We'd head down the road. Pray another village soon surfaced.

The sun set as we raced west in the faint orange afterglow of dusk. We felt defeated and the frigid breeze howling up the valley did little to console us. We trotted to stay warm, head hunkered down into the wind. Sadhu for once, just as intent in finding shelter, kept pace.

I couldn't help but chuckle, thinking, "Sadhu, ol' friend, we finally get to see how fast you can move when you want!"

For ten kilometers (six miles) there was no glimmer of village lights, no welcoming smoke from a nomad's fire. No tingle of *pung-gu* bells. No shepherds driving flocks home. Just an arctic glacial stillness as temperatures dipped below freezing. We jogged in silence; all energy was devoted to staying warm and pushing ourselves past sensible limits.

At last, after forty-five muscle-searing minutes, Cheryl exclaimed, "How long are we going to continue this death march?"

"Hey, I'm as cold as you are!" I replied, stalling and trying to guess how long the sun's afterglow might last at that altitude. "Another fifteen minutes."

"But it'll be so dark. We won't even be able to see those telephone poles to tie up Sadhu."

She had a good point. It had been days since we'd seen our last scrawny bush and securing Sadhu was vital if we planned to get any sleep. It was still one long trek with a backpack to Kathmandu.

"All right," I relented, pointing to the nearest post. "Let's set up camp over there."

Under the heavenly spotlight of a half moon, we struggled to pitch our tent on that bleak plain. It was a tedious and hilarious task. Tying knots was nearly impossible while wearing thick ski gloves, but without them our hands were numb and lifeless within minutes. So we endeavored as best we could. And eating? Well, any possibility of that vanished with the last light. It just wasn't worth the bother.

Meticulously, I checked Sadhu's ropes half a dozen times wondering, "Did I tie him tightly enough? Too tight? Is he close enough to the ground to forage for food? Will he still be there in the morning?"

Finally, convinced I'd done the best I could, we wriggled into already frosted bags. Still, sleep was fleeting, since those concerns kept me awake most of the night. That and listening to our wandering holy man crunch rocks, scratch for grass and take the occasional torrential whiz on Cheryl's side of the tent, just inches away from our heads.

November 5

It must have been 20°F the next morning when we stumbled groggy, famished and shivering out of our dew (and urine) soaked tent.

"Never again. No more hikes after dark!" Cheryl insisted.

"Fine with me," I snapped, angrily yanking tent pegs from the frozen turf. "You were the one so worried about some crazy lady knifing you in your sleep!"

We were a pair. Sometimes, though we hated to admit it, we were less like Lewis and Clark or Hillary and Norgay—and more like Ricky and Lucy or Boris and Natasha.

Clearly we weren't the only ones suffering. Even poor Sadhu shivered. From his typical nighttime meanderings, he was tightly wound about a hundred times around the pole and could barely budge his head. Nothing, not even breakfast, could entice us to stay one moment longer in that god-forsaken deep freeze. So, quickly stuffing our gear into packs, we scurried off down the road.

On the positive side, for once we had an earlier start than those diabolical trucks and their typhoons of dust and debris. Still, it was hours before we warmed up. By then we'd reached a small village. With typical charm, the ladies' morning *cha* klatch invited us to join them for hot yak butter tea. That cloudy, pungent drink never tasted better or warmed our very souls quite as much as it did that brisk autumn morning, and I don't think Sadhu ever appreciated a basket of hay quite as much either.

As the day slowly grew warmer and more welcoming, so did the villagers. We were greeted by smiling boys riding two to a shaky bicycle, honked at by supply trucks bound for Nepal, encouraged by couples clopping by on wobbly carts and waved at by kids driving goats to Lhazê market. Some even made us appreciate the humor of our situation.

One large but empty canopied truck spotted us from behind. Skidding to an abrupt stop beside us, the good-natured driver offered, "Ride?" waving to his vacant truck bed.

We shook our heads, choking back hysterical laughter.

"No? Hop in!" He insisted. "Hop in!"

"And what about him?" we asked, pointing at Sadhu.

"Oh…" he shrugged, chuckling as he realized the lunacy of his generous offer.

Our day progressed without momentous event until that afternoon. Entering a wide deep valley, it was as though we'd stepped into the Land of Oz. Startled, I pulled off my sunglasses, imagining I was seeing things. But it was the same without the shades. Everything, absolutely everything, had a turquoise hue: the horse's hoofs, trucks, packs, our faces. Shards of brilliant aqua were even embedded in the trail.

As Cheryl broke into a light-hearted melody from that kid's classic film, a tremendous blast exploded from the nearly parched riverbed below. "Ggggrrrrbbbooom!!!" The earth shook. "Ggggrrrrbbbooom!!!" The valley vibrated like a monster awakening.

With each shattering blast, a look of terror grew in Sadhu's eyes as he nervously strained at his reins, as spooked as we were by the explosions.

"Ggggrrrrbbbooom!!!"

They continued every ten minutes, while we drew ever nearer. Finally reaching the crest of the craggy hill, we encountered three apprehensive Tibetans taking stock in the spectacle below. Graciously those ragged strangers invited us to join them on that promontory for a *chang* break.

Grateful for the company and drink, we huddled in their intimate circle, sharing fermented brown brew from the same simple wooden cup, taking turns toasting each other, Tibet, the Dalai Lama, and now the surrendered beauty of that expansive valley.

In whispered tones, one whiskered man stated the obvious. "They're blasting ahead!" he confided, fearfully sipping from the communal cup.

Another grabbed the mug, stammering, "Very dangerous!"

"Yes," the third pantomimed, "You must be careful rocks don't fall on your head!" as he nervously slurped the numbing nectar through mustached lips.

At first, I was amused by what I suspected was just their naive fear. In the Western world, a new road is usually welcomed. Then with each sip of the *chang*, I slowly pieced together the implications.

"Those crews are blasting a new road on the other side of the river. But why?" Looking around, it became horrifyingly clear. "Mining. All this green dust! The area's rich in minerals, and since the present road is abysmal…"

To exploit this remote region, I feared the Chinese would plow over farmer's fields, blast apart remaining grasslands, divert water, turn pastoral villagers into miners at slave wages, then ship the riches back to Beijing.

Shocked, I remembered reading about China's pathetic record when it came to irrigation, mining, lumber, wildlife management and hydroelectric projects in Tibet. They were notoriously reckless and environmentally fatal. After already viewing vast regions of denuded forests without wildlife and having read about China's widespread mining of natural resources on ninety-four proven mineral reserves, including ferro-chrome, copper, corundum and magnesite, there remained little doubt. Then again, foreigners have always brought hardship to Tibet.

As early as 1903, Lhasa was invaded by English troops under the ruse of "trade problems." However, even then, Tibet was a precious pawn in a game of global conquest waged first by Britain and Russia, and then China.

Just then, as another blast echoed up the canyon, one wise wayfarer shook his head warning, "The Dalai Lama will be very angry with all this blasting." Clasping a sinewy hand into a clenched fist, he shook it crying, "The Dalai Lama will come down and squash them!" In frustrated rage, he pounded it into the shimmering green earth.

With that pronouncement, our impromptu party ended. The three kind-hearted men serenely blessed us and we begged the Dalai Lama's blessing on them since they deserved it, and perhaps needed it, more than we did.

Resuming our trek to Lhazê, rounding the crest of that hill, the valley exploded with Chinese soldiers. While several supervised the blasting, a few planted dynamite then scampered like frightened hares behind nearby boulders. Others, living roadside in olive drab wall tents, labored as cooks, drove supply trucks or kept that sorry mess of a dirt trail passable.

Spotting us, a couple soldiers brazenly cried out "Herro, herro!" in child-like glee, then giggled like schoolgirls when we answered.

Strange. For all those innocents, there were others who glared with obvious suspicion, wondering, "Who are those Westerners with a horse? What are they doing out here?"

We didn't tarry long enough for them to find out, since I grew more wary of that still unknown, pimple-faced teenaged soldier who'd shoot first—and mime questions later.

The blasting continued all afternoon. Between deafening explosions and gear grinding trucks, I chased after my long-consuming fantasy food. For hours I secretively dined on a feast of steaming, cheesy pasta, spicy oyster pizza, clams Alfredo, sweet chocolate cakes with coconut frosting and icy mango smoothies. When I caught myself actually chewing, I forced to confront the reason for my gustatory dreams.

"We're starving ourselves! My clothes are hanging. Glancing in the mirror recently, I hardly recognized the haggard face that stared back. I tried to tally what I'd eaten the past twenty-four hours. Five-hundred calories. The day before? Six-hundred. The day before that? Four-hundred."

"Here we are," I calculated, "walking thirty kilometers (18.5 miles) or more every day on 500 calories. No wonder we're so weak and light-headed. (Although trekking nearly three miles high never helps.) I just hope our strength holds up until we reach Lhazê and can restock supplies. Both our patience and tolerance are wearing thin, as slender as the air we breathe."

I don't know whether it was our slow starvation, the rugged conditions, our deteriorating health or a combination, but something in the very air itself amplified every emotion. At any given moment with the slightest provocation, we were either on the verge of crying with joy or seething with raw and bloody rage. Each success was glorious, every failure devastating. Worst of all, our arguments, usually over insignificant matters, had become more frequent. I worried we'd never repair that damage. Consequently, often scraping empty inner reserves, we'd trudge for miles without speaking or even seeing each other.

In my heart, I knew it was only a matter of time. With darkness falling, we silently prayed for a place to sleep, a warm house with equally friendly Tibetans.

"We just can't survive another night sleeping out," I admitted to myself. "We're too cold, too famished, too exhausted."

Almost immediately, as if in answer, we were approached by the tallest Tibetan I'd ever seen. With little talk, since Chinese soldiers observed us nearby, the giant discretely motioned for us to follow him to his hillside home.

Once inside his enormous private compound, Sadhu was quickly bedded down with a bevy of yaks, goats, sheep and donkeys, while we were led up a narrow handmade ladder to a covered porch on the second floor where we would sleep. As we prepared our bags, one by one his inquisitive family came out to inspect then welcome the strange foreigners. Mama, her face and arms blackened from years of cooking over a dung fire, greeted us with *cha*. Then Grandma, toothless but merry, shared nuggets of yak cheese that she'd dried on their flat rooftop.

"Hey, it tastes like Parmesan," Cheryl announced with glee, as we gobbled every precious morsel.

Still shaken by the afternoon's discovery, I pointed down valley entreating, "Grandma, what about 'Boom Boom?'"

In reply, she shook her braided, gray streaked hair and wrinkled up her otherwise pleasing face while secretively confiding, "Dalai Lama very mad." I supposed that was indeed true.

After Cheryl and I had enjoyed a cold jug of *chang*, our host returned for a little pre-dinner trading. Although we weren't really in the mood to shop, his generous hospitality was such a relief we agreed to play along.

First, he pointed to my feet then to his own Tibetan boots. They were beautifully crafted in black and red felt, running halfway up his shins and trimmed in brilliant embroidery with yak leather soles.

I was tempted to swap. "They'll be a great souvenir," I figured, so I tried them on. Unfortunately they were at least three sizes too large. "He's one huge Tibetan!" I thought. "I'd slosh around in these."

Genuinely sorry the trade wouldn't work, I tried to offer an excuse. "Walk…Kathmandu…Everest…Chomolongma," I explained, looking up the Tibetan name for the world's highest mountain on my tattered map.

Although he smiled and seemed to understand, he persisted, drawing a beautifully woven yak hair donkey bridle with brass bell off his cluttered wall. But to us, considering our recent experience, that seemed like a ridiculous traveling accessory.

"No, I don't even think that'll keep Sadhu awake!" I chuckled.

Eventually our host became resigned to the fact we had nothing to trade and the benevolent family invited us to join them on rug-draped beds circling their dung fire in their typical combination kitchen, living room and bedroom. It was nearly pitch-black inside. Their dung fire vented right into the room. That explained Mama's sooty face and why the entire family shared the same dry cough, a hack similar to our own.

"It must be caused by a combination of this thin Himalayan air and the thick black clouds billowing from the dung fire," I reasoned.

There in the dingy smoke-filled darkness, tiny round faces and black eyes filled with inquisitive awe peered up from the fire's glow. Mama dished generous portions of *thugpa* into tin bowls, while Papa, his hair braided and looking like a Hopi or Coppertoned Viking, contentedly sucked the insides from goat horns and ripped dark flesh from a whole dried sheep's leg. Dinner was unusually silent, interrupted only by approving grins, eager slurps and quiet gnawing. At last, after gratefully sharing meager sustenance around their fire, that former monk solemnly led us to his most special place, his meditation chamber.

The miniscule, musty room was softly illuminated by the glow of a yak butter lamp. Shadows created saints and demons upon primitive mud walls. The air was awash with sandalwood incense. Photos of the Dalai Lama, shrouded in sacred *khata* cloths, flooded the walls. Interspersed between these were well-worn snapshots of the Panchen Lama, former Dalai Lamas and even treasured photos of our host in his younger days as a monk.

A crowded yet simple wooden altar held other cherished objects of his faith: a *drilbu*, the silver ritual temple bell for summoning the attention of the gods, as well as a brass *dorje*, a thunderbolt for fighting the powers of darkness. It also cradled his prayer wheel whose metal cylinder, inscribed with prayers, was rubbed smooth by years of sacred devotion. Fastened to the end of a wooden stick, it would be spun like those in the Jokhang Temple, sending its holy missive *"Om Mani Padme Hum"* soaring to the heavens.

Sensing the gentle monk's need to be alone, Cheryl and I soon left him in serene meditation. Stepping outside to wintry stillness, we gazed toward a zillion stars. Silently I thanked God we found the holy man, or that he found us. And I earnestly prayed that his *dorje* still had some magic left in it.

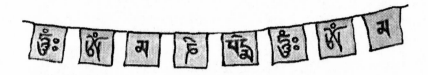

Chapter IX

Passes And Passages

Be courageous.
A mountain is always highest when you're climbing it.

November 6

O nly one obstacle stood between us and Lhazê, and the supplies that smudge of a settlement promised. Of course, compared to the others, that hurdle had to be truly formidable. Tsho La (Po La) at nearly 4572 meters (15,000 feet) was the highest pass we'd attempted and it was approached with humble trepidation.

Lately, I knew that even lower climbs had tested our endurance. While Cheryl was forced to pause every five-hundred meters to spit great green globs, I was doubled-over in bronchial fits until my sides seared and felt as though they were splitting.

I thought to myself, "This will be our acid test, since we'll face other even more challenging ascents over the next weeks. If nothing else, Tsho La will prepare us for those—or quickly prove their hopelessness and seal our fate."

As we began our approach, a barren cragginess enveloped us for over an hour until we started a steep, carefully measured climb. Although we struggled to keep a steady pace, at that altitude our hearts thundered. Breaths were short, wheezing gasps. A bitter wind shredded any optimism, while the summit teased, taunted and consumed every thought.

For over an hour little broke our concentration as we tenderly trod a never-ending series of switchbacks, a twisted heavenly highway to the clouds. That is, until we encountered that lone Tibetan roadcrew.

For days, highway workers had been our only companions on the ragged road to Nepal. We'd pass crews of ten men and women, hand-shoveling tons of rockslide from the pockmarked path. The distant, advancing drone of a small engine would develop into a tractor, the size of a riding mower, dragging exposed rusty box springs from the end of a flimsy rope. The crews, usually a boy driving with one crusty ol' geezer perched on the back, would often snap to a solemn salute as they passed and eyeballed our plodding progress.

Now, two men squatted alongside the road, warming themselves by a sheep dung fire. Their wives poured dried pellets of dung into the dancing flames, as they boiled a pot of *cha*. Spotting our ragged visage, they waved us over. And together, we huddled around that meager fire, sharing their strong, black tea and our sweet sticks of *Pao Pao Tang* bubble gum.

Perhaps in the scheme of major international events, it was nothing significant. But to us, it was more than a cup of hot brew on a brisk autumn's day. It was an act of unselfish human kindness shared between strangers—people with little more in common than a nearly insurmountable task ahead—scaling that formidable mountain pass.

Quickly fueled by their warm generosity, we tackled the peak itself. Struggling up its torturous switchbacks, we finally neared the crest. As our leaden bodies ached and groaned, our spirits soared on the wind. Reaching those faded, tattered prayer flags fluttering amidst the transparent, block printed prayer sheets atop that craggy summit, our eyes uncontrollably welled-up in divine gratitude.

And with that triumphant rapture, along with the thrill of success came the awesome realization that the crest wasn't nearly as daunting as the obstacle created in our own minds.

As if to join our celebration, a convoy of trucks appeared, blowing horns like ships in a regatta. Bus drivers waved and joined their serenade. Grinning Chinese passengers and Tibetan pilgrims gawked in disbelief at the two odd foreigners and their horse. Thundering past, they approvingly shot us an enthusiastic thumbs-up.

For the first time in ages, Cheryl and I tenderly embraced. Surrendering like two new lovers, our past arguments scattered in the breeze like those prayer sheets the faithful had left as offerings high on that peak closest to the gods.

Our victory celebration though was short-lived. It was already late afternoon and an arduous climb to the top became another marathon rush to the bottom. As the sun surreptitiously slid behind naked hills, its departure signaled the arrival of the unremitting winds that predictably began every evening at 5 p.m.

Putting Sadhu through his paces, I rushed ahead nearly jogging down the mountainside to locate a village before dark. Soon, it was obvious that Cheryl had fallen far behind. Since beginning our trek, we were often separated by five-hundred meters or more. However, we had both agreed early on, there was nothing wrong with that. After all, we weren't "joined at the hip" but at the heart.

Little could I imagine she was stranded and doubled over in pain.

I spotted three silhouettes below on the dusky plain, driving home their flocks. "We can't let them disappear," I thought. "There's no one else out here. Come on Sadhu, just a little farther," I coaxed my friend, as we sped ahead to intercept them.

Within minutes, breathless and nearing the shepherds, I gasped, "*Whey! Tashi delek!*"

Obviously a little shocked at the apparition appearing out of nowhere, they returned an incredulous, "*Tashi delek.*"

Light was fleeting and we were bushed, cold and hungry. So I didn't even bother to mime. Besides, our condition was obvious to anyone with eyes.

"Very tired," I choked, pointing up the road in Cheryl's direction. "Sleep? *Nga nyaysa gaw?*" Hearing my plea, the eldest herder nodded towards a nearly imperceptible village snuggled among the barren hills.

"So there is shelter here," I sighed, more than a little relieved. In this darkness, I'd never have seen it on my own.

As Cheryl finally appeared and drew near, the trio huddled and whispered among themselves. I could only surmise they were shocked to discover my companion was a woman. From that distance, they'd undoubtedly assumed she was another man since she was taller than Tibetan women and many local men for that matter. Plus she wore pants, unlike the local ladies garbed in those skirts and traditional aprons or *chogas*.

However, any joy, any sense of accomplishment I felt in finding us shelter was quickly dashed when she joined us. As we quickly crossed the path to the village with the shepherds in tow, she exploded.

"Damn it! Where were you? I was dyin' back there!"

"I ran ahead to find us a place to sleep," I innocently replied, not understanding her irritation or ingratitude. "Why? What's the matter?"

"You had all the water!"

She was right. I hadn't even thought about it, since I'd hadn't stopped for a drink or anything else while racing those last ten kilometers (six miles).

As we walked Sadhu clockwise around the village *stupa* out of respect for Tibetan religious custom, I quietly tried to douse the flame.

"I tried to keep an eye on you…"

Little did I know that simple comment would be like trying to put out a fire with gasoline.

"No, you didn't!" Cheryl snapped. "At one point, I even laid down in the middle of the road. Did you see that? Huh?"

Something told me I was being drawn into a fight. I refused to play.

"You know I can't watch you all the time," I admitted, lacking the strength or will power for yet another skirmish. "Look, I just wanted to find us a warm place to sleep tonight. Okay? So your cold would get better."

Although that quieted her momentarily, the incident was far from forgotten. We trekked in sullen silence. Gingerly leading Sadhu across a primitive, shaky, log-lashed bridge, we were soon joined by one of the shepherds, a fellow in his thirties, snugly bundled up in a fleece jacket. We followed him through a soundless settlement, dormant except for packs of prowling dogs. Together our stoic band wended toward distant peaks, skirting withered, ice-laden plants, frigid ponds and snowy pastures.

"Winter will be here soon," I realized and contemplated the implications of the approaching blizzards and the very real possibility of becoming stranded.

Meanwhile, out on the dead, frost-crusted, fallow fields, a dog appeared from nowhere. He streaked off in pursuit of a Tibetan woolly hare with its jack rabbit ears alert. The rabbit zigged then zagged, heart racing, then sprinted for cover as he ran for his life. But he was clearly no match for the hound who easily pounced on him. Re-emerging from the soil, the hunter held a lifeless trophy drooping between bloodied jaws.

Life in Tibet was that tenuous.

Our guide stopped. Thrusting a sinewy hand toward the snow crested mountain that towered on the horizon, he mumbled something under his fogged breath, then abruptly turned to leave.

"Where?" I asked. As he showed us again, we barely detected a faint, white adobe compound in the distance. "That? What is it? Monastery?"

He nodded.

"Come with us," I suggested, wondering why he was sending us all the way out there?

"Why couldn't we just stay in the village?" I wondered. "And why is he so afraid to join us?"

Reluctantly that melancholy shepherd led us a while longer as together we retraced goat tracks and slogged through deep mud and bog toward that lone, distant hut. Just as I began to think he'd lead us to its door, suddenly, the shepherd stopped stock-still, steadfastly refusing to go any farther. Tucking a crumpled one yuan note into my hand, he nodded toward that mysterious compound.

"What's this for?" I wondered, handing it back to him. "We don't want your money."

Looking disappointed, he begrudgingly withdrew his ragged bill. With a shrug, he turned to begin the long trudge back to his village. It was odd. No amount of coaxing could make him change his mind.

Discovering the remains of a vanishing dirt trail, we followed it until it trickled out at the heavy door of the strange compound. Leaning against

111

the rugged mud wall, a weathered old gent and his timid daughter suspiciously eyed us.

"Sleep? Here?" I pleaded, adding, "Villagers sent us," as if they'd understand, as if that would make a difference.

He skeptically peered up at us through half-blind eyes and shook his gray, bird's nest of a head, while his daughter silently studied the frozen ground.

Shuddering at the prospect of trekking all the way back to the village, especially stumbling in the dark, I begged, "Please. *Kuchi, Kuchi?*"

Upon hearing our magic words, the slight man furtively glanced about to assure no one was watching. Then he hesitantly led us to a crumbling adobe hovel. While we were shown to a vacant, bombed-out shell of a room only partly sheltered by the remnants of a roof, his gangling teenaged grandsons tethered Sadhu in the remains of a small courtyard. Once inside, our host graciously gestured to the dirt floor and what was once his stone fire. Matter-of-factly mumbling, "Sleep there," he shuffled out.

"Welcome to the manger..." I announced to no one in particular. Although we'd learned to be thankful for any kindness, that hovel tested our gratitude. The wind stealthily rushed through a portal with no door. Bitterly frigid air invaded through windows with no panes. We wedged stones into gaping chinks that made privacy as impossible as warmth. And then, just as we began to settle in, a grinning lad led two brown calves right into those derelict ruins, walling them up a few meters away.

Then, he awkwardly stood there staring at us. Shortly, six others joined him who seemed equally delighted to scrutinize us from the portal and peek in through remaining gaps in the walls.

Were they shy? Scared? Amazed? Hostile? It was anyone's guess.

"We might as well make the best of their company," I figured. So I pulled out our frayed translation book and started with a few fail-safe phrases. "*Tashi delek.*"

They said nothing, except snickered.

I tried another. "*Nga A-me-ri-ka nay yin.* I'm from America."

Still, nothing. Their silence was unnerving.

"Normally I don't mind the stares if people try to talk. But tonight, they won't even join our pantomime."

"And they whisper, too," Cheryl still fumed, flipping open our aluminum cook kit, "as if we'd understand anyway if they talked aloud?"

Any success in communicating, in becoming something more than two more animals sheltered in the family stall, failed. The boys eventually became bored and disappeared with the daylight.

Meanwhile, the cruel wind sweeping down off that frigid Himalayan sanctuary of the gods continued to howl unabated. Ice crystals drifted through our tattered roof. Our stubble of a candle blew out.

November 7

At dawn, we departed before the sun barely reflected its face off the reflective mirror of surrounding snow. Anxious to reach Lhazê and her comforts by sunset, we flew over frozen fields back to the main road. Although the village was just shaking itself awake, rag-bundled kids already threw themselves across silver ponds of glass smooth ice, butt sliding from end to frosty end.

Lhazê was closer than we'd expected. Remember that we just never could tell *exactly* where we were, given the inaccuracies of our map and indifference of that unmarked road.

But by early afternoon, we easily reached the dust bag of a town. Unfortunately, no sooner did we spot a few wisps of willows and vague outline of a village, than we were swallowed by a relentless sandstorm. Just to keep from blowing over, we had to lean far forward into that merciless wind, while dust, debris and Tibetan tumbleweeds blasted our faces with inconceivable force.

Through the din we discovered Lhazê's main drag, a motley assortment of general stores festooned in windsock-like hanging fox pelts, several Chinese or Tibetan restaurants, locals ducking for cover, and three less-than-hospitable hotels. The first one that Cheryl approached made it clear that they had no room for foreigners and they eagerly passed us to the one next door.

The second garden-style, whitewashed inn looked exactly like one of those 1950s mom & pop motels right out of Arizona's Mojave Desert. All that was missing was the humongous plaster cactus, garish, oversized

113

concrete teepee, a placard touting the "World's Largest Rattlesnake Pit," or the sign complete with skull and crossbones that ominously warned, "Last Stop For Water Before the Desert!".

A large courtyard faced the source of the town's running water, a muddy ditch where locals simultaneously squatted to drink, wash dishes, beat clothes, shave and bathe. That, it seemed, was the only bath Lhazê had to offer.

"Hey, remind me not to ask for water in the restaurant," I joked, as we blew in through the hotel's gates with the storm.

A robust Tibetan lady rushed to greet us and, after debating where to bed Sadhu, led us to a concrete chamber beyond a lower wall. With its steel-framed twin beds, wash basin and thermos, it was cut from the same cloth as our Shigatse hideaway. However, this time with Sadhu hitched to an adjoining door, he practically shared the room with us.

Pointing to our Tibetan eating machine, I asked our friendly innkeeper, "*Da?* Food?"

Already, Sadhu's snout rummaged in the dirt as he rooted for straw.

Laughing at his unbridled intensity, the manager passed us off to an older woman working across the courtyard.

Walking over, I began again, asking that weathered peasant, "*Da?* Food?"

Shrewdly, she grimaced, eyes squinting to black beads and croaked, "Five yuan!"

"Five? For one basket?" I wondered, shaking my head in mock-disbelief. "That's more than we pay for a place to sleep. No, three yuan, three baskets!"

She played along with the ritual that was an integral part of everyday Tibetan life, acting indignant that I was even haggling. "No, five yuan," she insisted, "Two baskets," shaking twin, reed-thin fingers.

"No, no. Five yuan, three baskets. And I carry!" I countered, thinking, "Here I am, standing in a sand storm, arguing about two yuan. But hey, they expect as much, right?"

She reflected a moment as we both stood squinting through the debris. Then she nodded and led me to the feed shed. There, she made sure I put exactly the proper amount of straw into each basket—and not a single blade more.

With Sadhu amply fed and bedded, Cheryl and I dodged flying, black-shrouded villagers in search of our wildest food fantasies. But finding no Italian bistros in that burg, we finally settled for Szechwan. One could have guessed it was a bad sign when the hand-scrawled menu disappeared along with the hospitality. But our waitress soon followed suit. After serving us cups of traditional fragrant jasmine tea, our Mandarin waitress ducked into a card game with a couple of truckers, never to return.

So Cheryl ventured into the murky kitchen alone, only to return a few moments later somewhat disappointed.

"Sorry. All I could find was fried noodles, rice and cooked peanuts. So I ordered a little of each."

"Well, at least we'll be able to "carb-up" for the climb tomorrow."

Then, with a sly grin she added, giggling, "Oh, I almost forgot," she teased. "I found us some cold *Pi Jius*."

Sure, it was just another small victory. But with *Pi Jius*, the local brew, we celebrated our victory over the first summit and faced our struggle up the next.

"This second pass," I warned, "is gonna be much harder than the last."

"Why's that?" Cheryl wondered, grabbing a fistful of greasy nuts.

"Well, Lhak Pa La's over 5220 meters (17,126 feet), the highest between Lhasa and Kathmandu. If we go slowly, I know we can handle that," I assured her. "Problem is, it stretches over thirty kilometers (18.5 miles) from here to the top!"

Cheryl gulped, visibly shaken. "But that's as far as we trek most days."

"Exactly. And it's suicide to camp on the crest with these winds. There may even be snow."

She bravely nodded as the challenge sunk in. "What choice do we have?"

I studied our tattered, useless map for a second, but it was just as I'd thought.

"None. We're gonna have to push uphill all day, then rush down the other side in what'll most likely be complete darkness. With any luck, we'll find a village or guesthouse over there." But our map wasn't encouraging. The other side of the mountain was empty.

"Let's try to get a decent start tomorrow," I suggested.

Since the sun rose later every day, we found ourselves sleeping-in like most villagers in order to miss the early frost and bitter cold. But even that was a luxury we could no longer afford.

In darkness and relentless blowing sand, we returned to our "bunker" and went to bed. At first, it seemed like a sound night's sleep might actually be possible. Then it started.

"Click, click, clack. Click, click, clack." Lead-footed crickets echoed through the frigid stillness of our tiny cell. "Click, click, clack. Click, click, clack," it continued unabated. For two hours I listened to Sadhu's relentless attempt to climb a flower bed wall, only to slip back down. "Click, click, clack. Click, click, clack," it persisted like a cantankerous grandfather clock.

Finally, I threw off the covers. Shivering and pissed, I tugged on my pants and stormed outside into the garden. "This has to stop. Now!" I warned, shortening Sadhu's lead by wrapping it around his leg. "Get some sleep...and stop eating...for once!" I kidded through chattering teeth. And I returned to bed.

It was silent for awhile. Then, just as I drifted off..."Click, click, clack. Click, click, clack. Click, click, clack. Click, click, clack." Sadhu, that amazing Tibetan grain thrasher, continued chomping and wall climbing all night.

November 8

Plans of leaving early disappeared with any hope of sleep. Our empty pantry forced us to shop for a few indecipherable tins of meat, more *761* bars and hard candies for the climb. After wolfing down a hearty breakfast of yak *thugpa* with red pepper sauce at an unpretentious Tibetan restaurant, we returned to the hotel courtyard only to discover it abuzz with over a hundred Jeeps and lorries.

"Looks like some sort of Chinese truck and auto show," Cheryl quipped. We hadn't seen so many vehicles in any one place since entering Tibet—or such a collection of military brass.

"Come on, let's get out of here," I said, hurriedly stuffing our bags into the packs. "All these tin soldiers make me nervous."

Outside, I quickly placed Sadhu's new "pillow" on his back. The kindness of the Tibetan people constantly amazed me. Thoughtfully, the hotel manager's young daughters, spotting the thinness of his cotton blanket, had stuffed a feedsack full of straw.

Nonetheless, after saddling our equine insomniac, we immediately faced a new crisis. There was only one way to the road and that was through the one gate. To reach it, we were forced to parade Sadhu right through the midst of that auto show, past gawkers and pointers, laughers and experts, and a hundred Chinese soldiers. We had no choice. But again, there was magic.

Looking back, it was similar to stories I'd heard of the great Indian leader, Crazy Horse. After religious ceremonies held prior to battle, people said he simply became invisible. Riding on horseback repeatedly across the line of cavalry gunfire, he was never wounded. So it was with us.

We slalomed through an army of green canopied trucks and cars, and scores of soldiers and officers, yet everyone politely skirted out of our way. A couple of startled young soldiers even saluted in respect. But no one asked any questions. And we certainly offered no answers.

After leaving Lhazê's core, it was amazing how soon those dust storms vanished. "How odd," I thought. "If people can build a town anywhere, why'd they choose the one location with terrible and, from what we heard, constant dust storms?"

Within moments, we entered a valley of pastoral riches. Once again, women winnowed barley. Men, decked out in jaunty felt hats, led donkeys trampling stalks around courtyards. Children tended flocks of goats and sheep, interrupting daily chores long enough to chase us, chanting, "Dalai Lama! Dalai Lama! Dalai Lama!"

"This is the first time," Cheryl keenly observed, "folks have begged us for pictures of him."

"You're right," I sighed, surprised by their change in etiquette. "It's as though someone has driven through and handed them out like candy."

"Are they reduced to being a status symbol? Is the photo perhaps worth more than the hope it represents?"

All day long we strained up that feared mountain pass. For long, painful hours we climbed through gray slate mountains, past naked granite slabs, along tundra-like pastures, down more dirt-choked red roads. Eventually, there was no glimmer of human life, no quaint adobe villages, no flocks of fuzzy goats or yaks, no empty stone corrals. Even the few rusted army trucks that begrudgingly droned by wheezed and bucked as they exhausted every gear. Not immune, we suffered the same fate, only worse. Bodies were never designed for that high altitude torture.

"This is more brutal than I ever imagined," I thought, trying to keep my blood from spurting out of my mosh pit of a brain. "My vision's blurred and I never remember being so alone, so insignificant."

Yet we continued slogging in searing, excruciating silence. Then unexpectedly, Cheryl was overcome by the heights. Doubled over in throbbing ice pick pains, she convulsed in deep heaves beside the road. I felt useless, unable to help. All I could provide was sympathy. We had to press onward. We had no choice. Or risk freezing to death with sundown.

As each kilometer post appeared and faded, the road constantly wound upward. The wind in mocking contempt whipped with a ferocity I'd never experienced. Dust, deadly at any altitude (let alone at heights nearing three miles), slipped past our kerchiefs and invaded our lungs.

Then again, suddenly, a soothing magic surrounded and bathed us. It made us ignore the pain, forget our bodies and ourselves. We shuffled in silent meditation, lost in deep circumspection. Trekking turned transcendental. Strangely enough, the wind, the cold, the height didn't matter anymore. For once, I stopped thinking of my needs, my life. They were as transient as the dust. Feet melded into earth. Breath combined with wind. Pace became a mantra. Heartbeat was one with the earth. My spirit soared free...free as the prayer flags that waved ahead. Prayer flags? Prayer flags!

"Cheryl, look!" I shouted, with all the grating voice I could muster. "Flags! The top!" Lhak Pa La's summit materialized above us.

Together, the three of us stumbled those last hundred meters to the *darlogs*, prayer flags, rising atop mounds of stones on the crest. With a final surge of adrenaline, grabbing Cheryl tightly in my arms, we hugged and for an instant it seemed like our very souls caressed.

We stayed that way for time-suspended moments. Until either our embrace, or the snowcapped mountains reflecting a burnt orange glow of dusk, dragged my consciousness kicking back into a more dire reality.

"Hurry. We've got to hurry," I cautioned, "if we're gonna find a place to stay."

It had been five or six hours since we'd seen any houses. But in my heart, I knew we'd find a place. "We're *meant* to be here. This trip *is* more than just another trek. And something or someone *is* watching over us. I have no doubt anymore."

We nearly sprinted down the mountainside. It wasn't till we were close to the edge of that high, arid plateau that we finally detected three shepherds decked out in their bushy fox fur hats and turquoise studded earrings. As we eventually limped up, it seemed they were as perplexed to see us as we were thankful to find them.

"Sleep?" I begged with ill-disguised urgency. However they only seemed interested in Sadhu, rattling on about his saddle, his bridle...

Cheryl impatiently interrupted, pleading, "Sleep?"

"Dalai Lama?" each asked, pointing to our stuffed nylon packs.

"Yes, Dalai Lama," I assured them, certain they were interested in our abridged tale. Nervously scanning the sky for traces of remaining light, I hurriedly mimed, "Dalai Lama...Potala Palace...Kathmandu."

"Picture?" one groggy shepherd suggested with a shrug.

Dusk disappeared, shrouding us in inky darkness. "Yes, yes. Sleep, now!" Cheryl insisted.

Finally, realizing our predicament, they pointed down the road.

"In the morning. Come. Dalai Lama," Cheryl quickly promised, eager to share a photo once she could dig one out of her pack in the light.

With a vague target, or at least a direction, we set off nearly running.

"Something down there?" I shouted.

"A building on the right?"

"You mean the left?"

Nothing was certain except the bone-bitter cold. It was already 20° F. But Cheryl thought she'd spotted a spout of smoke at a bend a half-mile farther below. So we flew down that mountainside through a wintry void, even waking Sadhu from his slumber.

"It is smoke!" There was hope.

Barely reaching the basin, the sheer willpower that had sustained us all day now vanished. Our utter exhaustion became nearly crippling. It was all we could do to muster the strength to feebly wobble over to the four silent figures huddled by a gated compound.

"S..sleep," I gasped, teeth chattering, shaking. "Tired... very t-tired."

"*Kuchi...Kuchi,*" was all Cheryl could whimper.

The shadows urgently whispered amongst themselves in strange tones then hustled us inside to their spartan, smoke-filled hut. Yellowed Shigatse newspaper pages wallpapered its one room, while two simple wood framed cots flanked a glowing potbellied stove.

Quickly recognizing our ragged condition, the sympathetic crew stoked our fires with strong *cha-deng* for the next three hours as we thawed by their fire. Hot as greenhouse tomatoes, we simmered in secure bliss in that roadcrew's simple shack.

"What a godsend these strangers are," I mused, "whether they're Tibetan *or* Chinese."

Eyes leaden, numbed and barely conscious, I drifted homeward.

top to bottom:
Traffic Hazards, Kathmandu
Young Lhasan Monk

top to bottom:
Wheels of Fortune
Fresco Temple Painting, Lhasa

top to bottom:
Prostrating Pilgrims, Jokhang Temple
Prayers Soar to Heaven, Lhasa

123

top to bottom:
Brandon and His New Buddies (photo by Cheryl Wilson)
Expansive Plains of Central Tibet

124

top to bottom:
The Potala Palace, Traditional Home of the Dalai Lama
1000 Yak Butter Candles, Jokhang Temple, Lhasa

125

top to bottom:
Yak Caravan, Same as it Ever Was
Pilgrims at Tashilhunpo Monastery, Shigatse

top to bottom:
Breathless in Tibet at 14,000'
Whip Master of Shigatse

top to bottom:
Tingri Quickie-Mart
North Face Mt. Everest from Base Camp

128

top to bottom:
Load Up the Yaks
Most Genial of Strangers (photo by Cheryl Wilson)

129

top to bottom:
Another Roadside Portrait
Tibet's Hope for the Future

top to bottom:
The Village People
Prayers From On Top of the World

131

top to bottom:
Tibetan Gothic
Cheryl at Drepung Monastery

132

In the Shadow of Mt. Everest (north face)

BRANDON WILSON

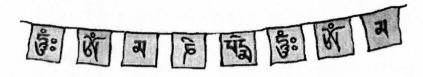

Chapter X

Keeping the Faith

Be happy.
Laughter and song are nature's tonic for adversity.

November 9

I cranked open my eyes. Smoke swirled around my head. My breath froze in mid-air since the dung fire fizzled out long ago. I struggled to glance at my watch. It was already 9 a.m., but the sun still hung low in the sky.

"We're getting started later with each passing day," I thought, "although it's far from laziness or even fatigue. These villages move with the sun and we're simply on their schedule. People rise later in the morning and often don't dine before nine at night. With a farmer's wise practicality, they refuse to adopt "Beijing Time," which artificially makes it the same hour in western Tibet as in the foreign capital, thousands of miles west."

Soon the potbellied stove was aglow. Everyone was groggy and whispering as they huddled over steaming *cha*. But as much as we'd have liked to stay and socialize, we had little time for such pleasantries. Eager to hit the road, we quickly packed, thanked our hosts and set-off.

After yesterday's grueling trek up the pass, we looked forward to an easy thirty kilometer (18.5 mile) day. However, we failed to take into account the 4,877-meter (16,000-foot) elevation, icy patches in the trail and near freezing temperatures lasting from sunrise to sunset. Usually by noon, I could strip down to just my fleece jacket, removing its nylon shell. But for the first time since we started, I was forced to leave both zippered to the top all day long.

All that morning and most of the afternoon, we trekked beside vast tundra-like plains. Lichen covered rocks, treeless hills, silent gray valleys, an ice-choked river and lifeless highway provided little reason to slow our pace. Besides, the wind continued to slice down past snowcapped peaks, slapping our faces with frigid air drawn from a bottomless fount.

Our cheeks were chapped. Our lips were cracked and bleeding, and hearts hammered with the intensity of Sadhu's hoofs as they glanced off the ice-studded road.

Although we spotted no one for fifteen kilometers (nine miles), occasionally, we'd detect discrete signs that hardy Tibetans braved that hostile land. Bare patches of soil sprung up, stark evidence of where slabs of sod had been cut for fires. On far-off crests, we'd spy herders' empty stone corrals, similar to Irish "fairie forts." But, all told, it did little to ease our loneliness.

We'd almost forsaken the hope of spotting another human, until we heard the distant, faint clatter of bells somewhere up ahead. Our pace quickened with wary excitement until, at last, we spotted nomads driving a straggling caravan of black, shaggy yaks overladen with hide-wrapped possessions along the distant bank of the racing river far below. Sighting us, two of the herders deftly slipped across the icy river and dashed up the hillside toward us.

"*Tashi delek!*" shouted a man perhaps in his fifties, looking as worn and weathered as his granite surroundings.

Slowing down, we replied, "*Tashi delek!*" Already I was intrigued that two people would drop their work and run so far just to intercept us.

As they jogged toward us, we could tell that one was a teenaged boy sporting a crop of wild, black locks and bundled in layers of threadbare clothes. His older companion was similarly wrapped in a well-worn, black wool robe ending above his knees in traditional Tibetan style. A dark leather pouch and minute bone phallic symbol dangled by a leather strap from his belt, as well as a miniature turquoise and coral studded silver knife. His toes poked through the end of beaten leather boots as creased as his rugged face.

"Dalai Lama?" that old fellow immediately suggested with a twinkle in his eyes as he drew alongside.

"It'd be great to give his picture to everyone who asked," I thought. "But it'd take another horse to carry that many photos."

We smiled, ignoring his request, explaining, "Potala Palace…" Then, pointing down valley, I added our seemingly *impossible* destination, "Kathmandu."

They nodded, seeming to understand. Then, with the enthusiasm of *blue light special* shoppers, they began to inspect our horse, our packs, even our bodies for items to trade.

Finally, spotting my leather tennis shoes anchored to Sadhu's wooden saddle, the elder stranger's eyes lit up. Excitedly he gestured, "What'll you take for these?"

To me, at that point, they were excess baggage. Cheryl always hated them, calling them my delivery driver shoes. Although I always imagined, when paired up with black socks and shorts, I looked like an Eastern European track star. As much as I considered just handing them to the grizzled herder, I knew it set a dangerous precedent for future travelers. So I returned his interest, carefully eyeing him up and down. Finally, intrigued by its suggestive shape, I pointed to the leather packet and ivory penis dangling from his belt.

Shooting me a sly glance, as if to ask, "You really want that?" he quickly untied his small pouch. Sliding it open, he displayed its meager contents.

Inside were four needles of differing sizes. A wide bone ring, a thimble, was tied to the outside, plus an inch long mystery implement. By its diminutive size, one could only assume it was another sewing tool and not some horny nomad's sexual aid. Since Tibetan men do all the sewing in their society, I'd heard those leather kits are as indispensable as their razor-sharp, jewel studded, silver daggers.

Well, a deal was easily struck. The curmudgeon was as pleased to get his feet out of the cold, as I was to have a meaningful memento.

Then the teenager faced us with a sad *what about me?* pout. Pointing to the Vasque boots on our feet, he suggested, "Trade?"

Shaking our heads, we declined. "No. No way. We still have a long way to trek."

He persisted. Lifting his foot, the likable kid showed us how the rubber sole was separating from the cheap canvass of his olive green Chinese sneakers. He'd soon feel the winter wind on his toes, too.

"Sorry," Cheryl sympathetically smiled, understanding, but helpless to end his plight. Who'd have thought? We'd never considered bringing shoes to trade.

After wishing the couple well, we continued heading down the road. Shuffling along, I congratulated myself that I'd found a traditional souvenir and pleased that we'd given the elder something he truly needed, instead of just candy or a cigarette. But we'd hardly finished patting ourselves on the backs before a voice desperately cried out from behind.

"*Whey, whey!*"

We wheeled around only to spot the kid still tagging after us, still trying to bargain for boots.

"No!" I yelled with finality. In truth, I was more irritated by my own inability to change things than by his dogged insistence.

Crestfallen, the nomad remained stock-still in the middle of the road until we and our shoes vanished from his life.

All day we continued our solitary trek, pausing only long enough for a rationed slurp of water and typical ten-minute lunch consisting of one or two *761* wafers or a few biscuits. It was meager, but intentionally so. After climbing Africa's Mount Kilimanjaro, we knew how difficult it is to digest food at higher elevations. Fortunately, our appetites faded with the stores.

Finding shelter replaced it as our utmost concern. After our freezing night in the manger, we grew more cautious. Since villages were seldom shown on our map, locating one became a race, a dangerous game of chance. Our daily goal was to reach the thirty-kilometer finish line and land in a settlement before sunset, which grew earlier each day.

About four that afternoon, we dragged into a small, squat cluster of buildings huddled by the roadside. As it was the first we'd seen in hours, we eagerly hobbled up to a slight man cradling a baby.

"*Tashi delek*," I offered, cordially grinning. He stared up at us with hollow eyes.

Cheryl suggested, "Sleep?" to which he grunted something more primeval than Tibetan.

"Friendly sort." Just as we decided to give him up as a lost cause, five or ten children who'd watched from a distance bounded up and led us by the hand to a nearby compound. Although they eagerly signaled for us to go inside, God, it was ominous. The massive adobe complex was surrounded by a ten-foot high foreboding wall and sturdy wooden gate.

"What is this?" Cheryl wondered aloud. "A school? Hotel? Someone's house?"

"Who knows? But it could easily hold twenty travelers and their horses. So it probably has room for us," I announced. Gingerly approaching its open wooden portal, I poked my head inside only to be greeted by the usual vicious, "Gggrrrr! Gggrrrr! Snapp! Gggrrrr!"

"Another guard dog!" I barked, retreating. I was tired of facing bared teeth every night; weary of gingerly sneaking down the road at night past snarling canines just to take a leak; fed up with rushing to gather stones in defense each time a pack of marauding, wild dogs approached. I'd had enough!

"Cheryl, give me...THE STICK."

My partner toted a high-tech walking staff throughout Tibet, much to the locals' constant amazement. Whenever we stopped, they'd examine it for hours, telescoping the black foam shaft in and out, screwing and unscrewing the polished wooden knob and removing its rubber tip to expose a steel point on the end.

Hoisting the weapon in one hand, I squatted to grab four stones from the rubble with the other. Then, standing to face my opponent, I snarled, "I'm gonna flatten this dog, if need be..." Ready to face the worst, I swaggered into the coliseum.

Well, they don't make lions like they used to. Once inside, I quickly spotted the mutt's owners. A squat fellow behind equally thick glasses and his diminutive wife stared aghast at the threatening specter in their courtyard.

Club waving, shaggy beard, filthy face, shredded clothes—I soon realized how frightening I must look to them. So I lowered my baton, if not my guard. Tossing several stones toward the snapping runt, I was surprised to see him chase after them, completely forgetting me.

"Ah, what the heck," I thought. "Sleep?" I apologetically mimed to the cowering couple. "We need a place to sleep."

Wary, not quite knowing what to expect, they led the Western wild man and his wife inside to a room garishly bathed in bright reddish orange paint and ringed by a band of cosmology symbols. A welcoming statue of the Chinese goddess of mercy greeted us from a bureau facing four beds, while a dour framed portrait of Mao, father of the genocidal Cultural Revolution, disapprovingly glared at us from a distant corner.

"Why," I wondered, "why is a holy golden *khata* cloth draped across him? Are these folks Communists and Buddhists like those carefully screened monks? Are they hedging their bets? Or is it just another example of 'political correctness,' like the woman we once met in Split, Croatia (then Yugoslavia), who'd hung a photo of beloved Tito in her kitchen, yet groaned, 'Tito?' in disgust, then spit."

No, unwilling "to look a gift dictator in the mouth," and ignoring the bizarre conflicting allegiances around us, we gratefully settled in. Famished, Cheryl began to unpack while I started fixing a simple dinner of dehydrated burritos.

"Hey, have you seen our fuel bottle?" I routinely asked.

"No, isn't it strapped to your pack?"

"No, not here…"

"Well, then it must have fallen off," she sighed, unfazed, pulling out our cook kit. "That's okay," she added. "We still have the spare." Then she realized the real problem. "Oh, no!"

"Yeah, our only fuel pump's on that bottle. We're sunk!"

With its loss there was no way to cook food for the rest of our journey. We couldn't even boil water to drink or add to our remaining foil dehydrated food pouches. Of all the things we could have lost, that hurt us the most. It was a blow at our very survival.

"From now on," I lamented, "we'll be even more dependent on the kindness of our hosts."

At just that moment, there was a hesitant rap at the door. As I stood to answer, it swung open and the manager's shy wife shuffled in, carrying a thermos of boiling water.

Our luck, our lives, had become just that magical.

November 10

It was late morning by the time we'd eaten, fed Sadhu, packed and handed our hosts some yuan and a photo of His Holiness. Although they welcomed the grubby notes, they looked rather unimpressed at the postcard of the god-king. It wasn't surprising given their larger than life portrait of Mao. But like our other kind hosts, I sensed maybe they, too, had a sacred altar deep in their living quarters and far from prying eyes.

It was still below freezing when we left, according to Cheryl's jacket mini-thermometer. Sadhu's timid pace matched the sun's reluctance to share its warmth. Already I longed for those days when we could expect the afternoon's blazing heat. I missed the frequency of villages and cries of children as they tagged along. At the same time, I grew bored with the blandness of scenery, the emptiness of the plain, the stoic mountain solitude and the brutal wind's torment no matter what direction we faced. Resolute, we trudged on toward Tingri. With its proximity to Mount Everest, I felt our spirits would be shored with our first clear view of the world's highest mountain.

By midafternoon, we reached the turnoff to Shegar (or, as its dubbed in China, Xegar) and its luxurious, multi-storied hotel at the crossroads.

"Hey," Cheryl suggested, "why don't we drop in for lunch," as if we had reservations at the Russian Tea Room.

"I know. I can't face another fatty graham cracker lunch, either," I confessed. "But the Chinese checkpoint's just ahead and it's still more than sixty kilometers (thirty-seven miles) to Tingri."

"Ah, come on," she teased, tugging my arm. "At least, we'll enjoy a hot meal for a change."

She had a point. Besides, Tingri was at least a day away and skipping lunch wouldn't make it appear any sooner. So, we led Sadhu off the road and onto vacant hotel grounds, foreboding in their strange silence.

"Pretty quiet for a hundred-room hotel," I thought. "Must be out of season."

Handing Sadhu's rope reins to Cheryl, I creaked open the glass front door and stepped into the lobby. No one was at the reception desk, the bar, or the restaurant. It gave me the willies, that abandoned ghost ship. Guests, staff and management had all mysteriously disappeared. Very weird.

Rushing outside, I was anxious to get out of there.

Well, as luck would have it, just as we turned to go, Cheryl spotted a gardener and wasted no time in sprinting over.

"Food?" she asked, drawing hands to her cracked lips.

Befuddled and wondering where we'd come from, the stooped worker nodded and whistled for the cook, who ambled over from a nearby building. Then, while Cheryl tied Sadhu in the hotel yard, the grotty chef led me to a kitchen, not in the hotel but in a separate barracks. It, too, was deserted and definitely not on Michelin's finer dining list.

"Now, I wonder what would they cook here? *Thugpa?*"" I suggested.

The cook shook his scrawny, crew-cropped head.

Of course not. This is a Chinese kitchen. "Fried noodles?" I asked, figuring it's a standard served most everywhere.

Wrong again. Leaning over the iron kettle, the fruitless gourmet tugged off its lid with a bony, hairless arm and revealed a seaweed and hot pepper concoction. Chunks of anemic fat floated in a slimy, translucent sauce, both reeking and repulsive.

But I was famished and willing to try anything once. "*Mifun?* Rice?"

Pleased, he nodded, since that was the only other food he had burning on the stove.

And then came that ever-crucial question. "Yuan?" I gestured, as if paying him.

Surveying me up and down, he quickly calculated how much his delicacy was worth to me. "Five yuan, five yuan," he squawked with a grand wave.

"Each?"

He nodded, grinning.

"That's outrageous!" I thought. "But it's hard to argue about money when you're half-starved."

So reluctantly, I agreed to pay his extorted price, about double the local cost.

Soon Cheryl joined me in that sickening, sorry excuse for a café, as we picked our path through the slippery dish. It was a struggle to lift thick ribbons of seaweed with chopsticks, while avoiding the foul, floating fatty bits.

Now, I'm far from a fussy eater. I've slurped sea slugs in Taipei, boa constrictor in the Congo and blubber in the Arctic with the best of them. Yet none of those quite prepared me for the surprise that lurked at the very bottom of the bowl—a bloated, corpulent white maggot.

"But it is hot..." Cheryl was quick to sarcastically remind me.

Swiftly leaving (much the wiser), we headed back to the main drag only to catch an equally curious sight—a bearded Japanese fellow squatting on his pack by the roadside. First, it was odd because we hadn't seen another traveler since Shigatse. Second, we hadn't seen any Japanese since entering Tibet. But they've been there since 1903 when Ekai Kawaguchi became the first foreigner to sneak into the forbidden city of Lhasa, disguised as a Chinese holy man.

Sidling up to the traveler, I asked, "Tingri?"

He tentatively nodded, just as shocked to encounter us there.

"Walk with us?"

Thrusting out his thumb, he doggedly shook his head.

"He's hitching?" I whispered in amazement. "Why, we barely see five trucks a day!"

Cheryl joined in, adding, "He'd probably make better time walking."

For once, we were left shrugging our shoulders at the craziness of someone else's journey.

Just beyond that "hotel of the damned" lurked our first Chinese checkpoint. Although far from disappointed, we had actually expected many others along the way. Neither of us knew exactly what to expect.

However, I'd read that early travelers, in order to avoid it, climbed nearby mountains in the dark—only to be chased by rabid dogs.

"Will they send us spinning back to Lhasa because we have the wrong stamps? What about Sadhu? We have no papers for him except a sales receipt. Will they search our packs? Will they find my extensive travel notes? Photos of the Dalai Lama? Confiscate our film? Jail us? Or just deport us?"

Those very real concerns flooded my mind as we approached the foreboding concrete hut, barracks and blockade "STOP" sign.

At last, pausing at the road's final crest, all I could suggest to my companion was, "Look. Let's walk down there…like we have every right to be here…out in the middle of nowhere…with a horse…And nothing…or no one…will stop us from reaching Nepal."

Knocking the dirt from our hats, pulling bandito bandanas off our faces, we marched toward the post with a certain defiant pride. As each step drew us closer, I chewed over again and again, "There are only two soldiers down there," while silently weighing our slim options. Simultaneously, those guards spotted us. They threw on their helmets and scurried inside their hut.

"Quick! Give me your passport, Cheryl," I suggested, yanking mine from my money belt. "You stay behind with Sadhu. Maybe they won't notice him. And," I added, as though it might help convince them of our innocence, "don't forget to SMILE!"

Grabbing both passports and ATPs, I donned the widest grin I could muster and approached the young, somber soldier seated behind the border shack's window. Tibetan probably won't go over too well here, I figured, so I stuck to English, offering a teenaged, voice-cracking, "Hello."

"Hello," he answered in perfect English, suddenly grinning.

"Is he grinning at my grinning, or grinning at us in general?"

"Passports?"

Whipping out our blue booklets, I placed them on the counter with a flourish.

"Americans?"

I nodded, then wondered whether that was good or bad?

He briefly scanned our documents, quickly comparing photos with the grim, ragged creatures facing him. Then he methodically entered our names, nationality and passport numbers on a grid. Looking up, he smiled again and inconceivably offered, "Tea?"

"Ah, no thanks," I cautiously replied, not wanting to seem discourteous, but not willing to push our luck, either. So far, he hadn't mentioned Sadhu.

Bowing slightly, eyes sparkling, that friendly toothless tiger wished us a good trip while his reticent companion swung up the heavy metal blockade.

As Cheryl and I waved so-long and led Sadhu southwest toward Kathmandu, my whole psyche sighed with overdue relief. With all the military posts we'd passed and all the military convoys that zoomed by, that Uzi waving soldier of my paranoiac nightmare had yet to materialize. Not yet, anyway.

Late that afternoon as the road flattened into a valley, we grew concerned about finding a place to stay. We hadn't passed a single village in hours. But considering our past luck and ease in clearing that checkpoint, I decided to try to stop worrying.

"We *are* meant to be here," I mused. "We're meant to walk to Kathmandu. Nothing's going to stop us now."

Spotting a roadcrew station, we were ready to test our theory. Two young men and two teenaged girls, donning official road worker hard hats, shoveled sand into a wagon. An older balding man, perhaps their father, supervised their tedious task. We stood watching for a moment. Then, as they drove their tractor onto the pitted road, we limped up, screaming, "*Tashi delek!*" above the ancient sputtering engine's roar.

In unison, they answered, "*Tashi delek!*"

Pointing to their walled compound down the road, I suggested, "Sleep here?"

Glancing at each other, they giggled like girls on their first dates and gestured to the older guy. "Guess we need to ask their boss," I shrugged.

As I walked over, their attentive supervisor paused with his shovel in midair. "Tashi delek?" I sighed. He nodded. Then reaching inside my jacket, I grabbed a treasured pack of American cigarettes saved for just such occasions, and cheerfully offered the guarded foreman the entire pack. "Smoke?"

He only looked away. Something told me he was going to be a hard sell. So I launched into our routine using the long version with full embellishments and mime.

"Walk...Potala...Kathmandu...pilgrims...tired...sleep..."

He remained unimpressed. Running out of key phrases that might get through to him, I invoked those two enchanting words that had seldom failed.

"Dalai Lama?" I begged, promising him a picture.

But no such luck. At the very mention of the banished Holy Man, the boss sternly shook his head with finality and returned to work. I was baffled, flabbergasted. Our efforts, especially offering a photo of that "Ocean of Wisdom," the literal translation of the title "Dalai Lama," had never failed to evoke a response, usually one of unbridled hospitality.

Desperate, we returned to the youthful roadcrew.

"Village?" Cheryl pleaded, "*Dhrongsay?*" as she pointed down a vacant void-of-a-road.

Collectively they shook their heads. Finally one chunky girl, offering us a morsel when we needed a meal, wagged a chubby finger toward nearby ruins and suggested that we sleep there.

Cheryl shivered at the prospect, exclaiming, "Cold! *Trangmo!*"

Laughing, the rugged crew now seemed to enjoy our little game. Yet they failed to realize how deadly serious we were. Nights recently plunged far below freezing.

"Why risk our health and tempt fate?" I figured. "Especially when a snug hut waits right next door? Besides, what would Sadhu eat?"

"Picture...Dalai Lama," I promised again.

Still reluctant to disagree with their boss, they shrugged as though to say, "There's nothing we can do," and the gang ambled back to their sand pile.

Defeated, we reluctantly turned to begin another miserable march, hoping it was all part of one of those Hollywood scenes where someone would stop us from leaving at the last second. Even though I reminded myself we were meant to be there, I remained convinced those things just happened in the movies.

"You know, Cheryl, it may be hours before we reach a village."

"Faith. We just have to have faith," she reminded me.

Right... Just as we began our deliberate shuffle down the trail, a lone scream like a whip cracked the air. "*Whey! Whey!*"

We paused, unable to determine whether it was real or only imagined. Then we heard, "*Whey! Whey!*" again, as others joined in. Turning, we spotted the youngest of the roadcrew girls waving us towards their home behind the compound's high gates. I was airborne with gratitude.

"Mama" appeared out of nowhere. She escorted us into the courtyard past a pack of yapping dogs to the immovable skeleton of an ancient tractor where we could anchor Sadhu. Then passing through a corridor of fragrant dried juniper, the kind woman brought us inside.

Certificates, roadcrew awards with ribbons and family photos provided a colorful blanket across adobe walls. A simple wooden butter churn stood in sharp contrast to an enormous, brilliant jade hued bureau just behind. As their potbellied stove quickly flooded the tiny chamber with warmth, Mama graciously seated us on one of four wood framed beds.

Soon the tiny room was aglow with excitement. The entire roadcrew, Papa, the stern supervisor, grandmother, sons, daughters and friends crammed onto beds doubling as sofas to inspect and socialize with the strangers. Three cute teenaged girls, obviously the village "maidens," crowded together on one bed and joined them. Flirtatious as sixteen-year-olds anywhere, they batted eyes and giggled at everything I garbled.

We had a captive audience. The family listened in wild-eyed wonder as we pulled out our map and relived our journey in detail. I guess they were surprised that we had made it that far. They plied us with homemade *chang* with the same bite as African millet beer, and poured it from one of those familiar tan plastic jugs. Meanwhile, we shared the only consumable we had left—cigarettes. No matter how politically incorrect, we took time to teach those coy ingenues how to blow smoke rings.

The boys, in turn, vainly attempted to teach Cheryl how to count in Tibetan, chanting, "*Jay, nie, song, shee, nga, zhu, doo, jiay, gu, choo.*" But she always seemed to get stuck on "*nga,*" as had I.

Chuckling, "My lips were just never made to get into that shape!" she tried teaching them to count in English, a task just as ridiculous.

147

"One, two, three, four, five, six, seven, eight, nine, ten," became, "One, zoo, sree, foar, vive, sex, zezen, aigt, noin, zen," sounding more like pulverized German.

Just as we began to laugh and unwind, another young girl flew inside shouting, "*Injis, injis, injis!*" Tugging my arm, she insistently dragged me out of the hut's toasty warmth and led me to another chamber several doors down.

"Has the Chinese Army discovered our hideout?" I wondered. However, ducking inside, I was even more shocked to see the person sitting before me—another Westerner!

"Ahh, bonjour!" the mysterious woman gushed, equally startled by my presence. In her flowing azure wool cape, stylish cap and weighty silver and turquoise necklace, the lady looked as though she'd just left a Parisian gallery.

"Bonjour. Where'd you come from?"

"We left Lhasa several days ago," she explained as she nodded at the bulky duo sipping yak butter tea by the door. "Zat's our truck outside. And you?"

"Ah…" There was a pause as I deliberated on exactly how much to divulge to the stylish stranger. "We've been gone a few weeks," I explained. "We're walking to Kathmandu."

"Wa-keeng? In zis weather? Forrr-mi-dable!" she cooed. "You must be verrr-y brrrave."

Flattery's been known to open a few reluctant doors.

"Well, I don't know about that…" I replied, slightly embarrassed and too tired to recall all the teachings of Miss Manners. "Some days I think we're just crazy."

"Zat ees wonderrr-ful! You are alone?"

"No, there are two of us and our horse."

"A horrrse?"

"Yes, Sadhu, our wandering Tibetan holy man," I exclaimed with all the pride of a Frenchman introducing his prized homemade brie.

"You are A-merr-ri-can?"

When two Westerners meet abroad, it's funny how one of the first questions that are asked is nationality, as if that helps to cram the stranger into a characteristic box. I've spent hours trying to convince Europeans that Americans are not all alike—anymore than the French and English.

"Yes. And you?" I asked, playing along.

"Frrrenchhh. Of course! But I live een Tah-hee-tee."

"Of course..." It suddenly dawned on me what the girl meant by *injis*—Westerner. Although our languages and culture are very different, to her we're all *injis*. I was equally stunned to find an obviously well heeled Westerner "slumming it" in a roadcrew house.

"How did you end up staying here?"

"Oh, je ne c'est pas...Zeese gentlemen decide wherrre we stay. Zey drive me to Tingri tomorrow to zee Mount Everest. Zen to Kathmandu zee day af-taire..."

For an instant, I was envious. If only it was so simple for us. In a few hours, she'd whiz past what it would take us days to reach. She could cover our two-month odyssey in a few days. Most of all, that continually tough decision of whether or not to take a twenty-five kilometer detour to another interesting monastery would be infinitely easier. It would be an hour's diversion, instead of a day's.

Still, I wouldn't trade our deliberate discovery of Tibet for all "zee tea in Tah-hee-tee."

As grateful as I was to share a few moments with another traveling *injis*, I was anxious to return to our hosts and the fire. By the time I'd returned, Mama and her daughter had simmered a delicious *thugpa* of radish, potatoes and yak cheese. It was a gourmet feast everyone gobbled with gusto.

After sharing their tasty banquet, for entertainment, we circulated our Tibet trekking book. The kids were especially fascinated since they'd never seen much of their country. Laughing and pointing, they flipped from one photo to the next, naming the location or asking what it was. Then they recognized several girls in one photo from a nearby village and giggled with unbridled glee.

As the hours sped by, everyone eventually began to doze off. The village lasses sighed, "*Ghale shuu*," and slipped away. One by one, the roadcrew disappeared. Then Grandma, pointing at two blanketed beds, ordered us to sleep next to the fragrant herbal fire, the most cherished spot in the house.

Chapter XI

Zen Answers

Be trusting.
Have faith that the trail knows where it's going—even if you don't.

November 11

I t was only 25°F when I stumbled outside. It was so bitter cold that Sadhu's butt was ringed with frost from his nighttime farts. Tiptoeing past half-awake, maniacal mongrels, I relieved myself with the hearty roadcrewmen in the family toilet, right on that one and only road.

Shortly after breakfast, yesterday's sweetly sympathetic *"Whey"* daughter abruptly transformed into a shrewd businesswoman. Pointing at her still-drowsy mother, the teenager blustered, "Yuan! You pay yuan now!" as if she half-suspected we were going to pack-up everything, casually skip out of their house, load Sadhu, sneak past hungry hounds and head down the road without paying.

So I gladly paid Mama her well deserved money. Then, the demanding diva declared, "Dalai Lama? Dalai Lama?" in an "Okay now, fork it over" sort of tone.

Extremely grateful, we passed her the promised treasure that she reverently slid under the edge of a rusted golden frame upon the wall.

Then swaggering up with arms akimbo, our persistent host nagged me for one more, "Photo? Photo? Photo?" This time it was to be of her.

"All right," I relented, noticing she'd spruced up just for the occasion.

Her ruddy face was scrubbed. Raven hair was braided with a red cord and wrapped atop her head. Chubby wrists were ringed with cheap, dime store turquoise, jade, red and silver bangles and a miniature silver locket rested on her purple woolen sweater. To top off her Tibetan runway model look, she sported a flashy, phosphorescent ski jacket and had even found makeup somewhere.

As I scanned the smoky, dimly lit room, it was clear there wasn't a chance of seeing more than the whites of her eyes inside.

"Where else?" I asked, eager to take her portrait and push on toward Tingri.

She pointed toward the tropically vivid bureau that filled one corner. "No, too dark."

So she led me next door to an even larger, more brilliantly painted chest of drawers. Yet that chamber was even darker.

"My camera flash is at the bottom of my pack," I thought, "and lighting this small kerosene lamp just won't make any difference."

"No light here, either," I groused again.

She just shot me a look of complete exasperation.

Finally, forgetting about her much coveted but impossible *Debutante with Dowry* shot, I dragged her out into the yard, exclaiming, "See, sun! Here. We'll shoot here."

Disappointed, she knew we were ready to leave and there was no time left to complain. So proudly donning her official road worker's hat, she struck a serious pose. Hand on one hip and chest stuck out like some Playmate of the Tundra, she struck a stern patriot's pout and scowled in front of the tattered cloth that covered her family's doorway. While I shot several photos in quick succession, she grew impatient and expected a photo immediately.

"You give me picture now!" she mimed. Evidently some previous Land Cruising traveler had passed through with a Polaroid.

"After we return home," I explained, swiftly packing my gear. And although she clearly wasn't pleased, she was resigned to waiting.

Surprisingly, of all the places we've traveled, I've never met people more willing to have their photos taken as the Tibetans, probably because portraits are rare. After all, where's a family going to have their picture snapped unless they travel to Lhasa or perhaps Shigatse? Discount department stores *$19.95 One Hundred Photo Kiddy Packages* still haven't made it to the high Tibetan plains. Consequently, treasured family photos are taped to living room walls for the entire village to appreciate as much as we display ours' on mantles or torture friends with our boring vacation slide shows. "Same, same," as they'd say.

All day long we trudged through an endless Monument Valley-like, volcanic coned canyon, as we beat a lonely trail to Tingri. It never warmed up above freezing. While the sand still whipped our faces, the desert played tricks on our senses. Whole villages appeared—then vanished. We heard the plaintive bleat of sheep where there were none. Occasionally, on distant hilltops, we'd spot the ancient crumbling ruins of a camouflaged fortress, the ones the Nepalese built long ago during their war with Tibet. But little else. We'd expected this to be one of the more scenic parts of our trek. Unfortunately, for hours, vast Himalayan screens ringed the south and blocked any encouragement we might have gleaned from viewing Mount Everest en route to the Tingri turnoff.

"Of all days to have to trek forty-five kilometers (twenty-eight miles)," I thought, "this is the worst. It's tough enough to trek thirty-five kilometers (twenty-two miles)... "

"Wait, what's that?" I wondered, freezing in my tracks.

What appeared at first to be just another mirage, magically transformed into stick figures. As it grew ever nearer, those pencil-thin lines on the landscape of life became a family of nomads bound for who knows where. Several bleating, bulging-eyed goats led the odd procession herded by the ever-present pack of yapping dogs. Burros buckled under the bulging load of family belongings. Father, a sinewy fellow in his thirties toting an ancient flintlock, brought up the flank. Gingerly carrying a long, wooden stringed instrument which she'd occasionally swing onto her back, Mother tended their six soot-faced kids who were spread out over five-hundred meters.

Approaching, we paused like mutts sniffing one another, eager to inspect each other's wares and maybe even trade. But the real hounds stood their ground and no command could move them out of chomping range. So regrettably, we parted with no more than a wish for safe journey shared among fellow travelers.

After the parade passed, I tugged on Sadhu's reins and shouted to get him moving again. But he just stood there.

"Come on, let's go!" I yelled, yanking his bit against the roof of his mouth. At last, he reluctantly responded with a weary plod that grew worse with each passing kilometer.

"Hey, Cheryl," I cried with tooth-grinding frustration, "can you please give our friend a little encouragement?"

Hesitant, mostly to appease me, my partner gently tapped our six-hundred-pound problem child on his furry rump.

"What's wrong with him, lately?" I griped. "He can't be hungry. He eats better than we ever do." In fact, none of our horse "experts" ever said he was underfed. His barrel stomach positively bulged.

"Maybe, he's just sleepy," Cheryl grinned, "from staying awake all night eating everything in sight," chuckling at the not-so-farfetched image.

"Look, I know swatting him bothers you."

"You're right, it does." She was convinced it was an act of cruelty, practically equine capital punishment.

"Well, I don't like it either," I admitted. "But almost every Tibetan who passes continually whips their horse. My guess is, since ol' Sadhu pulled a wagon for the past ten years, he sort of expects it."

"So?"

"I want to train him to walk beside us so we don't have to whip him." And so I won't have to pull him all the way to Nepal.

She shot me a skeptical *you can't teach an old horse new tricks glare*, but was willing to give it a shot.

So all afternoon, Cheryl led our wandering Tibetan on a short rein. Each time he started dragging his hoofs, I'd yell, "*Whey!!*" (Chinese for "Hey, you!"), then switch his rump with a rope until he trotted beside her shoulder. When he'd gradually slow down again, I'd scream, "*Whey!*" and bop him again. Eventually, a minor miracle occurred. He caught on to our routine. As soon as I'd shout, he'd glance the rope out of the corner of his brown saucer eye and lurch ahead. It was easier than I thought and heartening. Our trek assumed a new energy. Cheryl led Sadhu and overcame her initial wariness of our giant friend. Meanwhile, I found the faster pace more tolerable. Finally I could hike with Cheryl, instead of being forced to walk alone or take shorter strides.

Plus, as she sarcastically teased, there was an added bonus. "At least, if I'm leading Sadhu, you won't leave me behind."

That afternoon, sensing an approaching presence, we both stopped stock-still in the middle of the forsaken road. We spun around. Squinting through sand-crusted eyes, we could just barely discern two fuzzy figments floating across the barren floor three kilometers (two miles) away.

"What is it?" I choked.

"Beats me," Cheryl gasped, plucking her water jug from a net bag hooked across the wooden saddle.

The weird vision quickly drew nearer without a sound. Until finally, when it was little more than five-hundred meters away, we recognized the shapes.

"Bicycles? Panniers? Westerners?!"

We both watched with apprehensive excitement having only seen only two *injis*, that French lady and Tanji, since Shigatse. And we could rule out both of them.

Soon the duo reached us and coasted to a silent halt.

"Hey, y'all!" blurted the petite, dust-shrouded lady beaming from under a floppy, brown felt fedora.

"Billie!" Cheryl shouted in recognition, "and Marley?"

His baby dreads and dark mischievous eyes were unmistakable even under several layers of road debris.

Surveying us, the lanky novice Rastafarian quipped, "We figured it was you two. Who else would be out here walkin' their horse?"

"Hey, we thought you two would already be in Kathmandu and scarfing down apple crunch!" I joked. It was hard to believe that we'd run into them again out in the middle of nowhere. "What happened?"

"Well, we were forced to stay in Shigatse a little longer than planned. I was really hit by giardia," Marley explained, clutching his gut. "Still not feelin' too great."

Billie interrupted, sparing us the gory details. "Anyway, we stopped in Shegar, did some bikin' around and hiked up to the ol' fort. It was grrreattt," the wayward Looziana Coon Ass drawled.

"You still planning on trekking to Mount Everest?" Cheryl asked, worried about his condition.

Marley wheezed, "Sure, I wouldn't miss it…" Although as optimistic as ever, he looked worn-out and frazzled. "You, too?"

"We'd really like to," I explained, "if we can spare the time." It's not that our day planners were chockfull. The mountain snow and the time of year had me more than a little concerned. "Maybe we can pick up supplies in Tingri and head back with Sadhu to Rongbuk Monastery. Or, even hire a four-wheeler, or yaks and guide."

"Yaks…that sounds like a gas. Y'all, even though I've biked across China, I've never hiked very much," Billie confided. "And, well, I'm a little scared."

"Hey, if you can bike that far," Cheryl assured her, "you shouldn't have any problem."

"Look, we'll probably run into you guys in Tingri," I offered, since daylight was quickly slipping away. "You'll get there long before we do."

"Oh, we should reach it in another hour," Marley figured, "if my stomach quiets down long enough," he added, slumping over padded handlebars.

Cheryl was envious. "It'll take us another four hours at least."

At that prospect, we left the cyclists by that impromptu roadside rest stop and began plodding toward our imaginary oasis in Mount Everest's shadow.

"Look for us at the hotel," Billie bellowed.

Cheryl screamed, "Where's that?"

"Don't know. There's only one!"

"Well, save us a place and a cold beer!" I added, as they blurred into fuzzy blobs once again.

Hours later, just as the sun cast its fiery glow across the frigid desert floor, a stunning orange, snow-dolloped barricade of peaks rose on our left.

"Now," I thought, "*these* are the Himalayas I've always imagined."

"There it is, Cheryl–Mount Everest," I exclaimed, pointing south.

"Where? Which one?"

"Over there on the far left," I whispered in awe. Its jagged, frosted crest was partly obscured by nearly-impenetrable clouds.

"That can't be Everest. The one over there looks much higher."

"Well, it's just an illusion. Just wait till we get closer. Then, it'll seem all of 8,839-meters (29,000-feet) high!"

Suddenly, clearing a final dog's leg in the road, we spotted a vision in the distance nearly as welcome. It was the dusky lamplight and swirling smoke of a village—Tingri, whose name means "crystal."

Exhausted after trekking a new, masochistic span of forty-five kilometers (twenty-eight miles) and surviving on pure adrenaline, we swaggered into the only compound we saw off that dust bag of a road. Encouraged by the sound of faint voices, we detected a tiny room all aglow with the dim yellow light of a potbellied stove.

Hobbling over, I cautiously poked my head inside, stuttering, "Is…is this a hotel?"

A shadow snickered, "Yes."

"Have you seen two Americans on bicycles?"

"Yea, we're in here!" Billie screamed.

"Thank God," I thought, leaning against the cracked adobe corner of the inn. I couldn't stumble another kilometer.

Noticing our ready-to-drop postures, a lanky, easygoing Tibetan led us to a concrete cell that offered the same measure of comfort as all the rest. Identical in design, it was as though some Mandarin manual dictated that every room should have twin metal framed beds, thin mattresses, a tin wash basin and crimson liter thermos. It also boasted the usual broken window panes stuffed with newspapers, stub of a candle, cluttered floors and obvious lack of heat.

We stowed our packs. Meanwhile the manager, an older Tibetan who spoke English, anchored Sadhu to a rusted car wheel rim in a yard packed with goats. As he fed our wander horse a well-deserved basket of straw, we drew bucket after bucket of cold water for our thirsty *da* from the well. Then Cheryl and I hobbled in to join Billie, Marley, Hans and Jacob in the welcome warmth of the kitchen, which in true Tibetan style doubled as a restaurant.

Over the next few hours, we sat hypnotized by that dung fire's infernal glow, mesmerized by the bustling world around us. Five Tibetans hustled, toting plates brimming with *momos* back and forth to heavy wooden tables. Three lonely Peace Corps volunteers chewed everyone's ears, while four hungry cyclists chowed down and choked out conversations amid wolfish gulps. It was all part of an unfolding nightly drama. Only the visiting players changed.

I was just a spectator and too tired or willing to participate. "All I need," I thought, "is warmth, hot food, a cold beer and sleep. In that order."

Remarkably, that stove-stoked sweatbox boiled beastly hot, especially after we'd battled nearly arctic weather all day. Slowly I stripped away clothes melded to my skin; fetid layers barely removed in a week. First came the jacket...then the fleece coat...next a sweatshirt, until I was finally down to a long sleeved t-shirt.

While I performed my pilgrim striptease, the yak and radish *momos* kept arriving along with a delicious hot pepper sauce. Next came a steaming yak, radish and potato *thugpa*. Then some hot *chang* was poured.

"Sleep, wonderful sleep, is just a moment away," I mused...

Just then, Hans, who'd been jabbering on for hours about Everest to anyone who'd listen...how he was going to trek with Marley and Jacob to the advance base camp...trek to over 5,800 meters (19,000 feet) like his idol Reinhold Messner...famous Italian climber...who'd soloed to the summit with no oxygen tanks...blah, blah, blah...turned to me.

"And so," he began with that Teutonic, down-the-nose, in-your-face, condescending tone, "you are joining our little trek to advance base camp?"

Refusing to rise to the occasion, I vacantly stared at the table and mumbled, "Don't know..."

"Don't know?" he snorted. "Well, we can make it there, hike through the glacier fields and back in..."

"Don't know," I interrupted, "if we're going at all."

"How can you be this close and not go?" he demanded with a snide little chortle.

Something told me, this guy just wouldn't quit.

"Not that simple," I began, too boned-tired to enjoy being forced into that play. "We're exhausted."

"And so are we."

"Well, we still have 300 kilometers to trek to Kathmandu."

"Surely fifty kilometers to Everest is not going to throw..."

"It's not fifty, Hans. It's nearly a hundred kilometers roundtrip."

"Okay, one hundred," he conceded.

"Besides, it's not the distance. It's the time...the six days it'll take."

The room grew silent, as everyone examined their own unspoken fears. Meanwhile, I ENTERED STAGE LEFT starring in a reluctant role as the *Voice of Reason*.

"Look. Winter's movin' in fast. It's colder every day. There's ice on the road. Snow on the peaks. And we don't want to end up stuck in some remote village till May."

Snorting at what he considered our weakness, he countered, "Oh, I hardly think they'd close the road."

"Ah, but we heard they do." The odd March Hare, himself, warned us a while back.

The party mood turned to one of weary confusion, as the others tried to find answers in each other's eyes.

"Well, I don't know if I want to spend all winter with you, Hans!" Billie jabbed.

Oblivious to her last comment, like a frenzied shark, he went in for the kill. "So, if you need, you go a little faster..."

"We only have one speed. Remember Hans, we've been trekking with a horse for weeks all the way from Lhasa. Not casually riding our bikes!"

The room rang silent. That was a low blow. I immediately regretted my remark. Their trip was certainly no cakewalk.

"Look, to be honest, we're maxed out," I admitted. "Sure, it'd be great to trek to Everest. Even the higher camps if we had the right gear. And if it wasn't nearly winter."

Billie and Marley nodded in solemn agreement, while Jacob just stared into his *chang*.

"Reaching Kathmandu and finishing the pilgrim's trail—that's our goal. And I won't let anything, *anything*, jeopardize that."

Pushing out my rickety wooden chair and rising, I struggled a forced smile. "Look. We'll let you know tomorrow if we're going to join you, okay?"

November 12

That one question sat and festered all night, making me nauseous like a bad yak stew. Between it, the biting cold and Sadhu's nightly rummaging, I got very little sleep.

After inhaling a light breakfast of ramen noodles, I suggested, "Come on, Cheryl. Let's take a stroll through town." Secretly I hoped the change of scenery would clear our heads and help us decide which path to choose.

Cheryl cocked a sleepy eye. "Hey, I thought this was my day to rest!"

"It is," I grinned, pointing at the mountain soaring above the village. "We can both rest—on top of that."

"Why do we always have to go up?" she mock-groaned.

Grabbing our camera, we left the compound, its scavenging dogs, soldiers loafing over cups of jasmine tea, long distance trucks and hustling truckers. Just outside, beyond the gates of that traveler's paradise, we landed back in the other more real Tibet—that colorful tunic of black yak hair, nomad tents, green delivery trucks and fresh, pink goat carcasses strung across gray, gnarled wooden racks.

Tingri's one dusty, derelict street led us past a military garrison, then through a maze of neat whitewashed adobe walls and houses. Each was decorated with those ominously familiar orange and blue stripes. People flooded the streets. Women shopped. Old men in fox fur hats shared snuff and gossiped. Kids, as dirty and ragged as they were gregarious, chanted, "*Kuchi! Kuchi! Kuchi!*" begging for sweets as they tugged on our sleeves.

Partly to escape them, partly with the hope of restocking our meager supplies, we ducked into a series of closet-sized shops. But they only offered the same measly assortment of expensive canned delicacies: pickled mustard shoots, bamboo parts, more dace fish in black bean sauce, meat in olive green cans (with no picture of the beast for the illiterate traveler), cheap army sneakers, snuff, brandy, candy and dried goods. There was no cheese, no fresh fruit, no vegetables and no *Pi Jius*. None of our hiking essentials.

"If we do trek to Mount Everest," I thought, "it's going to be difficult to shop for supplies here. Plus, we're almost out of dehydrated foods. How do you prepare mustard shoots, anyway?"

Quickly we reached the end of the tiny settlement. As the road petered out, we traced a still smaller path along the base of a treeless, grassless mound. From the bottom, we spotted a painter's palette of colorful prayer flags, *lungdaa*, fluttering from bamboo poles against an unblemished azure sky.

"We'll have a perfect view of the mountains from up there," I proclaimed, as I scrambled hand over hand up the steep, craggy slope.

Meanwhile, Cheryl discovered a trail up a rocky ridge and jumped at the chance to rub it in. "Hey, it's easier if you take the path!" she hollered.

Within minutes, we rendezvoused at the flag-festooned summit. As we peered off in wonderment, the Himalayan vista rose more glorious, more enchanting than the evening before. A wide panorama of snowcapped peaks sparkled for an eon across the entire southern horizon. Indomitable, icy fortresses, the slopes of Mount Cho Oyu at over 8,138 meters (26,700 feet) and Mount Pumori at over 7,010 meters (23,000 feet) gleamed in the distance. But that was merely a prelude. Gazing at Mount Chomolongma, the Mother Goddess, as the Tibetans reverently call Mount Everest, unobstructed by any human creation, we were humbled by its exquisite magnificence.

Mutely beaming, we slowly sank down onto the silent crest. Transfixed, staring straight ahead, we were afraid to speak, reluctant to break its spell. Finally, I broached the question what had been on my mind for so long.

"Should we go to the mountain?"

"If we're meant to reach Kathmandu, we'll reach it," Cheryl whispered. In the simple Zen-ness of her answer, I discovered my own.

Suddenly, there was a sharp "PING!" Then another "PING!" whizzed by. Still another whistled past.

"Get down!" I screamed. "Someone's shooting at us!"

We both lay frozen for a few seconds, an eternity. Then we realized that whoever was firing at the mountaintop probably (hopefully) had no idea we were up there.

"*Whey!*" we screamed at the top of our lungs. "*Whey! Whey!*"

After we hurled rocks over the crest and down toward the gunfire, the firing finally ceased. Crouched, nearly crawling to the mountain's edge, we spied two Chinese soldiers, one with a pistol, quickly scrambling up the hill toward us. Frantic, we looked at each other.

"What do we do? They'll be here in a minute. Do we run? Hide in the rocks?"

As inappropriate or improbable as it might seem now, we calmly eased back down and stared straight ahead at Mount Chomolongma, meditating on its radiance and strength.

"If we're to die right here," I figured, "its image is the one I would most want etched in my mind."

Within seconds, a panting, scrawny Chinese officer approached. Obviously shaken to see us, he stuttered, "Oh, oh, sorrry," in broken English.

We gazed up. Trying to remain calm, we demanded, "What were you shooting at?" hoping he wouldn't admit to aiming at us.

"There's nothing up here," I thought. "Nothing but tattered prayer flags, a *chorten* and us."

"Birds," he chirped, with a fluttering wave of his hands. "I shoot birds."

Predictably, Cheryl stared a hole through him, demanding, "Why?"

"Many birds," he nervously giggled. "Sport."

Sport? I'd read how that great barren plain below was once alive with antelopes, gazelles, blue sheep and wild asses. Today, pilgrims and birds were all that remained. And clearly the days for both were numbered.

"Well, you need to be more careful where you shoot," I suggested. "People pray up here. Yes?"

The soldier nodded and again apologized before trotting back down the hillside.

We were again alone. However for us, the tranquility, the indelible uniqueness of the moment faded with that first bullet's echo.

"All right, we're in…" I hesitantly announced to Billie and Marley as soon as we arrived back at the inn.

"Grrreattt," she cooed, "it'll be fun."

"…As long as we can do it in six days," I continued. "Three days there, one at base camp and two back. That's it! That's all the time we can spare."

I hated to be miserly about it, but who knew how long the weather would hold?

"That sounds fair," Marley admitted. "It may be all we can afford, too."

"I was even thinking, maybe we can hire someone with a four-wheeler to drive us to Rongbuk Monastery. After we trek to the base camp, you can continue to the advanced camp while we hike back."

"That's always a possibility…" Marley answered with a toss of his matted dreads.

"That way," Cheryl explained, "we can still see Mount Everest but save three days."

"Well, let's go ask the manager, Mr. Big," I suggested, ready to set our plan in motion.

Grabbing Hans and Jacob, we located the innkeeper slouched in the perpetual darkness of his restaurant. He shared a brandy with a garrison officer.

Discretely drawing him aside, we confided, "Remember last night we talked about going to Mount Everest?"

"Yes…"

"Well, six of us are interested in going as soon as possible."

"Very good!" he replied with a conspiratorial wink. "I will arrange guides, yaks…"

"Well, we were wondering," I interrupted, "if we could hire a four-wheel drive, you know, a Jeep to take us up there? And we could hike back."

"No good. No good," he admonished our group. "No car will go back there this time of year."

Jacob skeptically stared at him. "No one in this entire village?"

Adamant, he shook his head. "Now, I can get you two or three yaks…"

We'd heard about yaks and all their problems. "Hey, what about a donkey cart?" I suggested.

"Very expensive and they take you in from Shegar. Weather no good for horse now. Too cold. Much snow."

"There's no way we're going all the way back to Shegar," I thought. "And the snow rules out taking Sadhu."

"I get you two or three yaks…" he plotted again, "and guides. They pick you up here in donkey cart," he assured us with a grin. "You get yaks in village. Only one hour from here."

We shot each other wary glances, wondering whether to trust him or try to put it all together ourselves. Time was so short.

Then Marley asked the one question foremost in all our minds.

"Can we leave tomorrow?"

He nodded as Hans whined, "Some of us will want to stay several days at Rongbuk instead of just two,"

"Okay. No problem."

"So, how much will all this cost?" the Münchner demanded.

Everyone braced themselves, waiting for the ultimate collision with reality.

"For six people, four yaks and two guides…seventy-five dollars."

"Sixty dollars!" Hans countered.

"No, no. Seventy-five," the outfitter calmly replied, standing firm. "Good price. You stay five days or seven—same, same."

"That's twenty-five dollars for the two of us," I quickly calculated. "That's fair and well within our budget."

Glancing around, I noticed everyone else appeared content with the price, even Hans.

"All right. We leave tomorrow?"

Our Tibetan host smiled broadly. "Tomorrow!"

After the others left, I turned to the innkeeper once more, asking, "What about our *da*? Can you feed and walk him while we're gone?"

"Yes. Don't worry."

"How much extra?" I asked, waiting for the other boot to drop. I was willing to pay anything, anything *reasonable* for his food. Over the past month, however, we had discovered that Tibetan families seldom charged for Sadhu's feed. With them, since he couldn't fend for himself, he was treated royally.

"Twenty-one yuan for seven days."

"Not bad," I thought. "Only four dollars."

"Hay and barley?" I asked.

"If you want."

"Yes, hay and barley then. We want to find our friend fat and rested when we return. You know," I confided with complete sincerity, "Sadhu…well, he's our brother."

The little guy chuckled, "Your brother?" perhaps failing to see the family resemblance. He cocked an eyebrow. But one glance told him I was serious.

"Of course."

Our expedition members spent the rest of the brisk afternoon scavenging enough food to last the next six days, while preparing mental inventories for the dangerous journey ahead. No one knew exactly what to expect. But no one was willing to pass up that once-in-a-lifetime opportunity, especially the chance to approach Mount Everest's North Face from the more remote, less "conquered" Tibetan side.

That night, as we tallied money and supplies around the dinner table, the kitchen flap unexpectedly flew open and a snow dusted, frosted apparition wobbled in. The tiny restaurant buzzed with curious excitement as everyone whispered, "Who or what is it?" until it shuffled into the dim light.

I'd seen that icy ghost before! Nearly spitting out my *chang*, I laughed in disbelief. "Hey! It's the Japanese trekker!"

Cheryl couldn't believe it either, slowly surveying the intruder from his knickered legs to his pointed goatee to his stocking-capped head. "We passed this guy two days ago, back at the Shegar turnoff."

Marley and Billie, having taught English in Japan, welcomed him in his native tongue.

"How'd he get here?" I wondered aloud.

The abominable traveler mumbled a few frozen words which Marley cheerfully translated.

"He said, 'The day you passed, he tried to hitch a ride all day. But no one would pick him up.'"

That wasn't surprising.

"Finally today, he paid a villager driving an oxcart to carry him here."

While we choked back guffaws at the thought of this character huddled on the back of a wagon, the shivering Nipponese snowman melted before our eyes, stuttering, "Cold…Very cold."

Billie spoke with him again in Japanese.

"I just asked if he'd like to join us and hike to Everest tomorrow?"

"And?"

"He said, 'Of course, if he ever warms up!'"

Chapter XII

In Quest of Mount Everest

Be loving.
Love all living things on the trail.
Love God, your fellow travelers, yourself.

November 13

A buzz rose throughout the compound as everyone made last minute preparations for their odyssey. Billie, Marley and Cheryl ran to the store, while Hans and Jacob stowed bikes and gear in an outdoor meat locker. Tanji, our Japanese snowman, purchased one of those brilliant red liter thermoses for the expedition. He had arrived without a canteen, cook kit, tent or utensils and I wondered how he'd made it that far.

Amid the bustle, I rushed among our companions collecting half of Mr. Big's fee to be paid in advance, the rest upon our safe return.

"Don't forget to take care of Sadhu," I reminded him as I counted it into his callused hand. "Remember, for that price he gets both hay and barley."

"Do not worry, sir," he replied, smiling. "I will take good care of your, your...brother."

It was noon by the time we'd loaded supplies and packs onto the awaiting donkey cart. As two gaunt Tibetan teens led our anxious procession through that settlement in Everest's shadow, villagers craned their heads and unabashedly stared from tri-striped windows and cloth cloaked doorways. There was no awe, only wonder. They knew where we were headed. Maybe they only wondered, "Why?"

For nearly an hour we tumbled across a marshy open plain at a relaxed, steady pace. Along the way, as if meant to confuse us, narrow dirt trails, no more pronounced than goat paths, crossed and headed off aimlessly in different directions. Ignoring these, we continued tagging behind the creaking supply wagon. Until finally, we dragged into the open courtyard of an even smaller hamlet known as Ra Chhu, hewn into the hillside overlooking Tingri Valley.

To welcome our arrival, swarms of curious, irresistible kids mobbed us, giggling and yanking at our sleeves. We loved the attention. Marley swung several in the air. Jacob, growling like a crazed yeti, chased others. A few more brazen fellas even mugged for Tanji, who swooped and circled like a persistent *paparazzi*.

After everything had been unloaded from the cart, our two guides "Don Juan" and "Ugly" finally made their debut and began strapping supplies onto four stout, black yaks.

Now, just to set the record straight, Don Juan and Ugly weren't uncomplimentary nicknames we'd given them. On the contrary. Those were their actual Tibetan names just mangled into English.

Don Juan was tall and muscular for a Tibetan, perhaps in his mid-twenties, although it was difficult to tell. His thick, black hair was slicked straight back with yak butter pomade. His teeth were stained ochre, the patina of a crumbling Italian facade. His face was slightly pitted to match.

Ugly, his shorter, more reticent partner, was perhaps a little younger. The herder was reed thin with slightly effeminate features. Laughing, almond eyes framed an angular nose, while his long black hair was carefully wrapped with a braided red rope and wound around his crown.

At first, it looked like they had yak packing down to a fine art. Employing a well-honed system, the first three yaks were easily loaded. Ugly steadied them by holding their braided yak hair bridles, as Don Juan saddled and cinched them. Then effortlessly, he tied packs, their bulky wall tent and sacks of supplies onto sturdy wooden saddles.

Everyone watched with a curious fascination. From a distance, whenever we'd encountered them, yaks looked affable in an oafish sort of way. They were Tibetan cartoon caricatures of hyperthyroid sheepdogs. But looks can be deceiving.

Our guides left the most recalcitrant one, an ornery, bucking black brute weighing nearly a ton, for their grand finale. First, eluding the saddle, the mad yak ran wide circles around the courtyard, chasing and inciting the others into a mad frenzy. Sensing an uncontrollable chain reaction, the herders quickly jumped into the fray. Ugly dove and caught the ivory-tailed behemoth's bridle like some Tibetan cowpuncher. Then Don Juan cautiously placed a wooden saddle on the unyielding yak's hunched, shaggy back, carefully cinching the wide girth strap.

That was the easy part. Now the beast simmered on a slow boil.

Pressing their luck, the guides gingerly eased the first two packs across his saddle. Well, the monster no sooner felt the weight than he lunged and bucked, sending the bags sailing! Unflinching, the guides regrouped and tried again. Then again. Each time with the same disastrous result. At last, an exasperated Don Juan carefully looped a yak hair rope around the obstinate yak's horns. Then grabbing him in a tenuous headlock, he tried to muscle him into submission—an action about as easy as flipping an SUV with a spatula.

Well, that certainly didn't help the yak's disposition. This time, as soon as the bags touched the saddle, Don Juan himself was thrown airborne.

Watching those escapades, it didn't take long to realize how lucky we were to find our overaged wander horse.

"Imagine us," I thought, "struggling to load him everyday?"

Finally, in a stroke of engineering genius, Don Juan tightened his rope around the animal's razor-sharp, gnarled horns. Yanking it down, he looped it around the yak's front hoofs and tied it off at the head. The demon glared with rage, steamed with fury. But convinced he was safely hobbled, at least momentarily, our guides moved quickly and tightened four packs against his sides. Then loosening restraints, they sprung out of his path.

The shaggy dervish tossed back his head, bucked and furiously stomped around the courtyard for a few tense minutes, a furious thousand pounds of steaming revenge. But the packs refused to fly.

In homage to that behemoth's noble defiance, it only seemed right to give him a name. So we dubbed him, "Bad Ass." Although it had taken Don Juan and Ugly nearly forty minutes to load him, we were finally off.

Tingri quickly became a speck on the horizon as we set an energetic pace, slogging through soggy tundra, crossing scorched gravel patches and leaping frigid streams and flooded irrigation ditches. Still, as much as we pushed, we struggled just to keep up with the yaks and guides.

For hours, the plain was barren, except for a lone adobe hut.

"Look, Cheryl," I gasped, pointing fifty yards ahead. "There's another one of those houses like the others we've seen with rivers running through them." We'd wondered whether they were badly designed or if someone just wanted a place with cold running water?

Vaulting over a stream, we approached a startled teenager leaning against the open front door. Bewildered by our request to peek inside, he obligingly led our group into his family's tiny, lightless room. Two massive stone wheels powered by the stream rhythmically turned around a rock basin grinding barley into *tsampa*. So that's what they are! The miller family's beds were just meters away, cradled between bulging barley sacks.

Curiosity satisfied, it took our ragged procession nearly three more hours of grass hummock hopping before arriving in Lungjhang.

Reverently, as though intruding, our group ceremoniously circled the village *chorten* and its stack of *mani* or prayer stones. Making the rounds, I was surprised to see their carved Sanskrit inscription, *"Om Mani Padme Hum,"* was identical to those painted on hillsides outside Lhasa on the giant prayer wheel and on other indelible holy billboards across the plains.

I, too, whispered a silent prayer. "On this part of our journey," I reckoned, "we'll need all the help we can get."

After advancing through the nearly deserted settlement, the last on the plain, we paused at a mud brick enclosure. While Don Juan disappeared to find the corral's keeper, we had a spare moment to study the bleak graveled terrain that started its stratospheric wind upward.

"Already, we're at 4,511 meters (14,800 feet)," I thought. "My God, there's another six-hundred meters (2,000 feet) to climb over the next two days just to reach base camp!"

As my mind staggered with those implications, an attractive village girl appeared, smiled bashfully and unlocked the gate to our dung-scattered animal pen.

Stepping in, we tried to avoid the more obvious piles while surveying our home for the night. For once, I could really sympathize with Sadhu.

"At least it's empty," I thought. "We don't have any goats to contend with. Plus, we'll be sheltered from this wind."

As if on cue, that breeze quickly grew into a howling tempest and plunged the tundra's frigid 30°F at least 10°F lower within seconds.

With growing urgency, we pitched our nylon two-person tent atop a flattened hay bin. Marley and Billie unfolded their tent next to Jacob and Hans's inside the main corral. Tanji was forced to share our guides' tent, since he had no equipment except the ever-present multitude of cameras bandoleered about his small frame like some Nipponese bandito.

After unloading our contrary yaks, a chore much easier than saddling them, Don Juan and Ugly unfolded their enormous, tattered canvas sheet. While Don Juan hoisted its center with a wooden pole, Ugly stretched yak hair ropes tight from each corner. Tying them off to nearby rocks, he sealed its sides with other stones. Then, while we methodically unrolled our modern, self-inflating foam sleep pads, down bags and nylon bivy sacks, the guides scattered blankets and hides across the dirt floor of their primitive shelter, careful to leave a narrow gap in between. There, they started a dung fire sheltered between two rocks.

First, Don Juan drew a homemade goat skin bellows from his sack. Then he lit a handful of slender juniper branches toted all the way from town. Once ignited inside that ring of stone, those fragrant needles crackled and burned intensely for seconds. As he feverishly pumped the swollen, wombat-like bellows, Ugly carefully fed the flames, breaking dried yak dung patties in half until a light glowed brightly.

It quickly boiled one pot of *chu*, another of *cha*. By then, our group had joined the hardy herders under their canvas. Realizing we were novices at the fine art of dung cooking, Don Juan and Ugly gently

pumped and stoked the temperamental flames while we wasted no effort
in cooking pasta for seven, wolfing it down and drowning our carb-fest
with *chang* and tea. Finally satiated, we relaxed shoulder to shoulder, butt
to butt in the cramped quarters.

With us out of their way, our guides contentedly guzzled liters of yak
butter tea and cups of *tsampa*; first alone, then blended together into a *pag*
they'd kneaded with their fingers.

Frequently as they ate, the fire threatened to sputter out. That's when
Don Juan, setting his wooden *tsampa* bowl aside, would rhythmically
embrace the bloated bellows again with Jacob chanting, "Pump, pump the
jam, pump it up, pump it up!"

Don Juan let loose a hearty guffaw. Then, like some Tibetan rapper,
he sang along and pumped to his beat. "Pump, pump da jam, pump eet
up, pump eet up."

Within seconds a blinding, choking cloud of dung smoke
ballooned, throwing everyone hacking onto their backs and our
devious guides into delirious laughter. He continued with renewed
vigor. "Pump, pump da jam, pump eet up, pump eet up." Again, black
smoke streamed from the fire, flooding the snug tent, stinging eyes and
singeing lungs.

Enough! We couldn't stand it any longer. Staggering from their toasty
tent, we laughed and shivered our way back to our flimsy shelters.

"He only...had to ask us...to leave," I coughed, as I struggled with
numb fingers to unzip our tent's frozen zipper.

November 14

It was late morning by the time we'd *tsampa*-ed, *cha*-ed, struck
camp and loaded the cranky yaks. Remembering Don Juan and Ugly's
heated battle the day before, Marley, Jacob and I offered to help load
Bad Ass.

"Sure!" Don Juan pantomimed. "Surround him in a circle."

So, standing guard, each armed with only a handful of measly
rocks, we watched for any sign that the unwieldy two-ton beast was
ready to break for the freedom of the open plain. Well, it didn't take

long. As soon as Don Juan approached with his saddle, Bad Ass sprung with a furious lunge in Marley's direction.

"Watch him! Watch!" I screamed.

Marley loped ten steps to his right. The angry creature swerved and spun the other direction. Jacob jogged to his left to cut him off. But the yak poured on speed like a charging bull. He paused. Then lurched toward me. I fired off a rock just in front of his flaring nose. He stopped in his tracks, spun, whipped around and charged back the other way. Marley cocked his arm and let a missile sail, SMACKING the beast on the side of his great shaggy head. He glared but he didn't attack again. Fierce, still fuming, he stood stock still while Ugly and Don Juan finished their task.

After the last packs were loaded and cinches tightened, Don Juan glanced over at us, obviously amused by our first awkward attempt at yak herding. Then, to our surprise, he sheepishly pulled open his jacket. Pointing first to his side then to Bad Ass, he made a horn-like gesture, hands atop his yak-greased head. Marley and I stared in wide-eyed disbelief at a grotesquely purple scar that zigzagged ragged down his side.

"He's already been gored?" Marley sighed.

"Now, he tells us..."

All day long we slogged through a bog-like tundra, trekked over rocky plains and trudged through stream-fed marsh. Occasionally, we'd spot the ruins of a crumbling *dzong* on a distant mountainside or a herder's stone corral enveloped in solitude. Otherwise, there was little evidence that humanity had ever invaded that lonesome end of the world.

For hours, Billie and I scampered ahead, scouts tracing the narrow dirt path that wound endlessly through those hills. After a while, as we ran out of conversation, I'd drop behind and strike up a new topic with another companion. As I barely knew the other five, any subject was fair game. And since I'd nearly perfected reading Cheryl's mind by now, having traveled together for so long, it was refreshing to inject a little new blood into our pilgrimage.

Still, no matter what any of us mindlessly gabbed about, everyone's rapt attention ultimately remained focused on the mountains and unknown challenge looming ahead.

For twenty-five kilometers (15.5 miles) we huffed and struggled up bone-wrenching slopes or were challenged to jump thawing, crystalline rivulets in the valley below. Only too soon we'd resume our dogged ascent along the vaguest of steep dirt tracks. Frequently, other trails would appear, merge and then splinter off in different directions. Confused, I'd pause, turn and crane my head for some reassuring sign from the diligent Don Juan, who pulled up the flank with his yaks. Invariably, he'd signal to continue straight ahead, usually up another heart-thumping incline.

We seldom stopped, nibbling on puny cooked potatoes and roasted barley as we hiked. Breaks were brief, just long enough to catch a miserly measured sip from water jugs. Everyone knew that their one-liter canteen had to last 'til sunset. Each trekker carried their own water buckled to belts or strapped across chests.

Tanji was the only exception. His huge crimson thermos, too bulky for any sensible trekker to lug, was lashed to the side of one of the yaks.

In early afternoon, just as we crested a summit overlooking a breathtaking gorge, Bad Ass spotted the tempting crimson gleam of Tanji's shiny thermos out of the corner of his eye. Magically he was drawn to it like a bull to a matador's sanguine cape. Sharply swerving to his left, he caught the other yak totally by surprise. As he gored its hairy side, there was a loud "POP!" and Tanji's glass jug cascaded in shimmering mirrored fragments over the cliff.

"What a hoot!" I thought. "Only now, he'll be more dependent than ever on the rest of us."

We made good time considering our various physical conditions. It was no race, but pacing was just as vital. Air became as precious as food. Supplies were limited, water rationed. We knew there'd be no more villages until we reached Rongbuk Monastery and everyone expected that near-freezing days, arctic nights, dwindling sunlight and heavenly altitudes would take their toll and test our very resolve.

Just that evening, as the sun escaped behind the snowcapped impasse before us, the day's greatest challenge soared overhead.

"Why couldn't this have come earlier?" I fretted, staring at the immense visage of Pang La towering at 5,212 meters (17,100 feet) ahead.

With intense, gut-wrenching deliberation, our very survival seeming to rest in the balance, our group made one last painful push up the vertical naked slope. Wind slashed across our half-frozen eyes. We trembled with inconceivable cold as sweat froze to our backs. As we stumbled in the fading light, sharp slag slid and shifted below our feet. Lungs burned. Hearts erupted. Heads throbbed louder than thoughts. Until finally, as the last whisper of strength was sucked from our shivering, expended bodies, we crawled to the crest.

Joined by our bemused guides and hungry yaks, we shuffled in a twilight haze across its bleak plateau and slid down the opposite side to an empty *drogpa* or nomad's camp surrounded by the fury of arctic gales.

We quickly pitched our tents inside the protection of the stone ring. However, whipped by that relentless tempest, our tents still shook with a fury and life all their own for hours. We were famished. Yet our meager meal of ramen noodles did little but brightly stoke our fires, then soon let them fizzle to ash like juniper needles upon dung flames.

Silently suffering from complete and undisguised exhaustion, everyone turned-in early. Alone, snuggled deep within the privacy of our down bags, we uncontrollably shook and struggled to keep warm. Our breaths rose and froze above us. Only the promise of reaching the Mother Goddess kept us going.

November 15

We awoke the next morning still shivering and wrapped in a wet shroud. Our breaths, at night a frozen mist lining the tent walls, had thawed, showered rain and drenched our sleeping bags. Normally that would be no major problem. We'd simply stretch them out in the sun to dry, as we had back in that potato patch.

"But today," I thought, "today there is no sun."

After a futile attempt to dry them in the still gusting, freezing wind, we reluctantly stuffed them back in our stuff sacks. Realizing those down bags were worthless when wet, it became more crucial than ever to reach Rongbuk Monastery and its heated rooms before sundown .

Try as we might, it was nearly 11 a.m. by the time we broke camp. Everyone was hesitant to leave that stone corral, reluctant to tackle the pass that had drained so much from them the day before. Don Juan and Ugly lingered a little longer over *tsampa* and *po-cha*. Hans and Jacob milked a third bowl of java. Cheryl and I savored a precious, withered apple squirreled away from Tingri. Tanji, as usual, contentedly shared everyone else's larder. Like clockwork, the yaks stamped, stalled and threw their usual conniptions.

Once we set off, our pace was brisk, as though to compensate for the late hour and temperature. In actuality, it was as lively as could be expected considering the altitude of more than sixteen-thousand feet.

Unfortunately, my breath was more labored than ever. Sucking noxious fumes from the dung fire morning and night for two days had reeked havoc on my bronchitis.

By midafternoon we reached several deserted stone corrals and decided to take a breather. From that pristine, rolling alpine pasture, we gazed down three-hundred meters to the valley and meandering river far below. Surveying our route, at first it appeared that an insurmountable granite wall blocked our path.

"Wait a second. We don't have to actually climb that," I thought, "do we?"

Then upon closer inspection, I could barely detect a faint path winding down the mountainside. Turning south, it seemed to skirt the shimmering river.

"*Kaaaputh! Chugrath, chugrath!*" Suddenly, there was maniacal snorting and rambunctious thunder behind me. I spun around. Bad Ass had thrown my bag into the air and Don Juan and Ugly were frantically barreling after him across the meadow.

"Stop! Stop him!" they bellowed, as the beast galloped full tilt up the embankment!

Snatching rocks with both hands, Marley, Jacob, Hans and I joined in that frenzied chase. As Marley whizzed stones across the beast's blazing eyes, the rest of us circled our prey like Neanderthals. The creature charged then slammed to a stop. Spinning 180°, he blustered off in the opposite direction. Then the demon madly galloped right at us threatening to ram us head-on. But we stood our ground. Waiting until we were nearly able to feel his foul breath, we shot off rockets that sent him spinning in another direction like some crazed fur ball. This mayhem persisted for at least twenty minutes. Until at last, Don Juan and Ugly were able to sneak up behind winded Bad Ass, lasso his horns and tie them again to his front legs. Safely hobbled, they loaded my bag back onto him.

Hoping everything was still in one piece, I ran through a quick inventory of breakables as I negotiated a gravel switchback down the slippery slope.

For twenty minutes we edged the water's path until reaching a broad, well-constructed wooden bridge festooned with gaily-colored prayer flags. Crossing halfway across the ice-choked, glacier-fed river, I abruptly stopped and gazed upstream. Mount Everest, home of the Mother Goddess, shone and sparkled on the snowy horizon with all the intensity of a million Hope Diamonds.

Then, for the first time since leaving, I knew we'd make it. At last, success was within our grasp.

Three more hours we wound along the dizzying, scraggy shore led by Chomolongma's lifeblood. Frequently, tidy rock mounds cropped up on the rugged hillside. Stacked by pilgrims throughout the centuries, they reminded me of home in Hawai'i and of offerings to the goddess Pele, who lives inside the erupting Kilauea Volcano on the Big Island.

As I became lost in memories of home, for once, like horses returning to the paddock, both guides and yaks shot past us.

"What secrets do they know? Are we that close?"

Walking hand-in-hand, Ugly sang a sweet Tibetan ditty in a high-pitched falsetto voice while Don Juan danced a jig. We were just content to stumble along in pious exhaustion, anxious to find our own respite in a valley once famous as a Buddhist retreat.

In the past, hermits had sequestered themselves in hillside huts or caves for years or a lifetime. In reverent meditation, they lived in humble seclusion. For some, food and water was even slipped to them through chinks in their cell walls. Sadly, although there'd once been as many as six active monasteries in the valley known as the "Sanctuary of the

Birds," only one remained after the Cultural Demolition. That lone survivor was Rongbuk Monastery.

Perhaps in joyful celebration by those long-solitary monks, the moment of our own arrival was brilliantly auspicious. We gazed upon the reassuring glow of Rongbuk *stupa's* golden spire at 4,983 meters (16,350 feet) just as the sun embraced the rooftop of Mount Cho Oyu. And although I'd heard there is actually a pass just up the valley called Changri La tucked between Mount Cho Oyu and Mount Everest, we were pleased to stumble upon our own private paradise.

Wandering inside the temple's gates, our group was hailed by a young, exuberant monk with short-cropped hair. He wore a traditional maroon Buddhist robe covered by an untraditional high-tech fleece jacket.

Whispering, "Follow me," in perfect English, the holy man glided past and led us up a flight of creaking wooden stairs to a five-bed dorm beside the temple or *lhakhang*. Although it was hardly a place some snooty travel editor would rave about, its rug-shrouded beds, broken window panes stuffed with wadded newspapers and potbellied stove protected us from the howling Himalayan winds—much more than any four-star monstrosity's complimentary shower cap ever would.

November 16

Hans, Jacob, Marley and I departed the following morning, bound for Mount Everest. Each harbored his own private reason. Hans hankered to reach the advance base camp at the edge of the East Rongbuk Glacier at over 6,400 meters (21,000 feet). Jacob seemed content now to just explore its glacier, realizing the limitations of his equipment only too well. He'd just worn out one pair of cheap Chinese hiking boots on the trail from Tingri. Marley and I were in it for the "experience," just wanting to get as close as we could and live to tell the tale.

Of their own choosing, Cheryl, Billie and Tanji stayed behind, basking in the warmth of the dorm's dung fire. They'd reluctantly decided it was better to recoup before starting our arduous two-day trek back to Tingri West.

For the better part of an hour, our foursome battled the frigid wind as we inched our way up the vast valley. The mountain itself served as our guiding beacon. Each step drew us closer to that extraordinary source of power.

For awhile, Heinrich, a lanky Austrian wayfarer whom we'd met back at that Tingri inn and again at the monastery, joined us. Fueling our imaginations with a vivid tale of his trek to Rongbuk Glacier the day before, he convinced us that it could, in fact, be done. For an instant, I chewed over the possibility again in my mind. But before I'd committed to brave it, he directed us to the best glacier viewing point then scrambled a nearby path to explore the ruins of Sherab Chholing Nunnery.

Over the next hour, we beat a furious pace toward the peak that had already brought us halfway around the world.

Like a beautiful woman, a "Lady of the Lake," she was elusive. For awhile, her snowy shawl rose almost close enough to grasp. Then, as we'd head back down into a gravel valley, she was totally obscured. Until finally, running over a craggy knoll, I stopped short in awe. Mount Everest sparkled ahead and flooded the horizon.

"Magnificent!" I whispered to the wind.

Similar meaningless epithets were all the others could sigh in a quiet chorus of praise, disbelief and wonderment.

Since I was a child, I'd fantasized about what it'd be like to gaze upon the world's highest peak, to feel the same air brush past my cheek that rushed along her ivory face. To me it was one of those sites I had to see in the world—more than any Taj Mahal, Eiffel Tower or Great Pyramid, all sculpted by human hands. Chomolongma humbles them all.

We crouched on that rise in silent, reverent appreciation of the unblemished beauty enveloping us. The aqua ice fields of Rongbuk Glacier flowed like a cape to her right. Her jagged-toothed, snow draped crown, for once free from any cloud, glistened against a royal sapphire sky. And her precious gilt-edged peaks radiated a pureness, twinkling in stark contrast to the slate gray glacial path of the ancient ocean floor below.

In her regal presence, I was disappointed that our pilgrimage, the season, or my own sensibility prevented me from climbing with the others farther into her lap. Although they planned on trekking another two days, I still wasn't convinced that it was wise, especially with their lack of winter gear.

"Maybe," I mused, "just maybe I'm gettin too practical for all this?"

But as the others stared at the dangerous passage ahead, they questioned their own sanity.

"I know Hans is crazy," Marley confided, lowering his telephoto lens for an instant. "And Jacob's got his moments. But this mountain and what it's capable of doing has me scared dungless!"

"Well," I thought, "that's a healthy attitude for this altitude in mid-November."

"Just don't do anything too stupid," I warned the ill-equipped musketeers. "We expect to see you guys back in Kathmandu!"

I slid down the steep, slippery descent to the 16,900-foot (5,150-meter) base camp and the world's highest concrete toilet. My companions were soon reduced to mere specks on the gravel overlook. I was content with my decision. As I felt that merciless wind slap across my chapped cheeks and sweep down my back once more, there was no doubt I'd made the right choice.

On the way back to Rongbuk, I paused to explore the crumbled nunnery ruins that Heinrich had diverted to earlier. Missing the path, I scaled a treacherous rockslide, then wove through a cavernous maze, unearthly in its silence. A miniature deserted village of stone huts was tucked deep within. Tattered strands of prayer flags fluttered mutely atop bamboo poles. Holy *chortens* sheltered pilgrim's *tsha-tshas* or clay offerings to the gods.

And for one strange moment, I swear I heard chanting; the echoes of a hundred thousand mantras wafting through the ruins, droning down deserted corridors, pounding with an eternal pulse over impenetrable boulders. A thousand sighs and heartbeats passed into another dimension.

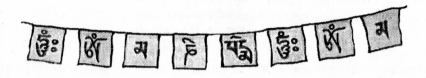

Chapter XIII

A Simple Act of Defiance

Be kind.
On the trail, even the smallest word of encouragement
makes a difference.

November 17-18

I t was a grueling two-day trudge back to Tingri with Billie, Tanji and Cheryl. At first, we were forced to face dreaded Pang La again. What was merely exhausting on the hike there became nearly bone-crunchingly impassable on our return. Yet that night we safely returned to the abandoned stone corral. This time, in hopes of relishing the added warmth, everyone, even Tanji, huddled together under our guides' heavy canvas shelter.

Since Bad Ass had crushed our short-wave radio during his earlier mountaintop tantrum, for once in our lives we were completely out of touch with the world, left to our own vacant stares and banal mumblings.

After fixing an early dinner of (what else?) ramen, we were ready to call it a night when Tanji shocked our band into a sensory overload. He nonchalantly tugged hoarded treasures from his pack. And what rare morsels they were: corned beef and real honey! We'd had very little meat in weeks and the mere thought of sweets set our mouths trembling. Every delicacy, each bite sized victory was slowly savored, as the scrumptious flavors exploded upon our long forgotten taste buds. Yet even that small delirious pleasure was short-lived.

Once the sun set, even with Don Juan's furious "pumping up the jam," temperatures remained well below freezing inside. Smoke from the dung fire blackened our already grungy faces and noxious clouds flooded every inch of the shelter.

Finally, unable to breath, I flew into an irrepressible coughing fit which only ended after I felt a "snap" and then an intense searing pain between my now cracked ribs.

Still, our tent flaps remained closed. Heat was too precious to waste. Dung equaled life.

Though our sleeping bags had dried at Rongbuk, near zero temperatures pushed them, and us, to absolute limits. The only way to get any sleep required scrunching down into a fetal position deep within our mummy cocoons. Although uncomfortable, that seemed to be just the solution. That is, until sometime late in the middle of the night.

Breaking the stillness, I suddenly bolted up screaming, "Ahhh! Ah yuchh!" Like some maniac shampooing with fire ants, I flung my head in fits and feverishly ran fingers through my matted hair.

"Whazza matta?" Cheryl mumbled, as she cocked a groggy eye and propped herself up on one elbow.

"Something just ran across my head!"

"You're dreaming," she sighed. "Go back to sleep." And with that she rolled over.

"No, I swear. It was mice!" I flopped back down and drew the bag's hood about my face. Then I tightly cinched it until only a tiny opening remained around my mouth. That's when a horrible thought crossed my mind.

"What if the mice find the hole and hop right in? Into my mouth?"

In the morning we made fast progress to Tingri. Its promise of hot *momos* and a good night's sleep spurred us on. For hours everything went smoothly until we reached the lower plains. Abruptly, Don Juan and Ugly whistled, barked and began herding the yaks toward Ra Chhu where we'd left the donkey cart. However, that slight detour would send us hours out of our way.

"Hey, wait a minute…We are goin' to town, aren't we?" I shouted over to Cheryl.

"Yo, Don Juan," my partner yelled, "you're taking us back to Tingri, aren't you?"

"No," he screamed, smiling, just eager just to get home. "Village."

"Wrong!" I reminded him. "You're supposed to take us all the way back to town!"

Unmoved, he just shook his yak butter slicked head, saying, "No. Village."

Just as dead tired, Billie finally entered the debate.

"Come on now, Don Juan," she gushed, "You don't want me to carry my pack all the way to Tingri now, do you?"

Ever since we'd met him, everyone suspected Don Juan had a soft spot for her and now that twinkle in his soulful eyes betrayed his secret. Sneaking one glance at her pixie face, he melted, shrugging, "Okay. Tingri."

Now that the plans were in motion, Don Juan and Ugly joined an old buddy for a swig of *chang* out on those plains. Meanwhile, for some unknown reason, Billie set-off trekking on her own toward Tingri which appeared on the horizon. She didn't seem to notice or care that we were still bound for Ra Chhu to drop off the yaks and pick up the cart. It wasn't until we pulled into that tranquil settlement that Don Juan even realized she was missing.

"Where Billie?" he cried, flustered. "Where Billie?"

"Don't know?" Cheryl replied. "Must have gone straight to town."

A look of disappointment, or was it concern, crossed his face. Swiftly piling everything from the four yaks plus the five of us onto one cramped, wobbly donkey cart, we set off trotting down the bumpy trail to town. As we bounced and jiggled along at double time, I figured our Tibetan Casanova was making that special trip just to see Billie one last time. But everywhere we looked, there was no sign of our friend.

As we grew nearer the village, Don Juan became more and more frantic, crying, "Billie? Where Billie?" as he craned his head, scanning the wild tundra.

183

Cheryl, her motherly instincts kicking in, grew worried as well.

"Wonder if she's lost? Maybe she couldn't make it across one of these streams?"

They did etch a hazardous, steel blue net of freezing water across the boggy landscape.

"Maybe she's stuck in one!"

For the next hour, all the way back to the village, we fruitlessly scoured desolate plains. It was if she'd simply fallen off the edge of the earth. That is, until we trotted into the inn's courtyard and spotted her, demurely relaxing in the shade as she sipped jasmine tea.

Greatly relieved, yet a little upset at her game of tundra hide-and-seek, Cheryl confronted our companion.

"Hey, thanks for leaving us behind...to handle all the details with your friend."

I wasn't sure if she referred to the budding romance or to the money that everyone still owed the guides.

"Sorry," she sighed. "Just thought ya'll were headed straight back. So I walked on ahead. Unfortunately, I ended up gettin' lost and havin' to cross a stream up to my waist. Boy, talk 'bout yer instant karma!"

To complicate matters, Billie couldn't pay our patient guide after he'd ridden so far out of his way. Hans didn't give her any money and Jacob didn't give her enough. Ultimately, she borrowed the balance and paid her ardent admirer without even an appreciative, "*Ghale phay!*"

A jilted Don Juan mounted his wagon seat, snapped his reins and clopped into the darkness.

November 19

Tingri quickly vanished the next day, soon reduced to a distant, dusty blur shadowed beneath a pristine panorama of frosted peaks. After six days under the innkeeper's watchful eye, our wandering Sadhu was a round, brown blimp. Unless it was my imagination, a long absent bounce had returned to his step.

Cheryl, however, was less enthusiastic about leaving. Suffering aches, pains and a throbbing head from the past few days, she was contrary as a yak. Although I, too, was physically worn out, I was determined to maintain our race to the last pass before those pure snows created an ugly impasse.

"It'll soon be December," I fretted and shuddered at the implications.

For several hours we continued west, hobbling across arid, scrubby flatlands toward Gutsuo, a day away. Having passed up Tingri's heinous selection of black dace or mystery meat, our supplies reached a critical stage. Since Gutsuo had a military base, we counted on them to have more food to spare. Any hope of finding supplies or rest before then was pointless.

There were few villages and even fewer people—except for the two Chinese soldiers toting an automatic weapon who lurked up ahead in the middle of the road.

"Oh, no. They've heard what you did last night!" I half-joked. "The Colonel's sent them to bring you in!"

"What I did?" Cheryl laughed. "Everybody else was in on it, too!"

Everyone had been hostile to five Chinese soldiers at the hotel's restaurant the night before. However, it all started innocently enough.

When we first walked in, we were a little surprised to see Billie "chatting up" the troops. She tittered and flirted with smiles and long glances exchanged on both sides of the table. She was eating up all the attention. But one thing really caught my eye. Those fellows seemed all too eager to share beers with her and it didn't take a mind reader to figure out that they were seriously trying to get her drunk.

"Billie?" Cheryl whispered, "How can you act like that with them."

"Like what?" she replied, becoming defensive.

"Making 'nice-nice' with these fools."

"I am not. They jest wanna buy me a beer," she coquettishly replied. "That's all."

"But," Cheryl reminded her, "you don't drink."

"So?" she giggled with a lighthearted toss of her shoulder length hair.

"So?" I reminded her, scanning the soldiers' hungry smiles. "So what do you think these guys expect in return?"

Her jaw went slack. "Oh…"

"There must be a way we can douse water on their plans," I figured. "I owe it to Marley. If we join them, at least Billie won't be alone. Who

185

knows? Maybe Cheryl and I can even drink them under the table. Hey, it was worth a try."

"Say, can we buy one of those beers from you?" I cordially asked one smirking soldier.

He looked over to his comrades, who nodded. So pulling a *Pi Jiu* from the wooden box behind them, he passed the cool bottle to Cheryl.

"How much?" I asked, knowing ours wouldn't be free.

"It'll probably be three yuan," I figured. "The same as in that Shigatse restaurant."

Glancing toward his friends again, there was a short animated discussion. Then chuckling over their decision, he faced me and announced, "Six yuan!"

"Six?" Why, in that land of constant negotiation, that was an insult!

"Keep your beer then," Cheryl insisted.

As the bottle was pushed back and forth several times, the friendly banter soon ended and the scene grew ugly. The soldiers kept demanding yuan and we kept refusing to be taken for naive tourists.

"Well, this is one sure way to disrupt their plans," I thought.

The whole episode dragged on several tense minutes. Until finally, frustrated, the troops screeched back their chairs and stood up en masse to retreat. As if that wasn't victory enough, Cheryl stubbornly refused to move her seat and allow their officer past.

"Why should I move for him?" she quipped. "I'm tired of always having to *kowtow* to the army here."

There was a hush throughout the room. All of a sudden, the scene took a startling, defiant turn. Tibetan waiters and cooks, encouraged by our simple act of resistance, joined in. They made playful, mocking faces behind the backs of the hated troops and even flashed that all-too-familiar crooked little finger indiscreetly in their direction. The only thing missing was the singing of "La Marseillaise," à la the film classic *Casablanca*.

The soldiers had taken all they could stand. At last, both humiliated and infuriated, the Colonel and his drunken troops grabbed what was left of their Chinese beer (and honor) and slinked out of the cafe.

As soon as they were out the door, the room erupted with glee and we were treated to a fountain of Tibetan *chang* by a victorious kitchen staff.

Now, as we approached the young soldiers, we forced a smile. They grinned back and waved their rifle in the air as we marched by.

"That's a good sign," I kidded. "You're lucky. They didn't recognize us." Then, casually glancing over my shoulder, I was chagrined to report, "They're following."

Figuring maybe there was something to our suspicions, we walked a little faster. They marched quicker. We picked up the cadence. The duo matched our pace. This tit-for-tat continued for several kilometers, until finally they drew alongside. For a few tense moments we pretended to ignore them. Then realizing that that made us seem even more suspect, I ventured to say, "Hello."

"Hello," they snickered back. At first, only that one word was uttered. Then one soldier haltingly tried to communicate with us for several frustrating kilometers. He asked us nearly unintelligible questions. In turn, I offered vague answers.

"Where you go?"

"Down the road."

"Where you come from?"

"That way."

"What village?"

"Very far."

The other soldier just nervously fingered his rifle.

Eventually, weary of the suspense, I whispered to Cheryl, "Let's take Sadhu over there for some water."

"But he just had some…"

"He's…thirsty…again!" I announced, winking. "Bye now!" I shouted with false bravado and a wave to the troops.

Well, of all days to be contrary, our horse just stood beside that stream. It only proves that you can lead a Sadhu to water but you can't make him drink.

Meanwhile, our two unwelcome companions marched two-hundred meters ahead. Then halting, one fell down on his knee and began shooting at some distant, unknown target.

As usual, that only spooked Sadhu more and we had to virtually drag our gun-shy gelding up the road past the gunfire.

"At least," I reminded Cheryl as we neared, "they're not shooting at us."

Upon reaching them, they ceased fire and resumed their uneasy, uninvited armed escort. One fellow, the soldier shouldering the automatic, marched on our right flank while the other brought up the rear. As we drew closer to the military barracks ahead, we grew queasier with each step. Conversation died. Our guards became sullen. The suspense built.

We stopped to pull water bottles from our saddle net. They waited. We paused to tie boots. They stopped. It was unnerving. That cat and mouse game continued for two...long...hours while we sweated bullets, concocting any reason to stop. We hoped to God, for once, they'd continue without us.

Until finally, we paused to study our useless map one last time, to stall, to secretly wish them away.

Call it magic, call it fate, or call it that mysterious force that had watched over us since our odyssey began. However, when we eventually, cautiously glanced up, I swear the two had simply vanished.

By late afternoon, just as we passed the ghostly ruins of an ancient, once palatial city on the windswept plain, a shout rang out from behind.

"Oh no, not again!" I cringed.

Startled, wheeling around, we detected a surreal image silently bobbing up and down the road. Experience told us it could only be one thing. Nearing, the vision glided to a halt.

"Hey, ya'll!" Billie coughed.

"What are you doing here?" Cheryl asked, knowing that she had planned to wait at the Tingri hotel for Marley to come down off the mountain.

The capricious cyclist pulled off her dusty goggles. "Well, I started thinkin'," she wheezed. "Why stick around till the 25th when I can be relaxin' in Kathmandu in just three days?"

"Three days?" I mused. "It'll take us another week or more at this rate."

"What about Tanji? Did he leave too?"

"Did he pay for another oxcart ride?" is what my partner meant to say.

"Get this...Tanji actually refused a ride in a truck all the way back to Lhasa!" Billie exclaimed, shaking her head. "Ya'll believe it?"

"Incredible!" Free truck rides were as rare as free *Pi Jius* and no amount of smiling and flirting would help.

"Yea," Billie smirked, "he said he was too tired to ride!"

"Too tired?" Cheryl groaned in disbelief. "He should try walking."

"Well, I gotta go, ya'll," Billie declared, remounting her well-worn seat. "But I'm sure we'll run into each other in Kathmandu."

"Right!" I was anxious to find shelter before it got too late. Then, remembering N.D., I reminded our buddy, "Hey, don't forget to deliver that letter, all right?"

"Don't worry!" she assured me as she pedaled off.

Turning, we continued our forced march into the wind just as the predictable, sandblasting midafternoon squalls surfaced. However, unlike other days, I had this intense feeling of dread, like something horrible was about to happen. Looking out to the horizon, my fears were easily confirmed. Ominously black, snow-bulging clouds gathered and headed straight for us; apocalyptic horsemen galloping down off the icy mountains.

"Time's run out," I thought. "And it's more than the weather. It's us. Our systems are shutting down. We haven't had more than a taste of protein in weeks. Diarrhea drains my energy. Every day it gets harder to hit the trail. Harder to hobble another thirty-five kilometers (twenty-two miles) on aching knees. Harder to choke on dust through sun-scabbed noses and peeling lips. Harder to sleep on stranger's floors. Harder to pantomime and deal with rejection one more time. Harder to stay disgustingly filthy. Harder to remain positive about what we're doing..."

While I privately wallowed in my own self-doubts, Cheryl toppled by the roadside.

"Damn you! I told you I didn't want to hike today!"

Why was her pain always my fault?

"Look," I reasoned, trying to stay calm. "As I explained before, we have to keep movin'." Couldn't she see it? Couldn't she see what was moving in right now on the horizon? Losing my patience, I screamed back, "We're runnin' out of time!"

"I'm so tired of bein' miserable."

For the first time in our arduous journey, overcome with acute exhaustion, hunger and fear, Cheryl sobbed.

189

"I know," I whispered, trying to comfort her without breaking down myself. "I know how you feel."

"What are we doing?" she whimpered. "Why are we out here?"

I'd asked myself those very same questions so many times. Yet only one thing could ease her pain; that same word she'd reminded me of so frequently before.

"Faith," I whispered, gazing into her mournful eyes. "We must have faith."

Gently gathering her fragile body in my arms, I pulled her up and together we stumbled toward a cluster of buildings a kilometer ahead. I hoped to God that it was either a roadcrew house or hotel.

Spotting the building's imposing facade, Cheryl quipped, "What do you think? Is it a Hilton?" as she smeared tears in charcoal trails across her dirt crusted face.

"Laughter's always a good sign," I thought. "She's already seeing the humor in our desperation."

"I don't know? Maybe Motel 6," I replied. "Are the lights on?"

It was obvious that the stark complex squatting beneath the stark hill was neither. "More likely," I thought, "it's a military base since twin scarlet Chinese flags frame its gateway."

Squinting, we detected a delegation standing in the middle of the road across from the compound. "Is it a road block?"

However, drawing nearer, we were relieved to discover our welcoming committee was just a group of kids playing and a plump Tibetan lady personally enticing guests to stay in her lodge. A hand-lettered sign in three languages dubbed the concrete bunker, "The New Restaurant and Hotel."

"When it's old," I wondered, "will they change the name? To what? 'The Old New Restaurant and Hotel?'"

Our timing couldn't have been better. With little ceremony or the usual meddling, we settled into another brightly-daubed concrete room that boasted standard spartan amenities.

Soon, Cheryl contentedly dozed off. As our candle melted, forming a milky pool on the cold stone floor, I offered a silent prayer for strength...since we, too, were fading and weak as our candle's dying light.

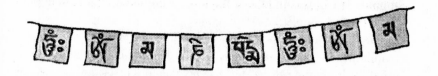

Chapter XIV

Words Of Hope

Be grateful.
Even the smallest things on the trail
are either a gift or lesson.

November 20

Gutsuo appeared by noon the following day. It was much closer—and smaller—than we'd ever imagined. A military garrison, menacing in its display of the Chinese flag, cast a repressive specter. Miniature adobe houses clustered on the hillside like a child's plastic train village. To our right, nomads' black yak hair tents sprouted from sparce plains. A few goats bleated and nibbled wayward tufts of grass. And as we approached the simple gathering of huts, the color drained from Cheryl's face.

"I thought you said Gutsuo was as large as Tingri."

"All I know," I admitted, shaking the useless maps, "is what I can tell from these."

Truthfully, I was just as disappointed since our prospect of finding supplies diminished with every step.

Spotting us, a carefree shirtless boy gave chase, screaming, "Dalai Lama! Dalai Lama!" while a Tibetan woman robed in a traditional black *choga* and striped apron approached us from the opposite direction.

Stopping her in the middle of the road, I implored, "Store?" hoping she'd help us find supplies. *"Tshong-khang ghapa yaw-ray?"*

She gave a curious, almost apologetic shrug. *"Mindu."*

"Nothing?" my companion sighed. "Ask her about a restaurant."

I tried again, hoping to get her to understand the seriousness of our question. *"Sa-gan du-gay?"*

"Mindu."

We grew more desperate. *"Thugpa?* Noodles?"

"Mindu."

"Pi Jiu?" Cheryl asked, willing to even settle for just a beer.

"Mindu," she chuckled with arched eyebrows.

Our consternation grew. "Even at half rations," I thought, "we'll be totally out of food in just three days. I doubt that that's enough to get us to Nyalam. And will they even have stores?"

As she examined us through melancholy eyes that seemed to reflect a lifetime of hardship, the slight, rosy-cheeked lady thought for an instant. Then she motioned for us to follow her.

The three of us tagged along in an uneasy procession, little knowing what she had in mind. As we passed that half-naked child, she paused just long enough to lovingly pull up her son's drooping drawers then turned off into the nomads' camp. Stopping in front of a yak hair tent, the woman brought a creased hand to her mouth to indicate that she would feed us. Then, before we could object, she ducked inside.

While we waited, famished, but embarrassed by our situation, we surveyed the simplicity surrounding us: five black wall tents flapping in a stiff breeze; a gaggle of scruffy, but lively children; several goats scratching in the dirt and tended by a venerable geezer looking as grizzled as his herd; and several teenaged boys who wildly snapped a yak haired whip in the air.

"Cheryl," I confided, "she can't afford to feed us. It's just not right..."

In an instant, that warmhearted Tibetan returned with a wooden stake. Grabbing a rock, she pounded it into the parched ground in front of her tent, then Sadhu was unsaddled, fed straw and finally hitched to the peg. Then, graciously holding open her tent flap, she motioned us inside.

Its cozy interior was illuminated only by light streaming through a vent in the roof and the open flap. Respectfully, as awkward as two teenagers picking up their prom dates, we settled onto well-worn rugs surrounding her dung fire as she gently fed its flames.

Her life was simple in the extreme. Glancing around that modest shelter, we noticed several colorful wooden trunks stacked at one end facing the door. On top of that makeshift dresser set a framed photo of her family and several precious shots of her.

Meanwhile, as shaken as anyone who unexpectedly has hungry visitors show up at their doorstep, she began opening one tiny tin box after another, asking, *"Thugpa?"*

We nodded in sincere appreciation.

Still, from her troubled frown, I sensed that her generosity exceeded her means. As she stood to leave, perhaps to borrow from friends, I stopped our host and convinced her to sit back down while Cheryl pulled two packets of instant ramen noodles from our saddle net.

Although a look of relief crossed her flushed face, she looked as though she'd never seen noodle packets before. That was quickly remedied. After showing our kind hostess how to cook the thin pasta, she enthusiastically boiled them, tossing in bits of petrified goat cheese. Then with all the aplomb of a sous chef, she spooned the satisfying stew into our grimy, plastic cups.

"Delicious," we sighed, slurping the steaming ambrosia. *"Tu jay chay!"* We quickly devoured two cups each and offered her and her angelic son who'd joined us the rest.

Afterwards, around the soft glow of her dung fire, we mimed the chronicle of our odyssey as they listened with rapt fascination.

Then, tenderly brushing her son's ebony hair from his eyes, she sadly shared her story…How she was our age—her husband was gone—she'd lost a child earlier on the road—we should be careful on that trail to Nyalam.

Upon hearing her tragic tale, we were even more deeply moved by her kindness; touched that a woman with so little had willingly shared it with two strangers and their horse.

Horse? From the corner of my eye, I saw a brown shadow silently shuffling pass the open tent flap.

"Sadhu? He's pegged," I thought.

Leaning over, I looked out to where he was tied. Nothing!

"Sadhu!" I screamed, flying out of the tent after him.

"Excuse us," Cheryl explained, chasing after me. "Our *da* is loose, again!"

Since ol' Sadhu had just wandered off in search of more hay, he was easily rounded up and saddled.

Afterwards, turning one last time to our sweet friend, we exchanged bows and asked the Dalai Lama's blessing on her, as she did on us. Then, succored more by her remarkable kindness than by any warm meal, we departed.

We couldn't help but wonder, as we had so often on this journey, why those Tibetans who had the least in material wealth were so eager to share with complete strangers? Would we ever become so generous, so trusting, so enlightened?

All day long, we battled boredom while trudging across a bland backdrop. It was impossible to imagine a more inhospitable region. Villages were as scarce as the few persistent patches of weeds that sustained meager flocks of gaunt sheep and goats. Naked hills replaced snowcapped peaks. The blustery wind was a constant, bitter adversary, reducing our pace, once again, to an exhausting crawl. However, as nighttime fell, we approached a small village with an incongruous look of prosperity.

Fat, healthy livestock abounded. Neighborly women and children filled a square, chatting, playing, and spinning wool and prayer wheels. Prayer flags, ever a welcome sign, flapped straight out in the stiff wind. Neither of us knew how far it was to the next village. Nyalam, the next town of any size, was still days away.

"This may be our only chance to find shelter tonight," I cautioned. "Wish me luck."

With that, I approached two ancient spinsters spinning wool beside a long adobe wall.

"They look like someone's grandmothers," I thought. "They'll understand—or at least have pity."

"*Tashi delek!*" I shouted, launching into my pantomime. "Sleep here? Walk...Lhasa...Kathmandu..." There was no response, just blank stares. I tried again. "Sleep here? Walk...Lhasa...Kathmandu. Then, I added, "Very tired," nearly falling to my knees.

They remained unimpressed. At the end of my performance, one old biddy, my harshest critic yet, sputtered, "*Mindu!*" through gaping teeth, as she jeered and waved us on.

Not willing or able to give up that easily, I approached another, spinning her wooden prayer wheel.

"Sleep here, Mama? Walk... Lhasa...Potala...Dalai Lama."

"*Mindu,*" she sighed, her sad, sagging eyes turned skyward.

I found it all hard to believe. That village with its immense courtyards, tidy houses, great flocks of sheep and piles of grain had no space? Couldn't they even spare their courtyard for two weary pilgrims? Still, convinced I'd just asked the wrong folks, I persisted along the wall.

Approaching one last group of girls and their mother, I begged, "Sleep here? Walk...Lhasa...Potala...Dalai Lama?"

Callously, they burst out laughing in my face. Wagging fingers, they made it very clear in no uncertain terms that we should leave immediately. So, dejected, we led Sadhu from the village square. Prayer flags continued whipping in the wind.

Fortunately, faith and fate were still our companions. Just three kilometers farther, we spotted another smaller cluster of adobe huts with a row of immense prayer wheels, as though to protect the hamlet from the swiftly coursing river. It was our last refuge. So, in the enveloping darkness, I teetered at the edge of the precipice and resolutely waved across the river to stick figures moving one-hundred meters below.

"Did they signal back?" I wondered aloud.

"Think so."

Placing hands to the side of my head in that familiar "sleep" position, I awaited a sign. Finally detecting some motion far below in the fading twilight, I asked, "Did they just wave us down?"

"Looked like it," Cheryl replied. "But it's so hard to tell from here."

Assuming they did, we vainly searched for a place to cross the icy riverbanks. But there was no place to ford. So we traced the road southwest a hundred yards until we discovered a stone bridge flanked by more prayer flags. Crossing it, we doubled back to the settlement.

There, a lanky, Navajo-looking fellow complete with thick, black braids met us. After glancing around to ensure no one was watching, he whispered, "Follow me."

Discretely he led us through the outer gates of his tiny courtyard where we unsaddled Sadhu, tethering him within reach of straw. Then the three of us hurriedly ducked inside to the warmth of his welcome hut.

It was similar in design to many others that we'd visited. Furniture was minimal. Three sturdy, wooden cots ringed a wall, each facing the dung fire. Stout wooden beams crossed the ceiling. Harvesting implements hung from mud brick walls. A side of yak ribs dangled from rafters. Looking around, we noticed the family's winter stockpile of potatoes and barley had already been stored in woven baskets and sacks by the door, alongside a bucket of brown, bubbling, fermenting *chang*.

While we settled into the comfort of his cozy home, the trusting stranger introduced his radiant wife and three small children. Then, in the finest tradition of all our other hosts, he drew a plastic mini jug of *chang*, that elixir of Tibetan hospitality, down from a shelf. Motioning for us to pull out our cups, since Tibetans expect guests to supply their own, he filled them for the first of many times that night.

"To your kindness," I toasted. *"Tu jay chay!"*

He joined our salute, adding, "And you."

I was mildly shocked. "Where'd you learn to speak English so well?"

"Oh, English no good now," he smiled, slightly embarrassed. "I go school in Nepal. Monk."

"How many years were you there?" Cheryl asked.

"S...S...Six," he stammered, searching for the right word.

Sensing the fellow's forthright honesty, I broached that one question we'd pondered for so long. "Maybe you can tell us," I started. "Why are some houses painted with orange, white and blue stripes?"

"Ohhh..." There was a long pause, as the monk struggled to answer our difficult question with only the simple words he could recall. His otherwise complicated reply was reduced to, "Those houses...people... Chinese."

That explained a lot. That was why people were not only inhospitable in villages where the houses were boldly decorated with those fearsome tricolors. They were downright hostile.

As we chatted further in broken English about drastic changes over the past decade in both Kathmandu and Tibet, his wife served us delicious roasted yak ribs with a crushed red pepper sauce, perfect for dunking. Then she turned on their small plastic radio. Its sounds were haunting; the melody and beat instantly reminding us of southwest Native American tunes.

"What type of music's that?" I asked.

"Tibetan," he sighed with undisguised longing. "Very old song."

The music eventually ended. In its place we heard the distant teachings of a man speaking Tibetan. Hearing that assured voice a world away, the former monk serenely beamed. "Dalai Lama! From India!"

Together we huddled with his brave family in that shroud of darkness, listening intently through every crack and sputter of the speaker. Each of us gleaned a different meaning from his words. The devout family feasted on and was sustained by the holy man's literal message. While we, not understanding Tibetan, heard a far subtler lesson—his words of hope.

"He will return someday," our host reverently assured us, as the broadcast crackled and finally faded into the cold night air.

November 21

We awoke thrilled and more than a little intimidated by the trek facing us. Thang La, at 5,200 meters (17,060 feet), was the last remaining physical obstacle before our dramatic descent across the border into Nepal. As we finished a simple breakfast of tea and hot cereal, our new friend, his braids flying, unexpectedly burst through the heavy wooden door.

"*Da* no eat today!"

"Why?" we wondered in polite amusement.

"*Da* eat! Eat! Eat!"

Dragging me outside to his corral, he pointed to where Sadhu, by craning his neck, had left a huge dent in the straw bin.

"*Da* eat more, he die!" he assured me.

I chuckled just to imagine Sadhu exploding in one giant fart along the road to Nyalam. Then noticing our host was dead serious, I assured him, as well as our Tibet thrasher, "No more eating!"

That settled, we turned to finish packing. Quickly we stuffed sleeping bags and cups into our unwieldy packs and zipped them shut. We were unaware that the youngest son eyed Cheryl's sneakers laced to her pack. At the last second, just as we hoisted our packs to leave, a brief, heated discussion burst out between the son and his father. It wasn't difficult to tell the subject. The scrawny kid persisted with the tenacity of teenagers everywhere.

Until finally, exasperated and slightly embarrassed, the monk pointed to her tennis shoes, suggesting, "Trade?"

"Well," Cheryl figured, "we're almost back to Nepal and I'm ready for new ones." Turning to the youngster, she suggested, "What do you have to trade?"

That signaled the start of another Tibetan "Let's Make a Deal." The monk's demure wife disappeared. Returning in a blink, she cradled a brass horse bell suspended from a broad, handmade needlepoint strap. It was decorated with traditional Buddhist swastikas and trimmed in black and red yak hair.

"Think this will keep Sadhu awake?" I joked, clanging the bell.

"At least, we'll hear when he raids someone's feed bin again!" Cheryl shrugged.

So, after the usual, "Yes," "No," "You want how much?" "Forget it!" "Okay, I'll take it!" trading gyrations, and after switching a tin tinkler for the more valuable brass one, the deal was struck. Sadhu gained a bell to rival the best we'd ever seen. And the monk's son proudly beamed an ear-to-ear grin as he modeled the village's finest sneakers.

Thang La is spread out fifty-seven kilometers (35.5 miles) from top to bottom, presenting even more of an obstacle than the last pass. Since ideally we could trek thirty-five kilometers a day, we faced another major decision. Either we could slow down and reach the summit in two days, or push ourselves to climb as near to the crest in one and camp on the saddle, descending the next. It was a tough choice. For so long, we'd viewed that pass with such trepidation.

"Are we ready to tackle one of Tibet's highest crossings? Do our bodies, our horse, our spirits have the stamina to meet the challenge? We'll just have to see how far we get this afternoon," I thought, postponing the inevitable.

Tempestuous winds and bone-numbing temperatures made our progress excruciatingly slow. For every labored step forward, we were blown half a step back. Chuckling as I remembered the comparatively easy first days of our pilgrimage, I wondered how long we could continue the plodding pace. And how long the weather would hold? Already it was the end of November and pregnant clouds might give birth to a dozen meters of snow any second.

By midafternoon, after struggling up that crooked, lifeless trail all morning, we spotted a roadcrew just ahead.

"Hey, maybe we can stay with them?" Cheryl proposed, ready to call it an early night.

"Maybe…" But from the looks of their shell of a house, we were too late. Four workers futilely fed a dismal fire in front of the burned-out ruins of a former road shack. It had no roof, no door, no potbellied stove, not even the mandatory yapping dogs. Just a hollow, vacant shell.

"Let's stay here a minute," my partner suggested, pausing. "You can ask them how far it is to the next town." So we led Sadhu into the yard. While my partner caught her breath, I approached the young, startled crew.

"*Tashi delek!*" I gasped, breathless. From the stunned looks on their grimy faces, they were obviously shocked to see us way out there. "Village?" I asked, pointing up the formidable mountainside. "*Dhrongsay?*"

After eyeing us up and down, a petite worker swaddled in layer upon layer of tattered jackets flashed a combination of seventeen fingers. Although I instinctively smiled and thanked her, her command of charades left me confused.

"Who knows if she means it's seventeen kilometers," I grumbled to Cheryl, "or there's a village at kilometer post something seventeen?"

"Can't we just stay here?" she pleaded. "It's too cold and I'm really tired."

"I know." I was worn out, too, though reluctant to admit it. "But we're just gonna be in worse shape tomorrow," I argued, "if we stay here tonight. There's no heat. We have no fire to cook." Just then, the ear throbbing wind began to howl and pick up again. "And this weather will probably get worse!" I yelled above the din.

"Well, I don't want to have to climb *that* today!" she countered, sullenly pointing to the dangerous vertical incline ahead which seemed to climb without end.

Something in my gut, something primal, told me we had to push on. As much as my head tried to ignore it, it was a feeling I'd learned to trust long ago. Perhaps our very survival depended on it.

"Well, damn it, we have to climb it sometime! And that sometime is now!"

"All right!" Cheryl bitterly choked. Grabbing Sadhu's reins, she led him onto the road. "Just keep looking back at us to make sure we're still there."

We continued our tenuous struggle up an endless series of switchbacks. The gale slashed our numb faces raw. Even with wool ski gloves, ear wraps and ski masks, we were half-frozen cadavers at the wind's mercy. My sides were splitting with every deep cough. My partner's pace grew increasingly slow, as she stumbled in a daze. It wasn't long before I realized that there was no way I could trudge behind her and Sadhu at half my pace, as in our earlier routine. No, we were long past those *truck ahead, truck behind* days. There was just no way.

So we endured a series of starts and stops. I'd forge ahead for thirty agonizing minutes, then wait ten more for them to catch up. And in those precious moments, I'd secretly wheeze and gasp shallow breaths.

For all its awkwardness, the system worked. We climbed higher and higher all afternoon onto desolate, rolling mounds. We raced the sun, desperately scouring deserted hillsides for a village before dark.

"Maybe we'll spot some sheep," I thought. "That's always a dependable sign that a village is near."

Still, our eyes continually played tricks on us. Stone shacks melded into steppes as we approached. Smoke from a dung fire became mist over the frozen plains. Once it even seemed that we'd reached the top. But there were no prayer flags, no mounds of stones, no *mani* stones, no offerings. Just disappointment.

"The saddle is only a plateau—higher, we must go higher..."

As the sun cast its magenta aura over the wilderness surrounding us, our dream of warmth became a nightmare of never-ending frigid stillness. Again, our pace quickened. Until finally, three or four kilometers away in the shadowed canyon below, we thought we spotted a minuscule hut. Smoke seemed to rise. And with it, hope.

"It might be a roadhouse," we prayed through frozen, bleeding lips. Our pace erupted, as we drew on every last ounce of our reserves. High on pure adrenaline, we flew down that serpentine, treacherously icy valley road.

"It is!" Cheryl exclaimed. "It's a roadhouse!"

Pouring on speed, we struggled to reach its gates before the light extinguished. Until suddenly, just two switchbacks from the finish line, our equine companion stumbled on the slick ice and fell with a bone shattering crunch on all four knees!

"Sadhu! Oh, my God!"

Rushing over, we helped lead him to his feet, more terrified than he was.

"Although nothing was actually broken, what would we do if he broke a leg out here?" I wondered. "What could we possibly do to help? Would we have to kill him? Could I find the courage? And how? A handy Swiss Army knife attachment?"

It turned out to be a roadhouse out in the middle of nowhere, complete with its own rumbling generator. As we approached the walled compound, for one mad second, I swore I heard Julie Andrews voice screeching off those glacial hills.

"Nahhh..."

While my companion sat down and caught her breath on a pile of rocks beside the open gate, I cautiously ducked inside. Armed with a handful of stones, waving the staff, I edged past a pack of snarling dogs and approached a window illuminated only by a gray flickering light. Gingerly inching open the door, I discovered eight Tibetans inside huddled in a warm video glow and transfixed by the "Sound of Music" dubbed into Chinese. The hills were alive.

"Sleep?" I pleaded, but I was no match for the singing Von Trapps and a cast of Nazis. An annoyed worker simply waved me outside. Assuming they meant another room, I knocked next door.

As it creaked open, I flashed the widest smile I could muster, made the usual nightly mime and coughed, "Sleep?"

After they too refused, for an instant, I flashed on that not so fond childhood memory of selling magazine subscriptions door-to-door. Then I tried the next, repeating my ridiculous performance. But they merely laughed and sent me down the line. This pitiful comedy continued another six times as I disturbed half a dozen more sleepy roadmen. With each rejection, they sent me reeling to their neighbor. Finally, only one door remained.

Nervously I knocked. As I shuffled to stay warm, a Chinese woman, her skin the texture of crack seed, eventually answered.

"We've just walked all the way from Lhasa…"

She only took one brief glance at me leaning in the darkness with my staff before slamming the door in my face.

I was paralyzed with shock. "What now?" I wondered. "Already, Cheryl's promised she's going to sleep on that rock pile if there's no room. Sadhu's famished, tired and frightened, and I'm definitely frazzled. God, if there is anyone watching out for us, now's the time for help…"

The door creaked open wide and a slight elfin character with short-cropped hair and huge ears swept me inside. Immediately noticing my severe condition, he shook his head and begged me to sit down.

I refused to get too comfortable too soon. "Please. Sleep?" I gasped, involuntarily swaying beside his glowing fire.

He nodded.

Then, pointing outside, I croaked, "Wife…*Da*…," in a voice still trembling from cold.

He nodded again and I stumbled outdoors to lead my stalwart companions past the hounds.

Although warned against feeding Sadhu, after his long, harrowing day, we risked it. Especially since our hosts insisted on feeding him a bucket of barley and *tsampa* water, his favorite. It was only my vigorous protests and silly pantomime of him exploding that kept them from stuffing him with an entire bale of straw.

We, too, feasted with the considerate strangers who insisted that we down bowl after bowl of rice *thugpa* and liters of hot tea. Willingly, they fed and cared for two exhausted *injis*. All without asking for anything in return. All under the watchful gaze of both Mao the elder and younger's portraits that hung on flocked walls.

"No, it's certainly *not* the Chinese people, after all," I mused, as I drifted off. "People are people, the good and the bad. It's just their leaders."

November 22

Only seven kilometers (4.3 miles) separated us from the top of Thang La Pass. "Only seven more," I thought, "and it's one long downhill slide into the tropical bounty of Nepal."

With that promise and the fire's warmth to sustain us, we buoyantly wished our kind hosts, *"Khale zhuu!"* and resumed an immediate ascent toward the summit at 5,200 meters (17,000 feet).

A sea of bleak, brown pebbled slopes ran in either direction, dissolving into peaks of sea foamed Himalayas to the south. Although the terrain varied little from the day before, our spirits soared. What appeared impossible in the night's anguished darkness, now seemed attainable.

Trekking became a walking meditation. Shuffling in silence, my mind emptied. It became as blank a canvas as the surrounding landscape. In doing so, thoughts and ideas flooded forward. Colors blended, then dissolved and emptied again. Food fantasies, erotic dreams, memories of relationships, childhood traumas, cherished loves, old problems, new solutions, even survival, were all reduced to brush strokes of a personal portrait.

One, perhaps two hours later, I finally spotted strands of prayer flags. Strung for a hundred meters, they undulated in a constant rhythm like waves ebbing against mountaintops. With that sacred siren that had lured us for the past few days finally before us, I jogged and jubilantly shouted the last hundred yards toward the crest.

At the summit, I swirled among scattered remnants of weather beaten clothing, onion-thin, block printed prayer papers and piled *mani* stones, all testaments to pilgrims before us. And I felt a joining of spirits with them, a mingling of hope.

"It is all down hill from here," I whispered, as my mate and I hugged on that heavenly summit.

Tears flowed, while in a flash we relived all we'd survived to get there. In heart-felt gratitude, together we silently remembered the gentle people who'd shared our dream, the faith we'd discovered and the powerful force that never deserted us even in our bleakest hour.

During our rapid descent, we dropped from 5,182 to 4,572 meters (17,000 to 15,000 feet) over a few kilometers. Hopes ran high. Nourished by another small victory, we eagerly looked forward to six days of easy trekking and a clear shot to Kathmandu. But that naive optimism wouldn't last long.

By early afternoon we reached the valley floor just as the daily dust storm began its scheduled howl, gusting up to 50 mph. Fighting a headwind through a twenty kilometer gravel pit has a way of burying any confidence beneath twenty layers of dust. Still, we struggled on. Until finally, just a day outside of Nyalam, as the first night frost fell, we encountered a small village. It was the only one we'd seen in many hours.

I waved to some fellows gathered across the river, five-hundred meters below. "Think they see us? I can't tell. It looked like they motioned us down."

Signaling again, I placed my hands to the side of my head while Cheryl squinted to see more clearly in the fading light.

"See the guy with the hat on...in front of the house?" she asked.

"Yeah..."

"Well, I'm sure he waved."

"I guess that means one of us has to go down there to check it out."

I hoped she'd volunteer since I didn't want to drag Sadhu into that ravine only, if rejected, to have to climb back out.

"I guess one of us does..." she demurely replied.

"Well, we did it last! The guys will sit this one out."

"It's weird for a lone woman to approach villagers."

"I know. But you have such a way with the old ladies."

"No way. This one's yours."

It was useless to bicker. Our chances faded with the light.

So, handing her Sadhu's reins, I scrambled down the gully switchbacks and sprinted over the wooden bridge to intercept the onlookers scrutinizing our every move. It was just my luck. Once below, I couldn't even find the one who'd waved earlier. So I approached the remaining five.

"*Tashi delek!*"

Launching into a mimed routine as worn as my callused feet, I pointed to Cheryl and Sadhu stoically waiting on the far shore.

Yet it was just as I'd feared. The shepherds only glanced at each other and chuckled. Inspecting me, they laughed even harder. Then with deliberate shakes of their heads, they waved us down the road.

"The next village could be five or six hours away," I figured. "There must be something I can say, some *abracadabra* that will make them change their minds."

"Dalai Lama, photo!" I promised, figuring that was the most powerful magic I had in my arsenal.

They shook their heads.

All right. "Yuan. Ten yuan. Money?" I countered, trying the capitalist approach.

They refused again. Then three of them, losing complete interest, returned to their work.

"Yikes! These guys strike a hard bargain," I groused. "And we're running out of time."

Quickly I made a rough inventory of all the items we still carried.

"Watch?" I offered, remembering the plastic one in our pack.

Both men showed me theirs.

"Cigarettes?" They declined again.

Then I hit upon it. What do people who spend their entire day out in the bright, glaring sun need most?

"How about SUNGLASSES?"

One stocky peasant's bloodshot brown eyes lit up. Without a moment's hesitation, he led me to his snug, stone cottage and I signaled for my companions to join us. Once inside the tiny room, we were soon joined by a curious entourage: his wife, their five young children, a gregarious six-year-old neighbor boy, two attractive village girls and the former monk's brother. While that shrewd holy man leaned back and took long snorts of snuff from a rusted tin, his cordial mate poured us cups of (what else?) home-brewed *chang*.

Raising my cup in a universal toast, I cheered, "To your health!"

He grinned and thanked us while his wife refilled our cups to the brim.

Well, that was only the beginning. That spry shepherd and I continued toasting and celebrating for the next hour. Until all their *chang* was polished off, as is the Tibetan custom (or, perhaps we just cleaned them out wherever we stayed).

Meanwhile, Cheryl was entertained or, should I say, captivated by a fascinating village boy. The lad with playful eyes and engaging grin had latched onto her like a long lost friend—or life preserver.

Seeing their obvious rapport, the herder asked, "You have children?"

"No," she replied, awaiting the lecture that usually followed. She was used to that question, especially in Africa and Asia. And tired of the haughtiness that followed. Egyptians even suggested I leave her if she couldn't bear children. "You can always find another wife," they'd advise, winking. They just didn't understand the lengths to which many Westerners go to prevent unwanted children. Of course, that's a hard concept to rationalize in a culture where a family's wealth equals its number of children or where infant mortality is high. It's especially true in Tibet where 127 out of every thousand children die, compared to only forty-three for its Chinese invaders.

"Why?" our startled host gasped, as he eyed us with obvious pity.

"Oh, I guess we travel too much," she quipped, choosing humor as an excuse. "It's hard to cram kids into our packs!"

The simple shepherd, a fellow close to our age, seriously studied the boy who showed more affection to my companion than any child ever had. And she unabashedly returned his love, glowing from ear to ear.

"You take him with you," the monk decided, drawing Cheryl's new buddy directly in front of her so they could look each other right in the eye. "You take him to Kathmandu!"

It made perfect sense. For an instant, I envisioned the boy perched atop Sadhu and riding across the border.

"Anything to declare?" they'd ask.

"Oh, nothing except this small Tibetan and a horse," I'd reply with a shrug.

That'd go over well. Then what would we do if we made it into Nepal? Drop him off in Thamel with a, "See ya later, kid."? And getting him back into the States would involve some sort of diplomatic miracle.

Cheryl sneaked a glance at me, as if actually seriously contemplating instant motherhood. But of course she realized in her heart that the obstacles were greater than the mountains around us.

"No, I'm sorry. We can't bring him with us."

"Then, you…" the matchmaking monk started again, turning to me. "Like one of them?" he asked with a scheming grin, as he glanced over at the two nubile village girls. They'd silently flirted, sweetly smiled, clung to my every word and shot lingering glances over the past hour.

Although I turned to Cheryl, joking, "Well, what do you think?" there was no use to wait for a reply. "Nah, I don't think they'd go over too well."

Our bewildered host merely shook his head, confused by his bizarre visitors and confounded by their refusal to accept his generous hospitality. Then deftly changing the subject, the uncle lifted a slender, guitar-like instrument from the wall. Cradling it, he plucked a sad tune.

Crestfallen, the sweet orphan and alluring Lolitas discretely disappeared, perhaps saved for the next traveling *injis* pilgrim.

Altogether, it was a magical evening, spontaneous and heartfelt. After dinner, the dung fire died down. We crawled into our bags atop sturdy cots, while the yak butter lamp was moved to the other side of the stone hut. As we reflected on our luck and the love shared in that home, the kids washed and splashed from a tin basin opposite the sputtering fire. Snickering and unfettered, they ran naked through the lamp's glow, then snuggled with their loving parents beneath a furry yak hide spread out upon the floor.

"In our short time in Tibet," I mused to myself, "we've already been offered a cow, a kitten, a child and even two attractive bedmates. We *could* always settle down here."

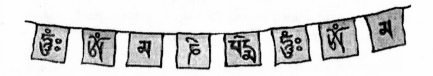

Chapter XV

The Snowy Road to Hell

Be content.
Savor the small victories now, along the way.

November 23

The next morning, we awoke to an eerie silence. That familiar stillness took just a second to register.

"No, it can't be!"

Throwing on some clothes and poking my groggy head through the wooden portal, I stared out at the one thing we'd feared most for nearly forty days—a raging blizzard!

Thick, downy flakes had already transformed Sadhu into an alabaster carousel pony. I, too, stood in shocked, stony silence. Just over twenty kilometers (12.5 miles) separated us from Nyalam. Only a hard half-day's hike, a fifteen-minute drive, kept us from the comfort of a hot shower, hot restaurant food and a warm bed. And Kathmandu waited just three or four days beyond.

Waking Cheryl, we scarfed down breakfast while weighing our only two options.

"What do you think?" I asked, lingering over my boiled *cha*. "Do we try to hike through this today and come as close as we can to Nyalam? Even though we don't know the location of the next village? Or, do we sit it out here another day?"

Our answer was obvious. It only took one glance at the kind-hearted Tibetan family still curled around the dung chip fire. Spending another night with them would be too much of an imposition. Besides, how much *chang* could I possibly hold?

"Let's go for it," I announced, my enthusiasm cloaking unspoken fears.

Appreciative, I slipped the shepherd his well-deserved sunglasses, but even they couldn't disguise his concern. Reluctantly he helped load our ivory horse. Then waving good-bye, we slid down the frosted hillside and skidded across the frozen wooden bridge back to the camouflaged road. With mounting trepidation we headed south, trudging face-first into the blinding snow and savage, slashing wind.

"We just ran out of time," I yelled above the deafening roar. "Now do you understand why I've been pushing so hard?"

"I take it all back," Cheryl's voice quivered, scared, through the shroud of flurries engulfing her. However, an *I told you so* would offer me no consolation.

Our progress was minuscule. Sadhu's gait was labored. With each cautious step, his hoofs slipped on thinly veiled ice beneath a blanket of snow. Terror blazed in his eyes. Until they, too, became frost crusted. Mine were little better. I couldn't wear sunglasses to shield them from the blinding glare. Shades immediately fogged up. But without them, powder pummeled so hard that our path was soon obscured. Then, like Sadhu, even my eyelids began freezing shut.

"This is miserable. How much more can we possibly take? After an excruciating hour we've only covered two-and-a-half kilometers (two miles). Now, as if to compound our torment, our path's starting to head up the mountain again."

"Hey!" Cheryl screamed above the howling maelstrom, "I thought you said it was all downhill to Kathmandu?"

I had no answer, no excuse.

As we struggled upward, the wind increased until we couldn't see more than six meters ahead. Thank God there was no southbound traffic. Practically no one was crazy enough to venture out into a blinding blizzard—except us. The only souls we passed for hours were two bundled herdsmen with yaks rushing the opposite direction and they merely gawked with incredulous stares and mumbled something unintelligible.

"I think they just said it's clear up ahead!" I joked, trying to remain optimistic.

"No, they just screamed how sick we are to come out in this!" Cheryl replied.

Any chance of reaching Nyalam faded with each footstep. We were pitifully pummeled. Icicles hung from my wool ski mask. Cheryl's boots were drenched. Sadhu's muzzle was caked with ice and he rubbed his nose against my pant leg to knock off frost. Still, the weather grew more intolerable.

For two and half-hours we intrepidly inched a tedious path through the blinding snowstorm. Until finally, from twenty yards behind, my white cloaked friend shouted, "Hey, there's a village up ahead. Let's duck in, at least long enough for this storm to pass."

"You ready to stop?" I demanded, indignant at the thought of surrendering.

"We're never gonna to reach Nyalam in this weather. NEVER!"

Unfortunately, she was probably right. Spotting a miniature grinning snowman guarding an icy knoll ahead, I suggested, "Hey, why don't you ask him if we can stay here awhile?"

"Sure. *Tashi delek!*" she shouted with relief to the stunned village kid.

"*Tashi delek?*" he mumbled, reluctant to believe his eyes.

"Go inside?" my companion pleaded, as she waved toward the hint of a hut materializing through a flurry of horizontal flakes.

Nodding, he led us scurrying through blanketed village streets to a small courtyard. There, under the wary scrutiny of the fuming family dog, we unloaded Sadhu and lugged packs, net and saddle into their adjacent tack room.

Horse, donkey and yak harnesses with brass and tin bells hung from rafters. A pile of straw cascaded in one corner, while a wall of dried dung patties flooded the other. No one was inside. But weathered rugs and sheepskins stacked along one wall told us that someone already lived there amid animal supplies and excrement. While the boy started a smoldering dung fire in a coffee can-sized pot, his older brother led Sadhu to a cozy stable brimming with straw.

"Well," I asked, as I surveyed our bleak surroundings, "better?"

Cheryl stomped her soaked, half frozen feet around the would-be fire and resolutely nodded.

"Let's hope this passes in a few hours," I prayed, gazing through the shed door, "and we can keep trekking."

But the forecast looked grim. That deadly white powder fell faster than ever, cementing itself to the ground as if it planned to take root till May.

At first, of course, we were just grateful to be out of that storm. But as the afternoon dragged on, it soon became obvious we'd never make it farther than that manger's frigid floor. At that prospect, I fumed in solitary frustration around the miserly warmth of the dung fire. However, even that peace flickered and faded when the family's teenaged daughter joined us.

The raven-haired girl brought a soot-stained hand to her grinning mouth and mimed, "Eat?"

"That's not a bad idea." We'd been running for hours on little more than hot tea and cereal. Reaching for my pack, I remembered we only had one dehydrated food packet, a few crackers and one can of long treasured meat left. "Look. We'd better save what we have," I cautioned, knowing it would have to get us to Nyalam or beyond. "Maybe we can buy some food here."

"Sure, that makes sense," Cheryl agreed, as she broke a yak dung patty in half and stoked the faltering fire.

Facing our hostess, I asked, "Store? *Tshong-khang?*"

She shook her head.

"Oh no." I figured. "Here we go again."

"Restaurant? *Zakhang? Thugpa?*"

She giggled and continued shaking her head *no*.

I tried again. "How about food? *Khala?* Any *khala?*"

At that her eyes lit up. She dragged me over to the corner and lifted the lid on several bushels of potatoes. Although the bland little tubers are my least favorite food, desperate times call for desperate measures.

"How much? *Ghatshay ray?*" I asked, expecting to pay a yuan or two. Suddenly serious, our enterprising hostess blurted, "Five yuan!"

"Five?" That seemed to be the price of everything in Tibet. Many times the going rate, it wasn't that it was such an extraordinary amount of money. It was the principle.

"Three!" I countered.

She shook her head, not budging. In that seller's market, we were forced to pay or starve. So we forked it over, as already our taste buds began to water.

"Cheryl, why don't we fix some sort of stew?" I suggested. "After all, we can add the tinned ham to the potatoes. That should get us through the night."

"Ah, what a treat," she sighed, plunking walnut-sized spud nuggets into the boiling water.

"Have you seen our can of meat?" There was no sign of it. What was at first a methodical search, soon became a frantic rummage through our net bag.

"It should be in there."

"Well, it's not!" It had vanished. We'd carted that precious Danish ham all the way from Mount Everest. Passing it over on many occasions, we'd hoarded it for an emergency. And this was rapidly becoming one.

"It was in the saddle net bag when we left this morning. So, it either dropped out in the snow—or that kid helped himself when he helped us unload."

"No, I can't believe that." Cheryl whispered.

Now in more normal circumstances, a can of ham is a can of ham; something neither of us would normally even eat. But to us, at that instant, whether it was the altitude, fatigue, the weather, or just the dung heaped situation, I was convinced it might mean our survival. It was not our finest hour. Physically and emotionally we were drained and the howling blizzard only made us more dispirited, more on the ragged edge.

After that sorry episode, we figured we'd seen the last of our hosts. But within an hour, just when the potatoes were finally soft enough to eat, the sneaky daughter slid back inside. Pretending to feed the fire, she fed her face instead with our hard-won spuds.

"I don't believe her brazenness," Cheryl fumed. "She's got bushels of potatoes over there, yet she insists on eating the only food we have?"

Hearing our heated conversation, the hungry teen paused and sheepishly glanced over at us.

"Ah, go ahead. Help yourself," I groaned, waving at the pot. "You will anyway."

She crammed morsels in her mouth until her cheeks bulged like an apple-stuffed Christmas pig.

All day long, Cheryl did an admirable job of keeping that dung fire burning with skills honed at Rongbuk. Since there were no bellows, it was a much harder task than usual. Although I kidded, "I think you've finally found your calling," I admired her diligence. That smoldering flame was all that kept us from freezing. Heating our hovel was a thankless, nearly impossible chore. At first, each time the teen ran out, she left the door ajar. Then, just as we convinced her how important it was to close that door, her older brother bounded into the tack room and left it open once again.

He swaggered over to our faint dung fire and critically inspected it. Then pointing to the pile of yak dung patties stacked as high as the hut's window, he warned, "*Mindu!*" shaking his head.

We were puzzled. "*Mindu?* No good?" Cheryl repeated. "What's he mean?"

Stooping beside our red-hot can, the fellow nonchalantly scraped sheep dung pellets, *luke-poo*, and trash off the dirt floor. Then he tossed those odd scraps into the flames with a "See there?" expression.

As our fire nearly fizzled out, we both gasped. Then it flickered a weak and dying flame.

Exasperated, Cheryl sighed, "He can't mean I'm only supposed to use what I find on this floor?"

Nodding, our dung monitor swept together another handful of mostly dirt and fed it into the can. Then with a grin, he sashayed out and left the door wide open. Snow drifted into the shed and with it the threat of slowly freezing.

"Look," I fumed, unwilling to play the intimidated *injis* any longer. "We'll use what *luke-poo* we can without putting our fire out. Then we'll just have to raid their good shit."

214

By early evening, the snow ceased its deadly cascade and we were thrilled to spot a patch of cobalt blue sky through the ever-open doorway. Still, we knew the futility of heading off through unknown drifts with just an hour of daylight left, only to take our chances at reaching another village.

"Maybe a meter or so fell in the village today," I thought. "There's just no telling how deep it is on the road."

Still, we ached to leave. Although the family shared their shelter, they wanted us gone as soon as possible. As usual, we were the local curiosity and each member of the family, all six or eight of them, paid us a visit. We'll never know whether it was out of reserved concern or just to make sure that we weren't raiding their dung pile. However, as the evening wore on, we wore out, and grew ever more weary of keeping the dying fire alive while gawkers continued to leave the manger's door wide open.

November 24

We fled the village shortly after daybreak, promising Sadhu, "There's plenty of hay at the end of this road." Although nearly a meter of snow had fallen with drifts reaching our waists, we promised ourselves nothing would prevent us from reaching a bed and hot food that evening. Fortunately, since nightfall, several persistent cargo trucks had already plowed their way through en route to Thang La. And for once, I was grateful for their tenacity.

There was a peaceful calm, since the thick, white powder also prevented other vehicles from rushing to Shigatse. No gravel flew in our faces. No horns blared. No dust engulfed us. There was just blissful tranquility. Azure skies assured good weather and white tipped peaks never glistened more pristinely. Bleak hills, stark villages and clumsy yaks were all dusted and purified with a powdered frosting, a serene blessing on once hostile surroundings. Ironically, like some fantastic vision, we finally discovered our long sought after mind's eye illusion of Shangri-La; one destined to disappear with the rising sun.

The snow, itself, did little to hamper our progress. It was the ice, hidden in shallow road ruts, which ultimately slowed us down. Cheryl performed an impromptu dance, a *glissade*, with our skittish horse. The instant his shoes hit a slick patch, Sadhu slid into an airborne arabesque on three legs. Meanwhile, I skated ahead and scouted hairpin turns for nearly silent trucks.

The surrounding mountains, those distant, ivory giants, ethereal homes of the gods, made our wary tango all worthwhile. Snow-capped Mount Lonpo Gang, Mount Dorje Lakpa and Mount Phurbi Chyachu, all over 6,706 meters (22,000 feet) high, led us southwest down the pass toward Nyalam.

The road was deserted except for the hourly truck and one elfin Tibetan clad in traditional black skirt over pants and turned-up yak hide boots. Long, braided black hair wrapped with a crimson rope encircled the elder's head and a turquoise stud shined from his ear. We met late that morning and hiked together much of the afternoon. While he admired Sadhu, we admired his aged strength and stamina needed to skate more than twenty-five kilometers (15.5 miles) into town.

Still, for hours we said nothing to the serene gentleman. There was no use. Trekking transcended the need for human uttering or feeble gestures. They merely stood in the way.

Only once did I ask, "Nyalam?"

"Nyalam," he shrugged, smiling with an inner peace.

As in life, somewhere along that road we lost our fellow traveler. We offered to share a quick snack of leftover potatoes with the stranger. But he politely refused and pointed down the road, as if we'd meet later. It wasn't long before we caught up to the spry fellow when he paused to eat. We passed. Then again, he rejoined us. Finally, stopping a third time, we watered Sadhu beside crystalline waterfalls. However, when we turned, the stranger was gone.

The afternoon passed uneventfully until hours later, as we rounded a quiet hilltop, a tiered city sprouted to our right. We'd made it!

There was no mistaking Nyalam with its multistory buildings, modern steel bridge and Chinese flags. It had the officious air of a border town, complete with a truck stop and military base. Music blared from open storefronts and restaurants offering a savory choice of Nepalese and Chinese foods. There were even a few of those "falling-star" inns.

Walking its main street, we wove amid a winding strand of trucks and military Jeeps waiting for the pass to clear. Until finally, we found the Snowlands Hotel. Although they had room and the price was right, our *da* presented a real problem. For an hour, that resourceful innkeeper and I waded through waist deep snow drifts before finding hay. Then we struggled another two hours in search of a place to bed our friend.

The squat innkeeper creaked open an equally low set door that led to a cramped storage shed adjoining the hotel. "How about in here?"

I poked my head inside. "Well, I'd say it's about a meter too short."

Then he led me to the inn's side yard blanketed in deep powder.

"No, I don't think it's too good for Sadhu to lay shivering in snow all night." We continued hunting around back.

"Maybe here?" the manager asked.

That ground was even more dangerous. It was covered with years worth of razor-sharp slivers of glass, a tribute to the Chinese penchant for smashing empty beer bottles against the nearest adobe wall.

"No, we don't want fricasseed horse, either."

Our genial host was stymied, as if we were the first guests to ever arrive with a horse. That seemed improbable, since Nyalam, or as its Tibetan name means "the Road to Hell," is on the old Himalayan trading route.

"Surely," I thought, "there must be somewhere he can stay out of this wind."

Just then, in a stroke of mad genius, I spotted the outdoor toilet. The hotel's only latrine, a slit in a cement floor, was set in a concrete shack that was wedged between two buildings and down a dark, narrow passageway. Having exhausted the other options, it was clearly our only logical choice. So, pleased at our *injis*-uity, we fed our wandering companion and hitched him to the outhouse door.

And anyone "going to see a man about a horse" that night, well, certainly did!

With Sadhu cared for, we immediately trotted across the street to the Nepalese restaurant. Although it was a far cry from our fantasy feast, the heaps of dal, rice, spicy tomatoes, curried vegetables, eggs, lamb and beer never tasted better.

One need satisfied, we ambled back to the hotel, anxious to fulfill another. Unfortunately, our room was nearly as frigid and drafty as Sadhu's. But even that was soon remedied with a little Western technology. After sealing strips of duct tape around the loose, cracked windows, our tidy bungalow offered temporary respite from the wind, rain, snow—and even dung of night.

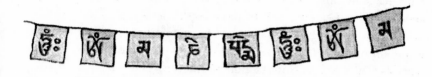

Chapter XVI

A Bridge to Freedom

Be human.
There is no harm in getting lost–only in staying lost.

November 25

Early the next morning, we shuffled out of that *Wild West meets Alpineland* sort of town that had given us momentary reprieve. We'd found a warm bed and decent food, including a mango drink that was pure nectar of the gods. But after forty days on the road, we still searched for the ultimate nirvana—that ever-elusive shower.

Our descent was rapid as we left Nyalam at 3,780 meters (12,400 feet) for the border thirty kilometers (18.5 miles) away at only 2,300 meters (7,546 feet). Contrary to popular belief, the "Road to Hell" is paved with more than good intentions. It's lined with inspired beauty.

Just on the outskirts of the rustic settlement, tall conifers and rhododendrons poked from the hillsides like budding cowlicks. There'd been so few trees for weeks. God, they were a welcome sight. But that was just the beginning of our sensual reawakening. Magically, we stepped through a looking glass of sultry perceptions.

The sweet scent of pine mingled with the relaxing rhythm of a cascading waterfall. Jade ferns gently wreathed clusters of rust hued boulders. Glistening steel blue waters rushed below us, engulfing us in their peaceful pulse, while the lonely cry of a spiraling hawk pierced the thin air above. But even that Eden was ephemeral.

Before long, those alpine forests transformed into a subtropical monsoon woodland of broad-leafed oaks and chestnut. A nose-numbing fragrance of tropical flowers flooded the air. The temperature soared, doubling from 35°F to 70°F in one afternoon. In gratitude, we shed layer after layer of fetid winter clothes, as if outgrowing our stifling chrysalis shells.

Awakening from a long overdue *Rip-Van-Winkle* sleep, we became energized. There was a bounce in our step and growing anticipation as each hour drew us closer to the border at Khasa and Tatopani's hot springs on just the other side. Then, just as miraculously as it had appeared, our illusion of a private paradise vanished.

We skirted past delivery trucks clogging narrow streets and were once again the center of unwanted attention. Children screamed, "*Da! Da! Da!*" like they'd never seen a horse before. Gnarled women gawked at us from open windows. Young girls glanced up from the dusty roadside where they washed tin plates in plastic buckets. Soldiers suspiciously eyed us up and down, as they gulped beers outside garish bars. Only the hustlers, scurrying from crowded storefront to packed blackmarket alleyway, were too busy to care.

With careful deliberation, we wove Sadhu through a hundred frenzied lives and approached an endless line of trucks and buses packed with partying, escorted tourists. Since a construction crane had stopped traffic, they impatiently languished bumper to bumper for nearly an hour. Curiously no one seemed to notice two white travelers out in the middle of nowhere walking their horse. This is, until a well-meaning, too-clean-to-be-believed American leaned out his mini-van window and yelled, "Hey, cute pony!"

"He's no pony!" we indignantly shot back in response to his unintended insult. "He's a Tibetan horse!"

"By now," I figured, "Sadhu deserves more respect than the word 'pony' implies."

"Come on," I snorted, tugging our companion's tattered reins. "There's no reason we have to stand in line. We can easily make it past."

At that, we casually waltzed on past the traffic snarl with our wandering holyman amid encouraging smiles and waves from the Tibetan roadcrew.

Although a maze of streets meandered down that mountainside for nearly ten kilometers (six miles), there was no telling where Khasa officially began. We only knew a Chinese customs post lurked somewhere amid the jumble, somewhere before a bridge marking the final frontier. It was already late afternoon. We kept a steady pace and hoped to reach customs before that hundred vehicle traffic jam was unleashed like bats—and we found ourselves stranded at the end of a day-long line. No, thanks. No need to subject ourselves to Khasa's nightmarish nighttime hospitality. Of all the villages we'd explored, it looked and felt the most "Chinese." It's sadly ironic, since for many travelers for many years it was the only part of Tibet they were permitted to view.

Just as the first revs of truck engines roared behind us, we spotted customs. I can't remember a time when I was more eager to reach a border. Already twenty fuming trucks and belching buses queued outside a white, two-storied building awash with red flags. So, intent on jumping what we assumed was the final hurdle, we wasted no time. We intentionally skirted the line and headed straight for the customs house.

For the past two weeks, I'd worried how the border bureaucrats would react to Sadhu. "Will we get by with paying duty? Or will they, can they, prevent him from escaping altogether?"

Just then, a pert customs official turned around and blocked our path. Decked out in bobbed hair, starched blue uniform and American running shoes, she could have passed for a flight attendant on some low budget commuter airlines, maybe Borderline Air? Casually, she eyed us up and down.

"Can we go through?"

"Anything to declare?" she asked.

"Nope." Why say anything about the horse standing with Cheryl just a meter away?

"Any purchases?"

"A few souvenirs." Sadhu, our brother, didn't seem like a purchase. "Less than fifty dollars worth."

"All right," she declared, smiling, as if she knew otherwise. "Here," she ordered, thrusting me a fistful of papers. "Just fill out these forms."

Now, nowhere did they mention "horse" and I certainly felt no obligation to state the obvious. It wasn't like we were sneaking him out. He wasn't disguised as a yak or mini-van. He was just a horse who stood there in plain view for all the sniveling paper pushers to see.

"Why complicate everyone's lives with details?" I figured.

So, I quickly completed the necessary forms and handed them to another officer lounging on the porch.

"Can we go now?"

With a lethargic nod, the comrade raised the white gate blocking the road and we gleefully set-off down the dirt trail towards the bridge at the final border.

"Great! Now there's nothing between us and Nepal!" I proclaimed.

Just then, a voice from a nearby shack wailed, "Wait! Wait!"

"Who? Us? Do we stop? Just ignore him? Or is that pushing our luck too far?"

While we weighed those options, a wiry little guy tore after us, screaming, "Quarantine! Quarantine!"

"Quarantine? Wait a minute. We're leaving the country. Why would China quarantine Sadhu?"

Stopping, I calmly walked over to that still yapping poodle-of-officialdom and in my best Luke Skywalker imitation I deadpanned, "This horse is going to Nepal."

"No. Quarantine!"

"This horse is going to Nepal," I insisted, not missing a beat.

He lifted up his dark glasses still sputtering, "Quarantine."

Staying in Tibet was not even a possibility for ol' Sadhu. Pulling off my shades, I looked deep into his narrowed eyes.

"This horse...IS going...to Nepal," I pronounced with finality.

I don't know why. Maybe it was that strange magic again. But that officer blinked as if he'd been hit in the head. Then nodding, he matter-of-factly proclaimed, "This horse *is* going to Nepal" and he waved us on.

Defiant, we congratulated ourselves on breezing through the bureaucracy and on liberating our friend.

But any celebration was premature. Rounding the next bend, we ran headlong into another long line of trucks with a contingent of a dozen soldiers stalled in the road.

"Now what?" Cheryl whispered, exasperated by the constant delays.

"Let's just go around," I suggested. "And keep smiling."

Sometimes playing the stupid tourist can be an excuse for almost anything. So Cheryl nonchalantly led Sadhu past the motionless throng of vehicles and continued through an anxious crowd of villagers and troops.

Suddenly, one Chinese soldier sprang from the pack. He reached out and slapped my partner across the shoulder!

"Ahhh!" She wheeled around, shocked and unaccustomed to being struck by anyone. "Why'd he do that?" she demanded, glaring holes through the smirking bully. As one might guess, she wasn't smiling anymore and I was trying my best to behave myself.

"Because he could! Come on, let's get out of here!" I suggested, as we tried to edge past him before things got truly nasty.

But the soldier motioned for us to stay, giggling, "Boom-boom!"

"Oh, so they're blasting another Tibetan hillside." That explained it. "I thought we were out of 'China!'" No such luck.

Cheryl led Sadhu over to the wooden facade of a grocery. She was taking a break on its creaking steps when the same idiot soldier swaggered up and leaned back, kicking Sadhu in his flank with full force! And he laughed again!

"That's it!" I bellowed, forgetting my pacifist leanings, ready to flatten him. I shook my fist just inches from his smirking grin and glared nose-to-nose. "If you touch my wife again," I seethed, barely containing my rage, "or my horse, I'm going to wrap this whip around your wretched neck!"

He stood stock still as the blood drained from his face in terror.

"Relax," Cheryl admonished. "Remember what you told me?"

"Right," I snarled. "Keep smiling."

The blasting subsided, as did my fury, and we sped off with only the vaguest idea how far no-man's-land stretched or where the Nepalese border truly was. Within moments though, our question was answered. We heard the reassuring rush of the river. Peering down through the mass of verdant flowers, we spotted Friendship Bridge (an ironic moniker) hundreds of meters below. Nepal awaited on the opposite shore. All that separated us was a series of switchbacks. Exactly how many wasn't clear. Yet it was obvious that the light was quickly fading. A faint glow already radiated across the obscure, rocky path to the bottom. And although we'd tried to avoid leading Sadhu at night, especially since his topple a week earlier on the ice, tonight we had no choice.

As she zigzagged across the road, veering close to the edge, Cheryl naively asked, "How well can a horse see in the dark?"

"Not well enough to keep from taking you over a cliff!"

"Oh."

The last rays of the sun disappeared. We plunged into a blind darkness with only the roar of the river to lead us nearer the bridge. For nearly an hour, we groped through the void of a moonless night. Finally, we hesitantly approached what we hoped was the final checkpoint. Not a soul was in sight. All we heard was the steady "clop-clop, clop-clop" of Sadhu's hoofs echoing off the pavement in front of the border station. Call us crazy, but for one mad moment we considering just walking across that bridge in darkness.

"Who's there to stop us?" I reasoned. "Maybe the guards are all in bed? Or involved in another drinking game."

At just that moment, a soldier toting an automatic rifle rose from the shadows only two meters short of the span. He screamed, "Pass-a-port!" above the river's din.

Hurriedly, I struggled to tug out mine. I even supplied him with a flashlight to compare the more sensible face in the photo with the ragged visage facing him.

However, instead of focusing on us, he had his sights on our four-legged friend and shrieked up the hill to his superior, "Come quick! Horse! Horse!" (Or, without subtitles, that's what I thought he cried.)

Smiling, always smiling, I admitted, "Yes. Horse."

Soon, an older, rumpled gentleman appeared and immediately started poking our packs lashed to Sadhu's sides.

"In here?" he motioned.

"Camping gear. Sleeping bags, air mattresses..." For once, I kept the story of our journey to myself.

That shadow of a man, whose face I never saw, examined Sadhu from shaggy mane to meter long tail. Then muttering something in Mandarin, probably "Crazy Americans walking their horse in the dark!" he waved us on.

I felt a shudder through my very soul as we crossed that bridge into Nepal; a sense of pride in what we'd accomplished, something finally measurable. And I felt a sadness that we'd only been able to help one Tibetan to freedom.

We staggered in the darkest of shadows toward Kodari, Nepal's border town. Our flashlight was only switched on long enough to make sure that we weren't headed over the cliff. Its batteries were nearly as dead as we were. After forty days on the trail, only the promise of hot springs kept us moving when more sane minds would call it a night.

Trusting our map, I figured the border was still two kilometers ahead. Still, I worried about Sadhu. "Will the Nepalese refuse him entry? Will there be another snapping quarantine officer? Could we be lucky twice in one day?"

"Now, keep him quiet when we reach customs," I warned Cheryl. "I'll just go in with our passports. I won't mention him."

All of a sudden, Sadhu let out the loudest, longest neigh I'd ever heard. It was quickly followed by an inquisitive voice whispering, "Hello?" from the nocturnal mist.

Whipping around, we faced a stocky, robed figure.

"You will please come with me," the man ordered. He brushed past us toward a hut that seemed to materialize out of the shadows.

"So this, in all its glory, is Kodari? Why, it's hardly five-hundred meters from the bridge," I protested. "Cheryl, please stay here with Sadhu," I suggested, as I followed the apparition. No need to get both of us in trouble.

The hooded elf led me to a cramped wooden shack, the first of thirty lining the dirt road. There, for a few tense minutes, we played twenty questions by candlelight.

"Bringing in any carpets?" he began.

"No." At least he didn't immediately ask about our horse.

His eyes gleamed in the flickering light. "Have any gold?"

"If I did, would I arrive like this?" I joked with a shrug.

"I see what you mean," he chuckled. "Now, about your horse..."

"He's Tibetan. We bought him outside Lhasa." I explained, thinking "Now we're finished."

"Lhasa?" he asked with wide-eyed wonder. "You walked all the way here?"

"Yes, we're pilgrims. On our way to Kathmandu."

"Ah!" To him it seemed incredible someone would walk so far, especially with a horse. "And the lady, she is your wife?" he asked, flashing a broad, betel nut-stained smile.

"Of course." That pleased him.

"And how many babies do you have?"

"There's that age-old question again," I thought. "But that means we're nearly out of the woods. He's moved on to more personal questions."

"None," I admitted. Since he looked disappointed, I added, "We're too busy walking across Tibet!" And we both had a great laugh.

At that, the genial fellow, everyone's favorite uncle, handed back my passport and pointed up the road to Immigration.

"I think he's closed for the night," he cautioned, then added the subtle suggestion that he might open—with the right offer.

Buoyantly we stumbled down that frontier main street. We were guided only by a dim kerosene lamp haze that flickered from the dusty windows of rickety restaurants and ramshackle storefronts. Cautious, hopeful to remain somewhat incognito, we edged past long-distance trucks, lackadaisical dogs sprawled across the road, and the usual assortment of gossiping onlookers. However, our presence was far from unnoticed.

By the time we reached the front steps of a shanty marked "IMMIGRATION," a whole curious cadre joined us. While a few eagerly rushed to fetch the authorities, we stood waiting in the shadows. Several tense moments later, a lanky fellow, who was dressed in a square collared Nepalese jacket and modified fez, lazily approached us.

"The border, it ees closed until 6 a.m." he announced in that Nepali singsong accent.

"Thanks."

"Who *is* this expert?" I wondered. "I'm not up for mindless banter right now."

"We're just waiting for the Immigration Officer, " I replied. I was still hopeful that we could work something out.

"I *am* the Immigration Officer."

"Ah…," I choked, relieved that I didn't say what was first on my mind. "We'd really like to continue to Tatopani tonight."

"The border is closed now. Besides, it is too dark."

"I know. But we've already walked two hours in the dark from Khasa. Tatopani's not much farther and we've got a flashlight." (Little help that it was.)

"No. You find a room here tonight."

"But there's nowhere to keep our horse."

"There's nowhere in Tatopani either."

My mind grasped at straws. "Maybe…but it's a smaller town. We can find hay there."

"That makes sense…" I thought.

"Ah huh…" He still look unconvinced.

"And he'll be safer."

That had to be true. I didn't like the looks of his seedy strip of shacks.

He wavered an instant. "Possibly…I'll go ask my boss."

Unlocking the door, he ducked inside. I still felt that we had a chance.

However, a few tense minutes later he returned, declaring, "No. My boss said, 'No. Absolutely not.' You stay here tonight."

I was desperate. We'd rushed down that mountain all afternoon and I wasn't ready to trade one degenerate border town for another, especially when my fantasy hot springs were only two kilometers away.

"Look," I said, lowering my voice, glad that he spoke English. "We've been on the road for nearly forty days. We're pilgrims and we've just walked almost 1,000 kilometers from Lhasa." Since he seemed vaguely interested, I continued my sob story. "We're goin' to Kathmandu.

We're tired. Hungry." Then I added for good measure, "And I haven't bathed in over a month! My wife tells me that I reek!"

Although that was something he certainly couldn't ignore, he argued, "I know, but…"

I cut him short. "Look, if you could issue our visas tonight, we'd be VERY grateful…" I practically added, "Wink, wink, know what I mean, know what I mean," ala that old Monty Python routine.

Well, that was the key phrase he'd waited for. Smiling mischievously, he creaked open the weathered door to his office and led me inside, closing the door tightly behind us. He motioned for me to sit down, then pulled the proper forms from his desk. After I'd quickly filled them in, the mustachioed official finally laid his cards on the table.

"That will be thirty dollars U.S. each!" he pronounced with a grin. Then he disappeared with our passports and forms behind a set of doors.

"Each? Visas are only twenty dollars at the Kathmandu airport," I thought, "but what choice do we have?"

Within moments he returned. While he stamped our documents, I placed a neat stack of ten dollar bills on his rusted metal desktop. Then after some small talk, a pack of cigarettes was shared and he finally leaned over and grabbed the pile of tens, expecting to find sixty dollars. But so far, I'd only anteed up forty.

"There's only forty dollars here," he complained, disappointed and a little angry.

"Oh, didn't you say twenty each?" I replied, playing the stupid tourist once again. "That's what we paid in Kathmandu."

"No, I said thirty each," he grinned, adding, "Special night time rate."

"Oh…" I stalled, trying to guess how much it would take to make him happy.

"We don't have too many dollars with us." That was certainly true, since it was nearly the end of our trip. "How about twenty-five dollars each?" I suggested. "That's good, isn't it?"

He scrutinized me for a second, then bobbed his head side-to-side in that unmistakable wobble which meant, "All right. If that's all you can do."

Quickly rising from our chairs, business completed, that border entrepreneur and I shook hands and he warmly wished us, "Good trip."

Opening the door, I burst out into the street entreating to Cheryl, "Come on! Let's get out of here before he changes his mind."

Truth is, I was very grateful he'd bent the rules. It was a relief to be back in a place where the "impossible" was always possible—for the right price!

Leaving the ragged kerosene glow of that one street town, we soon tumbled back into oblivion. It was pathetic. The three of us comically stumbled and swerved down the pitch-black road. We hiked through ankle deep muck that was the consistency of freshly poured concrete. We forded streams across a mud caked stretch that our guidebook had described as "sealed." For nearly an hour, there was no other illumination, no car headlights, no faint glow from a house. Only occasionally did we dare shine our flashlight and then it was just long enough to make sure that we weren't headed over a cliff.

Finally, we spotted one slight flicker from a window up ahead. Reaching the doorway, I poked my head inside. It appeared to be a store or restaurant. A balding fellow in a cook's frock was cleaning up behind a glass counter that was chock-full of sodas and cookies.

"Too bad this isn't that hot spring town," I sighed, as I salivated at the sight of all those goodies. "It still must be an hour away."

"Tatopani, how far?" I asked.

At first, the fellow just beamed in amusement. Then with a flourish, he simply pointed down.

"Tatopani, here?" I gushed, surprised that we'd reached it so soon. He just nodded. Then remembering that we could speak English here, I mumbled, "Can we sleep here tonight?"

Confused at my knack of stating the obvious, he eloquently replied, "Well, of course. This is a hotel."

The kind innkeeper took charge, since our exhaustion was unmistakable after our record forty-four kilometer trek. While he fixed Sadhu a feast of bamboo leaves in the yard, his son led us on a long-awaited hot springs sojourn.

As we slid down those slippery stone stairs to steamy bliss, I began to think how long it had been since I'd seen myself naked. "Well, we've been staying with families...monks...in potato patches...tack rooms...

freezing hotel rooms…Shigatse…Lhazê…Nyalam…God, it's been a month or more!"

Beside the inviting pool, in the cool solitude of the night air, we stripped off our ragged clothes then gazed down in horror. We were emaciated. Skin hung from my bones where muscles had been. My body had aged thirty years in as many days. We were in a pitiful condition.

"Still," I figured, "Kathmandu and all its food isn't very far away now. It *is* all downhill from here."

Ducking under the intricately carved mossy spouts, that simmering water quickly soothed away all our aches and bone chilling cold. It quickly renewed our weary spirits.

Later, after shuffling back up that tranquil village street, we paused for a second in front of the hotel. "What's the name of this place, anyway?" I wondered aloud.

"I've no idea…" Cheryl replied, anxious to finally get some sleep.

Squinting at the weather beaten sign hidden in the shadows, we could just barely discern the name of the inn where fate had delivered us— TIBETAN GUEST HOUSE.

"Here we go again," I mused. "Magic…"

Chapter XVII

"Ghoda! Ghoda! Ghoda!"

Be hopeful.
Tomorrow is another day awaiting with the possibility of success.

November 26

The next two days blended into a blurred palette of greens and pastels during our steep, continual slide to Kathmandu at only 1,297 meters (4,265 feet). Spurred on by a sensory explosion, our pace was steady and days were longer than ever as we pushed to put that final 112 kilometers (69.5 miles) behind us, as quickly as our feet would carry us.

The saturated color and rich vibrancy of the tropics insisted on cradling us in a heady perfume and tender embrace. Lush terraced farms, hugging steep hillsides, bathed us in unending splashes of emerald. Unbridled waterfalls, as many as six at a time, spouted from craggy cliffs. The sweet fragrance of brilliantly exotic flowers encircled us. Poinsettias as large as oaks splashed crimson across our path. Broad-leafed banyans cascaded across a vermilion mud avenue. Expansive pandanus shadows provided hours of shade from the scorching sun. The brilliant orange beaks of Birds of Paradise pointed our way, while banana, avocado and breadfruit transformed Nepal into one continually moving equine buffet.

"See, Sadhu," Cheryl joked, "we told you you'd like Nepal. Everything's edible."

231

Our Tibetan eating machine took full advantage of his mobile smorgasbord. Trotting just three steps at a time, he'd pause then swivel his head around to grasp another mouthful of grass or leaves.

Sadhu was an instant celebrity in those hinterlands. Whenever children spotted him clip-clopping past their simple huts, they'd cry, "*Ghoda! Ghoda! Ghoda!*" (Nepalese for "*Da! Da! Da!*"), then scamper down to the dirt road just to sneak a peek at him. Sometimes fifty or more kids tagged along behind us from one end of a village to the other. Giggling, they'd goggle in wild-eyed fascination, as though they'd never seen a horse before. A few more brazen ones even tried to pet his shoulders or stroke his tail.

Their rapt attention was usually appreciated, except for one moment on our first day outside of Tatopani. Having just cleared our first roadblock and crossed another bridge, we ran into a group of girls, braids flying, skipping down the road. Decked out in blue uniforms and starched white shirts, they were obviously headed to school.

As we finally drew close behind them, Cheryl, ever the genial traveler, chirped, "Gooood morning!"

Well, they nearly jumped out of their hides, startled by our horse and shocked at seeing us. One timidly asked, "Where are you going?" in perfect, textbook English.

"Kathmandu," I replied, as though it was the most natural thing in the world.

"Ohh...," they gasped in wide-eyed wonder, as they cautiously sidled up beside our horse. Sadhu certainly had a way with strangers. A few of the more brave kids gently stroked him, while others still looked a little afraid. But together, they all began softly chanting, "*Ghoda! Ghoda! Ghoda!*" in a strange equine cheer which grew ever louder as they escorted us all the way to their school.

I was beginning to think that we were to become their classroom *Show and Tell*, until Cheryl ominously hummed, "Ah, Brandon..."

"Huh?" I replied, distracted as I kept an eye on the kids and horse.

"Ah...just keep moving. Quick-lee."

"Why?" I whispered, confused by her mysterious tone.

"Tell you later."

A kilometer farther down the road, upon reaching the schoolhouse, the girls gleefully waved and trotted off.

Curious, I turned and faced my wary companion, wondering, "Well? What was it?"

"I didn't want to say anything back there, but we were passing the NEPAL VETERINARY CHECKPOINT."

I hadn't even noticed.

"Well," she pointed out, "it's just a little hard to be discrete with kids cheering, *"Ghoda! Ghoda! Ghoda!"* at the top of their lungs.

At first, I was shocked, then so relieved. We'd cleared one last hurdle without even realizing it.

"Now Sadhu's in Nepal to stay," I thought with pride. "Nobody can send him back to Tibet or detain him. And if anyone asks where we're going, we'll just say we're headed south towards India. Kathmandu just happens to be on the way!"

It wasn't exactly "all downhill" to our final destination, as Cheryl was eager to point out. But with the pleasant weather, stunning scenery, frequent roadside shops offering cool sodas, and the gregarious Nepalese, we were in ecstasy. By late afternoon, twenty-four kilometers (15 miles) outside Tatopani, we stopped in Barabise just long enough to change money.

Cheryl suffered through creeping bank lines and triplicate exchange forms. Meanwhile, Sadhu and I were engulfed in the middle of the main thoroughfare by the local "equine experts" who acted as if horses were rare in those hills. Only slightly curious about me, they positively fawned over my four-footed friend. One shy villager, who'd sized Sadhu up and down with obvious admiration, finally approached asking, "Where do you go with the *ghoda?*"

"Kathmandu."

"And then?" he demanded. "What do you do with him? Sell him?"

"How can I sell my brother?"

Although he chuckled, I was serious. After all we'd all been through together, I'd wondered for weeks what we were going to do with our sleepwalking companion. Unfortunately, it was impossible to cart him home, although we actually considered it. No, once we hit Kathmandu, we'd begin our search to find him a foster home—with lots to eat, of course.

"Maybe," I thought, "maybe he'll be more at home out here in the countryside."

"Why?" I asked. "Are you interested in him? Do you have other horses?"

He nodded, confidently.

"That's a good sign," I figured. "He'll know how to care for him."

"And where do you live?" I asked, continuing my interview of the prospective father.

"Not far from here," he replied. Then he continued with, "How much did you pay for him?" hoping to seal the deal before we hurried on.

"Too much." I hated to play coy, but the $285 we paid was probably close to what that farmer earned in a year. So I directed our conversation to more serious matters.

"What exactly would you do with him?"

"Oh, he would work on my land."

"A farm horse? No, not at any price," I thought.

"Sorry," I explained, walking over to the bank. "He has to come with us to Kathmandu. You see, we haven't finished our trip yet!"

I'd decided I wouldn't put Sadhu under the yoke again, not after all we'd been through. Our loyal friend had made our pilgrimage possible. Actually, we'd thought more along the lines of finding him a home with a tour company or donating him to a children's organization.

"That'll be like retirement for him," I figured, "after this journey."

We traced the deep river canyon all afternoon, trekking a dirt road barely a lane and a half wide. With recent flooding, it was nearly as torturous as Tibet's had been. Rockslides had careened across the highway. Roadcrews, working at less than a feverish pace, had heavily laden dump trucks backed up as far as the eye could see. But again, unfettered by wheels, we easily sauntered around.

As nighttime approached, we strolled into the first village of any size we'd encountered since Barabise. Although hesitant to interrupt his daze, I approached a policeman. He surveyed a constant stream of trucks, carts and pedestrians from his phone booth-sized traffic nook beside the highway.

"Langomasu?" I asked, as I wiped the dust and sweat from my brow. He cocked a jaded eye, as if to say, "Where else?" and nodded.

Since we'd already covered thirty-four kilometers (21 miles) there was no sensible reason to push any farther. Who knew where the next hamlet was?

Ambling down Main Street, we searched in vain for a place to spend the night and stable Sadhu. Although we were far from picky, within ten minutes we'd walked the entire length of town.

"Cheryl, I just don't see any hotels."

"There must be something here," she sighed.

"Well, let me check over there."

Sauntering over to three fellows relaxing at a sidewalk café (minus the sidewalk), I wished them, "Namaste!"

Local executives, looking somewhat out of place in their starched white shirts and ties, glanced up from their brandies.

"Is there a hotel nearby?"

"Right next door," one giggled.

Noticing the puny sign we'd missed in the fading light, I thanked them and wove my way toward the inn. By then, as usual, a crowd had gathered. Curious kids reached out to pet Sadhu. Swarthy, mustached men meticulously inspected his unique wooden saddle and packs. While women, whose blubbery waists bulged over magenta and fuchsia *saris*, nonchalantly sashayed down still-hustling streets.

Anxious to get settled in, I approached a petite, beautiful child who stood shadowed in the hotel doorway.

"Can you get your father? We'd like to rent a room."

She skipped off to find the innkeeper. A moment later, a rotund, hairless fellow all wrapped in a white, gauzy suit appeared—a virtual egg man.

"We'd like a room," I gasped, choking back a chuckle.

"Take him upstairs," Mr. Humpty commanded with a languid flutter of his flabby hand.

On cue, his lithe son led me to another comfortably austere room atop the four-story, terraced building. Other than having to maneuver sixty stairs while toting all our gear, it was pure luxury.

Flying back down to the street, I puffed, "That's fine. Now, where can we keep our *ghoda?*"

"*Ghoda?*" the egg man proclaimed with an "harumph" and puzzled glare.

"Yeah, this huge, four-legged, pointy eared animal that's been standing on your doorstep the past twenty minutes!" I wanted to shout! Instead, I politely introduced him to our fellow pilgrim. Pointing to the hotel's empty stairwell, I suggested, "Maybe we can keep him in your hallway?"

Staring as though I was completely out of my mind, he stubbornly shook his head.

"If this was Tibet," I thought, "*they'd* make room for him."

"Put him there, then!" Humpty announced. He waved toward the side of his concrete tenement, an alley heaped with trash and broken bottles.

This time I shook my head. I didn't want to expose Sadhu all night to the probes and gropes of fifty villagers who already swarmed him like flies on a fresh carcass.

Sensing our predicament, a lanky teenager wearing an American baseball cap approached through the circle of spectators. "May I help you, sir?" he softly asked.

"Where'd you learn to speak English, so well?"

"I attend the English school here," he proudly replied, "so eventually, I may get a good job in Kathmandu."

I was impressed. "Sure, we're trying to find a place to keep our horse tonight."

He thought for a moment. Then sighing, "Please follow me, sir," he escorted me down the darkly somber street.

For what seemed like an hour, we maneuvered back and forth between ramshackle shops and dilapidated shacks as we asked merchants and his friends where we could possibly keep a horse. It was difficult. Villagers already inhabited even the most decrepit shanties that lined that squalid street.

Finally, the town's restaurateur, located practically next door to our hotel, relented. What remained of his building was warm—even though the back wall had been crumbling so long that trees had taken root inside.

"How much does he want to keep our horse here?"

"Oh, nothing," the Anglophile grinned. "Just eat at his restaurant."

"We'll be happy to."

"That's great," I thought. "The Nepalese are just as generous as the Tibetans when it comes to keeping animals."

"Now, where can we get some *tsampa?*" I asked. I planned to surprise our buddy with his favorite dish.

"*Tsampa?*"

"You know, barley flour?"

The teenager glanced down, embarrassed. "Oh, we don't have that here."

"How about barley then?"

He looked confused. "Barley?"

Obviously his English book didn't cover food very thoroughly.

"A small, white grain."

"Rice! Yes, we can buy rice."

"It'll take a heap of rice," I figured, "to feed this hungry horse."

"No, barley," I insisted, showing him the size of a grain. He resolutely shook his head. "Straw? You've gotta have straw."

"Not in town," he shrugged. "Maybe you can get some from a farmer in the country."

Oh, I'd forgotten. This is "town."

"Nepal may be lush," I thought, "but it's going to mean a change of diet for ol' Sadhu."

"So, what exactly do horses eat in Nepal? *Ghoda-Chow?*"

Sometimes, you just have to ask the right question. Our guide's eyes lit up, happy to finally offer a solution.

"*Corni,* sir!" he exclaimed. "Dried yellow corn and bamboo grass."

"Well *corni* it is!" I decreed and we hurried off to buy a kilo from the dried goods shack across the street.

Sadhu was delighted to discover the pleasures of *corni,* as he circled his wide, wet tongue around the tin bowl. With all his slobbering, half of it landed on the floor of his stall. But he was content for hours, nibbling each golden kernel from the dirt with agile, fuzzy lips. Meanwhile, we were equally pleased to sample the pleasures of dal, curry, peas and chapatti—all washed down with homemade brandy at his host's restaurant, as promised.

237

November 27

Hospitality has its price in Nepal. The next morning, the restaurateur's kind offer disappeared. His shrewd wife presented us with a bill for keeping Sadhu in their bombed out shelter. Bizarrely, it was even larger than what we'd paid for our own hotel room. This, of course, erupted into more negotiations until a compromise was reached.

At last, relieved, we saddled up and headed back into the more charitable countryside.

All morning, we wended along a path stretching down verdant valleys. It was wonderful to hear birds again, to feel warm air brush past our skin, to smell the musky tropical blend of syrupy blossoms and fermenting mangoes. Most of our day was spent in peaceful solitude. It was only briefly interrupted by our entry into tiny villages where the fascinating processions of children began once again; some barefoot, some in flopping sandals, others on creaking one-speed bikes. They were curious and thrilled at the sight of two strangers and their horse. Mobs of friendly kids were satisfied with just an *injis'* smile, a brief conversation and a fleeting chance to join our impromptu parade.

We were equally proud to have their company; someone to interrupt our loneliness and share our exploits. Older boys even cycled beside us for miles, providing mounted escort until another village was in sight. Then, with a friendly wave, they'd spin around and head home.

Our progress was relatively tranquil all afternoon, until we were awakened from our daze by a familiar "Hey!"

Turning, we recognized two familiar forms quietly bobbing in our direction. "Hey, it's Marley and Jacob!" Cheryl exclaimed, pleased to see our old friends.

Coasting toward us on mud covered, 18-gear mountain bikes, they glided to a silent stop.

"Hi guys!" Marley coughed, knocking dust from his goggles.

"Glad to see you survived advance base camp!" I laughed.

"Well, we didn't quite get there," our old friend admitted. "The fuel line on our stove froze. It was just too damned cold."

"Did you get stuck in that snowstorm on Thang La?"

"Just the tail end," Jacob smirked. "We holed-up in a roadhouse just below the summit. The lady even served us rice *thugpa*."

"Sounds like the same place we stayed. The one with larger-than-life Mao photos?"

"Yea, that's the one, all right," he chuckled.

"Say, when do you think you'll reach Kathmandu?" Cheryl asked, as she tried to gauge how far we still had to trek.

"Tonight, if we're lucky," Jacob replied, although he appeared doubtful. "There's still one long, last pass to climb. But it's not too bad."

My partner shot me her familiar, "So it's all downhill from here?" glance. "Maybe we'll reach Kathmandu by tomorrow night too," she offered. "If we hustle."

"Well, that's pretty optimistic for a change," I thought. It was still nearly one-hundred kilometers (sixty-two miles). Trekking that far in a day and a half would push us to all new heights or pains.

"Guess we'd better get cruisin'," Marley said, remounting his bike.

"Oh," I mentioned one last time, "will you please remind Billie about the letter to N.D.?"

"Sure. She's probably already given it to him," he assured me. "But I'll give her a nudge."

"Thanks. Hey, why don't we all get together on Monday night to celebrate at that Austrian restaurant? The one those Peace Corps volunteers raved about back in Tingri?"

"Sounds great," Jacob shouted. "Eight o'clock?"

"Yea, see you then!"

All day long as we trekked, the slowly decreasing numbers on the infrequent kilometer posts measured time. Perhaps it was our impatience. But I could swear Nepalese kilometers seemed twice as long as those in Tibet. And we should know! After hiking nearly a thousand, we had a pretty good idea how far a kilometer was. So, when we passed only three posts in an hour, we suspected more than Nepal's beauty was to blame.

By sunset ninety-five Nepalese kilometers (fifty-nine miles) still separated us from Kathmandu. Because of that and the lack of any villages in sight, we made the only obvious choice we could. We'd continue hiking in the dark.

God watches over fools and travelers, right?

For two hours, our slow pace was reduced to a crawl as we inched up the pass Jacob had warned us about. With no light to guide our way except for one dim flashlight, we were reduced to feeling our way through the soles of our boots. Our useless torch was only switched on long enough to keep passing buses and trucks from plowing into us.

Finally around 9 p.m., we recognized the rough-and-tumble main drag of a bus stop village, illuminated by a dusky kerosene lamp glow.

"Here we go, again," Cheryl sighed, as we shuffled down the gloomy road.

I was just as eager to collapse, especially over a delicious ten-course dinner at the greasy spoon I'd spotted across the street. "Let me try in there," I offered, ambling toward the eatery.

"Hotel?" I asked, clearing my throat.

The grizzled, curry spattered cook looked up, as he plopped thick, steaming dal into a customer's plastic bowl. Unfazed, he pointed across the road.

"At least," I thought, "it's not any farther down the road."

Simultaneously, Cheryl was approached by another local English student who eagerly led us across the street to the town's only hotel-cum-restaurant-cum-liquor store. Its dining area opened right onto the street. Climbing down groaning stairs, we were introduced to a chunky fellow who played cards with his family right on the cafe's dirt floor.

"Do you have a room?" I asked, anxious to wrap my tongue around some of that spicy dal across the street.

"One hundred rupees," he huffed, without interrupting his game.

"Fine. But where can we keep our *ghoda?*"

At that, the innkeeper simply shrugged, not even bothering to look up from his hand.

"Well, we can't stay here," I confided, "if you don't have a place for our horse." I figured that statement might spur any sort of real businessman into conveniently remembering a place.

Indifferent, he called our bluff, snorting, "Sorry, then."

"Sir," the genial student suggested, "I know a family very near. They will probably keep your horse for the night."

"Great," I sighed, anxious for some food and shut-eye. "Let's go talk with them."

So while Cheryl eagerly flopped down on a stiff wooden bench, that teenager and I led Sadhu through a dark void toward the neighbor's inviting open porch. For an instant, it seemed as though everything might work out all right after all.

Then suddenly, just as we headed off the road, Sadhu's front hoofs missed the rusty oil-drum bridge spanning an open sewer in front of the adobe house. Down he went! A four-foot trench swallowed his front leg!

Frantic, I scrambled to yank him out, screaming, "Sadhu! Come on, boy!"

Terrified, eyes ablaze, he struggled until his front leg stumbled out—only to have his back leg take its place in the steaming, putrid mire! Now, he was even more distressed! Whinnying, nostrils flaring like a steed possessed, he jerked and twisted, battling to climb out of the mire.

"Come on, Sadhu!" I yelled, trying to coax and tug him loose.

"Damn, what if he breaks a leg now?"

I pulled, grappled and lifted again! He hopped, dug and pawed while I yanked. Until finally, after several tense moments in that dung slinging tug-of-war, our wandering holy man stumbled free. Quickly, I ran my hands up and down both of his legs and was relieved to discover nothing was broken. He'd live, but it was anyone's guess who was more scared or whose legs wobbled more.

Looking back, I should have considered it a sign.

With that grand entrance, we stepped up onto the porch where we were met by a young guy the same age as our guide. After our escort quickly explained the problem in Nepalese, the kid ran inside to fetch his mother. Silently we waited there in the darkness until a somber mysterious woman, shrouded in a faded sari, surfaced from the shadows.

Suspicious, bird-like eyes peered out at us from beneath a wild veil of raven hair and I felt a slight chill go up my spine. At first, she was as reluctant to be Sadhu's host as I was to trust her with our companion. But after some solemn calculations, she eventually agreed to let Sadhu stay on her porch for fifty rupees, half the cost of our hotel room. Still, it seemed fair and we were desperate.

241

"Will she include his feed for that price?" I asked. "He's very hungry."
Our guide mumbled our request to her and she nodded in agreement.
"All right," I figured, "what choice do we have?"

So, while I hitched Sadhu to the porch railing, her son fetched him
water and a meager bowl of porridge. Then he set a basket of cornhusks
in front of the famished gelding. At first, Sadhu seemed pleased with his
feast. Diving nose first into the woven basket, his head bounced up and
down like a child bobbing for apples. But he kept coming up empty.

"He'll never settle for cornhusks," I figured, "now that he's tasted
corni. Plus their house is wide open with no door to prevent his walking
right inside."

"See, we need to find more food for him," I patiently explained to the
mother, son and curious group of town folks who'd gathered.
"Otherwise," I laughed, "he'll break these ropes and come looking for
food in your house!"

I was only partly joking, since I already knew a hungry Sadhu is a
roaming Sadhu.

Although a quick translation was whispered, they ignored my advice
and insisted on trying to force-feed him corn husks by sticking handfuls
under his nose.

"Now, Sadhu is not a finicky eater," I thought. "He'll munch almost
anything, edible or not. But I can already tell that corn husks are not to
his liking. All this nonsense is just keeping me from my only meal of the
day and a waiting bed."

"Look, take me to the store," I suggested. "I'll buy him some *corni*."

After walking next door, getting two kilos of the golden nuggets,
feeding our nose nuzzling friend, checking his ropes one last time and
considering him "tucked in" for the night, I returned to the inn with our
helpful go-between. That's when the proverbial "dung hit the fire."

Just as I prepared to savor a long awaited beer with Cheryl, the
lady who boarded Sadhu stormed into the cafe, wailing at the top of
her lungs! Although I couldn't speak the language, her problem was
soon clear. In the few moments since we'd left, someone had
convinced her that she could get eighty rupees for keeping Sadhu and
she'd come to collect.

"We agreed on fifty," I wearily replied, catching her between ravings. "Assure her that I'll pay her in the morning when we pick up the horse."

To me, it was a done deal.

To her, it was the start of a twenty minute Nepalese diatribe, best described as a "fit" with a capital "F." As she ranted and railed, the innkeeper and his wife stood stock-still, staring in disbelief. We refrained from screaming back, while the English student tried to reason with her. But it was all more than he, or any of us, had bargained for.

Eventually growing more and more impatient, in disgust, the boy clucked, "She is a very ignorant woman!"

Before long, that tiny café flooded with an audience of engrossed villagers. Meanwhile, the banshee barked, screamed, shrieked, screeched, hopped up and down and wept in the performance of her life. Until ultimately, noticing only startled, slack jawed looks of shock duplicated on each our faces, she ordered our horse out of her house!

It was nearly eleven at night. The parade followed her back to her shack where Sadhu patiently waited, unaware of all the fuss he'd caused. Of course, I was determined not to move him until I found a new temporary home for him. After all that, our hotel was still out of the question and I could just imagine both of us camped out in the middle of Main Street all night.

For long, tense moments, everyone tried their best to find a workable solution, to accommodate, to compromise. Huddling together in the murky light, the villagers tried to reason with the raving lunatic and tried to convince her that fifty rupees was fair and certainly better than none at all.

At last, I had enough of her silly game. In the midst of another one of her harangues, I quietly slipped out my flashlight and shined it at her seething face.

"I just wanted everyone to see the face of a greedy woman," I stated matter-of-factly.

Well, at that, she flew into a thundering rage. Swinging at me in a flurry of fists, she had to be restrained by the fellows who had been cowering behind her. Oh, she was livid, spitting out words that barely made sense even to those who understood her shrill patter.

Then, incredibly she crowed, "Ninety rupees!!"

"Ninety?" I shook my head in disbelief. "She still doesn't get it, does she?"

Frustrated, our guide simply repeated, "Ignorant woman, ignorant woman…" as he shook his head.

Meanwhile, the harpy continued ranting, flailing and insulting me. At long last, sensing an impasse had most definitely been reached, one audience member meekly interrupted our passion play, suggesting, "We can just keep the *ghoda* down the street at my friend's stable."

"Why wasn't that mentioned an hour ago?" I wondered. "Is this some local midnight madness? Is this village starved for entertainment? Or, is this all some strange Hindi melodrama only lacking the final musical chorus with falsetto singing maidens."

Sadhu was moved.

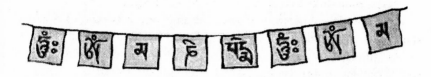

Chapter XVIII

Flags Of Solidarity

Be aware.
It is the journey that ultimately matters,
not the destination.

November 28

After a sound sleep, the sad events of the night before faded with the morning mountain fog. Anxious to push on to Kathmandu, still over forty kilometers (twenty-five miles) away, I was determined that nothing, but nothing, was going to prevent us from reaching it that day.

As we trekked an easy cadence, I fantasized about our "message in a bottle" that had washed away with Billie and floated to N.D. I dreamed that he actually *did* receive it, that he actually *did* have influence with the Royal Family and that half of the bustling metropolis was already lining our route, eager to cheer us on those final few kilometers.

While lost in that sweet illusion, mystically, a distant snow frosted Himalayan crest sprung from banana fields and captivated us one final time.

"Well," I sighed in disbelief, "that's where we just came from!" It looked so far off. It seemed impossible that we were there just days before, thousands of meters higher and bundled beneath thick layers of clothing.

"You know," Cheryl lamented, "I miss it already."

"I do, too."

"It's all downhill from here!" became our running joke, as we continued a gradual climb for hours. Yet compared to Tibet, we were seldom alone. Boys, as thin as the air, still led us through villages in simple bicycle escort. However, that afternoon a more officious, far less hospitable motorcade became our unanticipated companion.

High in the mountains above Kathmandu, a local traffic cop appeared out of nowhere. He waved for us to stop.Then he directed a fleet of twenty black Mercedes flying miniature Chinese flags into a luxurious restaurant nearly concealed behind bushy palms.

"Excuse us," I asked, stopping in the middle of the road. "What's happening here?"

"Oh, very important," the policeman replied. "Very important," he stressed, waiting for our reaction as though we should be impressed. "Chinese dignitaries are here to meet with Nepalese officials."

Although never too excited about meeting bureaucrats, the implications of Chinese-Nepali talks at a little mountain hideaway had us intrigued.

"Is King Birendra in there?"

The officer suspiciously eyed us and studied our rough appearance, probably wondering why we asked.

"Yes," he snapped with finality, as though he'd revealed too much.

"He's right," I thought. "It would make a great political statement to present the Lhasan prayer flags to the monarch here in front of his Chinese audience. But we're hardly dressed for the occasion. They'd never let us through the front door looking like this."

Then out of the corner of my eye, I spotted something that guaranteed we wouldn't make it past that wary guard. Sadhu, deciding that he'd had enough waiting in that stifling humidity, began to collapse onto his knees.

"Cheryl, get him up!" I warned. "He's gonna roll!"

Reacting instinctively, she yanked him up by his reins. Oh, it was definitely bad form to be seen in front of such "very important" dignitaries with a horse flopping on its back.

Irritated by our lack of respect for this solemn occasion, the trooper brusquely waved us on.

All day long, stone kilometer markers drew us down the verdant mountain as we clip-clopped past exclusive gated resorts and hideaways tucked into hillsides. Taxis, a long fare from the city, carried genteel Westerners to stylish mountain retreats for cool gin & tonics. Curiously they all whizzed past, hurrying for God knows what?

"You know, Cheryl," I breathlessly panted, "since we left Lhasa...all those four-wheelers...full of Western tourists...have never stopped...no one's ever asked what we were doing...out in the middle of nowhere...with a horse!" No one, of course, except that wayward Parisian back in that lonely roadhouse.

"You're right...It's always been the villagers...Never an American or European."

As we reflected on that bizarre anomaly, we suddenly rounded a lush promontory and peered through the smoggy, amber haze towards the most incredible sight we'd seen in weeks. At first glance, it was so difficult for either of us to believe, until Cheryl cornered a bewildered passerby and giggled, "Kathmandu? Is that really Kathmandu?"

The startled fellow grinned, as though to say, "What else would it be?" and she nearly kissed him.

We dove into each other's eyes, grins sweeping across our dirt smudged faces. Hugging tightly, I whispered to my mate, "Almost there," and for once it was really true.

Giddy with exhilaration, we glided and nearly flew down that final hillside. Villages became frequent and crowded. Traffic was heavy. But with the outskirts of the capital finally sprawled before us, those last fifteen kilometers (nine miles) seemed within reach. Still, no matter how much we tried to hurry, no matter how much we were tempted to rush, no matter how much we wished ourselves there, it was impossible to exceed our constant four to six kilometers (four miles) an hour. It was at that moment I realized what a blessing our mode of travel truly was.

Often travelers of the road, and of life, are so anxious to get somewhere, that the getting there, the actual journey, takes a back seat to the "reward" at the end. That wasn't for us anymore. The ultimate beauty of walking, of "traveling deliberately" one foot in front of the other, was the opportunity to observe and wallow in the minute details of everyday life surrounding us. There was time to share a moment of peoples' lives, their hopes, their triumphs, their fears, and to truly live the path leading to the destination. It was a blessing. Our lives were reduced to raw essentials.

Like Henry David Thoreau's noble quest to "live life deliberately," *deliberate* travel forced us to confront each day head-on. By traveling one step at a time, we were exposed and vulnerable. We reveled in the life surrounding us, the gritty beauty others missed by barreling through. And that dogged deliberation made our odyssey across Tibet more special than any we'd ever taken before.

Although Kathmandu taunted and teased all afternoon, it was late in the evening by the time we navigated its still swarming streets. Cars honked. *Tuk-tuks* sputtered. Brightly colored buses buzzed by. Still, resolutely, we led Sadhu in single file across traffic choked bridges and down dark, frenzied streets toward a familiar beacon, the Mount Everest Hotel.

Contrary to my far-fetched fantasy, there was no royal reception line. No parade. No welcoming committee. We were just three weary wanderers, a trio of mad marathoners. Yet like long distance runners, we were propelled by a wildly powerful surge of adrenaline like none ever felt before.

We wended through hordes of traffic for two frantic hours. As we headed into the heart of the pulsating city, we were accompanied by an ever-changing entourage of kids walking and riding their bikes; shouting a hundred questions.

"Where have you come from?"

"What are you doing?"

"What do you think about Tibet?"

Funny, the more they shared their infectious curiosity, the more triumphant we felt.

"Maybe we have accomplished something," I thought. "Maybe our trip will make them think about Tibet, their neighbor, its people, its struggle. Maybe someday they'll pressure their government to open borders. Maybe they, too, will have the freedom to set-off on their own private pilgrimage."

All of a sudden, within the passing pandemonium, a black sedan swerved, abruptly stopping just yards ahead. Rolling down her window, a lady excitedly poked her head out and gushed, "We heard about you, two! I'm so glad you made it!"

We were shocked and so elated. All we could stutter was a heartfelt, "Th-thanks!" as we choked back a tear. Moments like that played just as fine a tune as any regal brass band.

Our runner's high swept us mapless past a marauding wedding orchestra and through a confusing maze of murky streets. Finally, Cheryl spotted Kanti Path. It was that one section of the city that we knew as well as any stranger might ever hope to know.

Turning down one last reeking alley, it was a straight shot to Utse Hotel and not a moment too soon. After trekking almost fifty kilometers (thirty-one miles), we were burnt out and down to our last reserves.

"I hope N.D. got our letter," I worried aloud. "Sure hope he hasn't let us down again."

"I wouldn't count on him," Cheryl remarked.

Unfortunately her prediction was right. The Utse had no reservation for two weary pilgrims. Although they agreed to find us a room, they laughed at the prospect of keeping a horse.

"Well, if they have no room for Sadhu, they have no room for us!" I stubbornly vowed.

Dejected and unwilling to accept defeat, we begged at several other hostels in Thamel with no greater luck. We even tried the Tushita Rest House where we'd stayed before leaving for Tibet. Although they were sympathetic to our dilemma, they too had nowhere to keep a horse, except in their garden.

It was so frustrating after trekking so far. "Doesn't anyone in Nepal ever travel with a horse, anymore?" I wondered.

Scanning the gloomy alleyway, we spotted one last light. The sign read, "LHASA GUEST HOUSE," and on its door was hand-lettered a welcoming, "*Tashi Delek!*" Placing our trust in fate once again, I gingerly stepped inside its comfortable lobby. As if a good portent, a photo of the Dalai Lama serenely gazed down from behind the counter.

Filled with hope, I silently approached a bear-like fellow at the front desk. Sensing my presence, or perhaps just smelling my *l'air de yak beurre*, the innkeeper peered up from his guest register.

"Yes?"

"Do you have a room for two very tired pilgrims. We've just walked all the way from Lhasa and Potala Palace."

"Of course!" he replied with an expression of complete astonishment. Spinning the guest book around, he handed me a pen.

"Ah...we have one small problem," I admitted. "Our horse. Our *ghoda*...er *da*," not knowing exactly what to call him, since he was a Tibetan in Nepal. "We need a place to keep him tonight, too."

The bewildered Tibetan was lost in thought for just an instant. Then, sailing past, he swept me back into the street where Cheryl and the usual audience of kids watched Sadhu swivel his head around to munch the hay that we'd tied to his broad chestnut back.

"You've just walked from Lhasa," the manager guffawed, "with him?"

I didn't quite know how to take that.

"Yes, he's Tibetan," I answered proudly, "and he's been with us all the way!"

"Then you are very welcome here!" he pronounced, leading all three of us back into his sparkling lobby. We were stunned at both his generosity and compassion. Upon the innkeeper's command, two Tibetan ladies fetched food for Sadhu, while he and another fellow cleared a cozy place for our wandering holy man right beside the lobby staircase!

"Now, he can stay right here," the innkeeper promised with a twinkle in his eye, "but only for one night. In the morning, you will find another place for him, okay?"

"Yes, of course!" I beamed.

While the gentle women mixed our companion a bowl of his favorite, *tsampa* and water, Cheryl carried in armfuls of hay. Then for one long moment, as Sadhu slurped his gruel with undisguised gusto, everyone watched in humble admiration, each feasting with our *sadhu* in a celebratory glow.

The next morning, after moving our famished friend to a feedlot across the street, we began a feverish week spent searching for his permanent home. Who'd have thought it would be so difficult?

At first, we placed an ad in *Nepal Rising*, the country's leading newspaper. While at their offices, we were pleased to give them an interview about our journey, hoping to stimulate interest in both Tibet and our friend. After speaking frankly about the desperate situation we'd witnessed throughout Tibet, you can imagine our shock to read their censored version. It was remarkable to see how cautiously they padded around the Chinese. They invented statements we never made, ignored observations we did, and even forgot our plea to find Sadhu a new home.

To make matters worse, N.D., in one last-ditch effort to redeem himself, allowed us to publish his telephone number in our newspaper ad. However, as it turned out, it was his fax number! So, not surprisingly, we received no adoption calls.

Stymied, we set off on a different course. Remembering how much the Nepalese kids loved him, we contacted children's charity organizations. But that was less than fruitful. Save the Children outright refused him. Although UNICEF was interested, they didn't have time to contact their members before we were scheduled to leave. Frantic, we even contacted the Peace Corps and the American Embassy, hoping some equestrian expat would show interest. Although we had no luck there, they referred us to the Nepalese Cavalry.

Now, personally, I'd never seen Sadhu as a "military type." But we were desperate. With all the concern of parents placing their first-born in school, we inspected their first-rate facilities. The Major who supervised the stables was interested in Sadhu, particularly since he was opening a riding academy. So we were encouraged when he offered to take our friend sight unseen. But his enthusiasm was short-lived. Upon inspecting squat, shaggy Sadhu tethered in the feed yard, his interest waned. Compared to the regiment's mammoth, sleekly shaved Persian mounts, well, our companion was the disheveled runt of the litter. Besides, when the officer approached, Sadhu reared up, kicked in the air with his front legs, snapped and whinnied in protest or fear.

251

"All the better," I thought. "We've never seen gentle Sadhu react so violently to anyone as he did that soldier."

Although we'd exhausted the military, our search didn't end there. We asked every Tibetan businessman we met in Thamel. Unfortunately, they had no interest. Nor did the few touring companies offering horse excursions or the city park's defunct stables.

"Cheryl, folks in Kathmandu just don't have the space or use for a horse anymore, I guess."

"I know" she lamented. "Everyone tells us to take him to Pokara, as if we could just stuff him in the back seat of a car and drive him there."

That mountain village was another week's trek or more and none of us were up to that. We were both recuperating or making a serious attempt. Although I wasn't heavy when we started, I'd lost thirty-five pounds in forty days, and I was battling a third bout of giardia. Cheryl was the slimmest I'd ever seen. While Sadhu, of course, still gorged on everything in sight, edible or not.

At last, in a final hour of desperation, I returned to the Tushita Rest House. Its manager, a slim relocated Tibetan, was one of several fellows who'd inspected Sadhu earlier that week. He'd made us a standing offer. We'd passed on it initially though, reluctant to pass our friend off to a "city" person who hardly knew one end of the horse from the other. But by now we were growing desperate.

As I entered his lobby, he peeked up from under a sheaf of papers.

"We're still trying to find a good home for our *da* before we leave. And," as I was hesitant to admit, "we're running out of time. Still interested?"

"Yes, do not worry," he quipped, trying to ease my fears, although no one really could. "Of course, he will not stay here. I will be happy to take him to my family's new mountain lodge in Nagarkot." The luxury resort was near completion and they planned to offer one day treks into the surrounding hills.

"I just wanted to make sure that our brother has a good home," I explained.

Now I was convinced that we'd done all we could, except for reminding the Tibetan manager once more, "We never would have made it without his help!" I hoped that his equine pilgrimage might command extra respect in that Buddhist innkeeper's eyes. "He'll get mountains of hay, right?"

"Of course," he assured me with one of those Nepali head wobbles. "My family will make sure he is well fed. Write to him whenever you wish."

"All right. He's yours," I relented with an immediate twinge of regret and betrayal. As I turned to leave, I remembered his mostly French clientele and their fondness for "*cheval.*"

"And I don't want to see any horse added to your menu either, my friend!" We both had a good laugh.

The following day, with great remorse, I led our loyal friend to the hotel and solemnly tied him in the garden. Trustingly he glanced up at me as he'd done so often before. Only this time, I knew there were no more days to hoof together down dusty roads. No more lessons in walking side by side. No more slides across Tibetan ice. No more midnight food binges. No more pauses to share a *761* bar together. No more attempts to slip across borders. Or sneak a whiz in unison off the road and do "a guy sort of thing," as Cheryl joked. Through all our difficult times, through all our moments of doubt and fear, Sadhu had remained our one trusted companion, the very heartbeat of our journey. In memory of our shared adventures, I did the only thing I could. I prayed for the Dalai Lama's continued blessing on him. And I walked away.

On December 7th, 1992, we presented the strand of multi-colored prayer flags we'd carried all the way from Lhasa to His Majesty The King of Nepal's Private Secretary, Mr. Chet Bahadur Kunwar. Given their long journey, we'd have preferred to hand them directly to King Birendra. But the monarch, a Hindu, was away on a pilgrimage to India.

"What perfect timing," I mused. "If he's been on a holy journey himself, maybe he'll have greater empathy for those Nepalese and Tibetan Buddhists who are prevented from crossing frontiers on trips of faith to their own sacred sites. Maybe he'll use his wisdom, power and influence to set politics aside."

A brief note was enclosed with those precious pendants. It read:

Your Majesty:

Please accept this set of Tibetan prayer flags with our kind wishes. As one of the first Western couples to walk the pilgrim's route from Lhasa to Kathmandu, my wife and I have carried them all 1,000 kilometers from the Potala Palace, especially for Your Majesty.

I am very sorry we were unable to present these in person. We understand that, presently, you and the Queen are on pilgrimage to India.

In consideration for pilgrims of all faiths, may we humbly suggest that you fly these simple prayer flags from Bodnath Stupa.

If Your Majesty flies them there, they will wave as a symbol of solidarity and religious freedom for all people—especially for the many kind Nepalese and Tibetans who remain unable to make pilgrimages to their holy sites, as we have done.

Their prayers shall fly with these flags. Namaste.

That same day, Cheryl and I left the Himalayas behind. However Tibet, her gentle people and their courageous struggle to be free, will remain a part of us—as much as the Dalai Lama remains a part of the sacred land and spiritual consciousness of a people who await his blessed return.

We traveled deliberately. And in turn, we were rewarded with a bit of enlightenment—one step at a time.

The student learns by daily increment.
The Way is gained by daily loss,
Loss upon loss until
At last comes rest.

By letting go, it all gets done;
The world is won by those who let it go!
But when you try and try,
The world is then beyond the winning.

-Lao Tzu

Afterword

This pilgrimage actually felt completed when a copy of this book in manuscript form was presented to His Holiness the Dalai Lama for his blessing at Wood Valley Temple on the Big Island of Hawai'i two years later. Since then, much has changed in Tibet. Unfortunately, not for the better.

Today, the Tibetan people suffer great hardships as prisoners of occupation in their own country. Over the past four decades, since China's brutal invasion in 1950, Tibet has withstood turbulent changes, bringing it to the brink of "cultural genocide." Although not an Iraq or Bosnia, the crisis is just as severe, the suffering is just as real.

During our journey, we witnessed the breadth of injustice for ourselves. But don't just take our word for it. The cruelty has been well documented.

According to leading international newspapers: Communist Chinese have killed over 1.2 million Tibetans. There are hundreds of political prisoners. Freedom of speech and the press is but a memory.

During the Cultural Revolution, thousands of Tibetan cloisters or temples were pillaged, tens of thousands monks or nuns were killed or sent to concentration camps. Remaining lamaseries no longer admit school-aged children and China limits monk recruits to novices who "love the Communist Party."

Tibetan public schools teach only in Chinese. Yet most villages have no schools, electricity or running water, and the Tibetan infant mortality rate is abysmal: 127 per 1,000 vs. 43 per 1,000 for the invaders.

China's logging denudes Tibet's forests. Their mining rapes the land.

Perhaps worst of all, China actively promotes resettlement of ethnic Chinese into Tibet, creating tension and disintegration of traditional Tibetan values and way of life. Presently there are over more Chinese living in Tibet than Tibetans. The new railway connection from Beijing to Lhasa will be completed in 2007 and will hasten the assimilation. Soon the Tibetan will be a foreigner, a stranger in their own land.

Not surprisingly, China doesn't want the public to know about this. Since the humiliating atrocity at Tiananmen Square, the last thing they want is more attention brought to their flagrant violation of human rights. In fact, China is currently waging an active propaganda campaign to correct the world's opinion about Tibetan oppression.

The Western "free" world needs to speak up for freedom before it's too late. Political pressure must applied. We must link trade with human rights, friendship with freedom. We must make it clear to the Chinese that the issue of human rights, dignity and national sovereignty is not simply an "internal matter." It is a global imperative.

Otherwise Tibet's future is bleak. Soon it will only remain a memory, an instance of a people held hostage in their own country while the world looked away.

We, who cherish freedom and self-determination must write, phone, e-mail or fax our congresses, parliaments and world leaders today...before it is too late.

To become involved in the global effort to free Tibet, please contact:

The International Campaign For Tibet
1825 K Street, NW, Suite 520
Washington, D.C. 20006 USA
Tel. (202) 785-1515
E-mail: info@savetibet.org
www.savetibet.org

International Campaign for Tibet Europe
Keizersgracht 302, Amsterdam
P.O. Box 3337
1001 AC AMSTERDAM
The Netherlands
Phone: +31 (0)20 3308265
Fax: +31 (0)20 3308266
E-mail: icteurope@savetibet.org

International Campaign for Tibet Deutschland
e.V.Marienstr. 30
10117 Berlin
Germany
Phone: +49 (0)30 27879086
Fax: +49 (0)30 27879087
E-mail: ict-d@savetibet.org

Amnesty International
322 Eighth Avenue
New York, NY 10001-4808 USA
Tel. (212) 807-8400
E-mail: admin-us@aiusa.org
www.amnestyusa.org

Please visit www.PilgrimsTales.com for other Tibet links.

Suggested Reading

Bayonets To Lhasa, Peter Fleming, Oxford University Press

Freedom in Exile: The Autobiography of the Dalai Lama
His Holiness the Dalai Lama, Harper Perennial

Heartlands: Travels in the Tibetan World
Michael Buckley, Summersdale Publishers, UK

Lost Horizon, James Hilton, Macmillan and Co.

Mountains of the Middle Kingdom: Exploring the High Peaks of China & Tibet, Galen Rowell, Sierra

My Journey to Lhasa, Alexandra David-Neel, Beacon Press

My Land and My People, His Holiness the Dalai Lama, Potala Press

My Tibet, text by the Dalai Lama, photos by Galen Rowell, UC Press

Peace Pilgrim–Her Life and Work in Her Own Words
Friends of Peace Pilgrim and Ocean Tree Books

Seven Years in Tibet, Heinrich Harrer, Tarcher/Perrigee

The Art of Pilgrimage, The Seeker's Guide to Making Travel Sacred
Phil Cousineau, Conrari Press

Tibetan for Beginners and Travellers
Melvin C. Goldstein, Ratna Pustak Bhandar Bhotahity, Kathmandu

Tibet. A Travel Survival Kit,
Michael Buckley and Robert Strauss, Lonely Planet Publications

Tibet Handbook, A Pilgrimage Guide, Victor Chan, Moon Publications

Tibet: The Bradt Travel Guide, Michael Buckley, Bradt Travel Guides

Trekking in Tibet. A Traveler's Guide, Gary McCue, Mountaineers

About the Author

Brandon Wilson is an award-winning author and photographer, explorer, internationally published adventure-travel writer and expert light trekker. A voracious explorer of over ninety countries, he's particularly passionate about inspiring others with the possibility of discovery through long-distance trekking.

Walking in Tibet and Africa first opened his eyes to the deep satisfaction of traveling 'one-step-at-a-time'. By slowing down, he believes, we absorb the hidden 'magic' in the world. We travel outside— while traveling within.

Besides crossing Tibet, the author has twice hiked the famed Camino de Santiago across Spain, the St. Olav's Way across Norway, and he was the first American to complete the 9th century, 1150-mile Via Francigena trail from England to Rome. He also enjoys wandering long-distance GR trails across Austria, the Czech Republic, France, Tuscany, the Pyrenees, Dolomites and Alps. These physical, mental and spiritual journeys help fuel his irrepressible wanderlust.

Yak Butter Blues has won an Independent Publisher IPPY Award and his photographs have won awards from *National Geographic Traveler* and *Islands* magazines. He is a member of The Explorers Club and Artists Without Frontiers. And, as one might expect, he is an ardent supporter of Tibetan and human rights.

For color Tibet expedition photos, exciting links,
ordering information, and a free preview
of his critically acclaimed book
Dead Men Don't Leave Tips: Adventures X Africa,
please visit: www. PilgrimsTales.com

Other Books by the Author

DEAD MEN DON'T LEAVE TIPS: ADVENTURES X AFRICA

What does it take to follow your dream? Quite a bit, if your dream involves crossing Africa. That's what Brandon and Cheryl Wilson discover when they set off on a seven-month, 10,000-mile overland journey from Morocco to Cape Town. As independent travelers, they'd traveled around the world. But was a trans-African odyssey too much for even them?

Against their better judgment, they join a do-it-yourself overland safari and are flung into a bewildering band of companions and clueless guides. As their dream of crossing Africa turns into a nightmare, they set off across the continent alone. And that makes all the difference.

Join the adventurous couple as they meet mountain gorillas face to face. Melt down during a blistering Saharan breakdown. Hunt dik-dik with Pygmies. Climb Africa's highest mountain. Feel the raw power of the Serengeti. Hop the "gun-run" through a civil war. Rush down thundering Class V Zambezi rapids and dive into South Africa's cauldron of turmoil.

"Dead Men Don't Leave Tips is an adventure journal only the craziest traveler would take as a guide. But we can dream, can't we? I was swept away by the drama and storytelling in Wilson's book...Brandon Wilson is never a tourist. He travels heart-first with both feet solidly on the ground and his curiosity always in high gear. He is exactly the right person to be writing travel books for the rest of us." ~ Joseph W. Bean, book reviewer, *Maui Weekly*

"Brandon Wilson jacks the vehicle of trans-African adventure for a ride so real you breathe the dust and drip the sweat while trundling down off-the-beaten tracks outstanding in the number and quality of their ruts. If adventure drives are a genre, Wilson has created a smarter, more brazen, more sweeping subspecies. This is a masterful crossroads of characters, exotic places, history and human drama in a rig that never stalls, and allows the devil to drive his own ill-behaved backyard." ~ Richard Bangs, adventurer/author of *The Lost River* and *Mystery of the Nile*/executive producer Yahoo Media Group

"There's a magic about Africa that few are privileged to enjoy first hand. Author Brandon Wilson, however, allows readers to share in all that. Wilson masterfully takes the reader along on a seven month trip across the African continent to meet its people and enjoy its breathtaking beauty in ways few have written... He writes a magical story, indeed, laced with humor and tragedy. Well worth reading, it brings Africa to readers on an intimate level not found elsewhere." ~ Andrew F. O'Hara, author of *The Swan: Tales of the Sacramento Valley*/journalist

Give the Gift of Adventure Travel
to Your Friends, Schools,
Libraries and Colleagues.

~ Order Here Today ~

❑ Yes, I want ___ paperback copies of **Yak Butter Blues: A Tibetan Trek of Faith** signed by the author for only $16.95 each.

❑ Yes, I want ___ paperback copies of **Dead Men Don't Leave Tips: Adventures X Africa** signed by the author for only $16.95 each.

❑ Yes, I want ___ paperback sets of **Yak Butter Blues: A Tibetan Trek of Faith** *and* **Dead Men Don't Leave Tips: Adventures X Africa** signed by the author at the discounted price of only $30.00 per set.

Include $3.95 shipping and handling for one book and $1.95 for each additional book. Hawaii residents must include applicable sales tax. International orders must include payment in US funds. Payment must accompany orders. Allow 3 weeks for delivery.

My check or money order for $ _____ is enclosed.

Name_____

Address_____

City/State/Zip_____

E-Mail (in case there's a problem with your order)

_____

Special signing instructions_____

Make your check payable and mail to:
Pilgrim's Tales, Inc.
P.O. Box 791613
Paia, Hawaii 96779 USA

Or order a signed copy via our web site at:
www.PilgrimsTales.com

Printed in the United States
47060LVS00002B/157